IMAGES
of America

THOMASTON

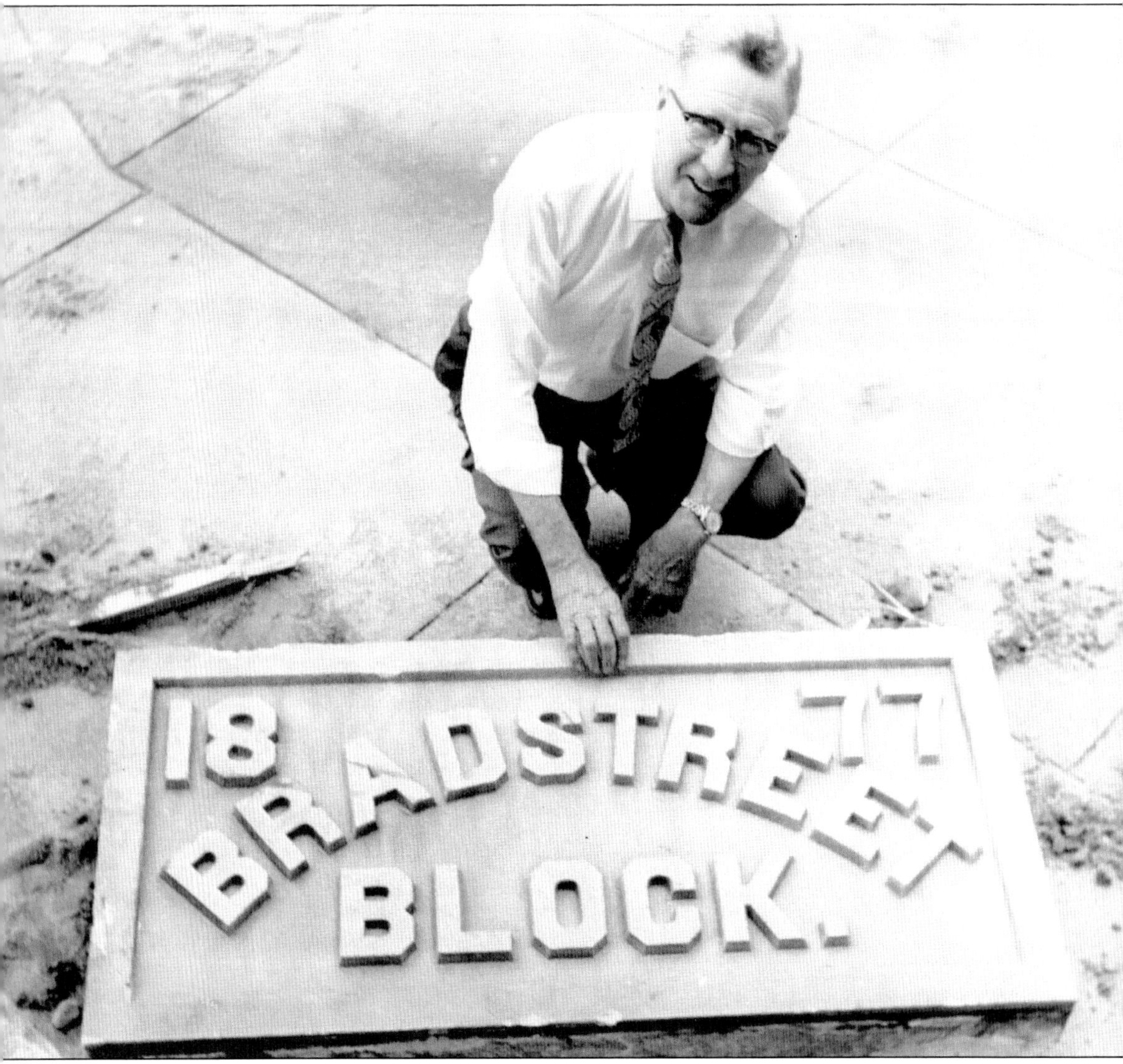

The gentleman pictured here was known affectionately as "Papa." From 1941 to 1984, Robert Robinson (1897–1984) was the treasurer of the town of Thomaston. A native of Stockport, England, he came to the United States before his first birthday, and to Thomaston in 1913. He worked at Plume & Atwood and at the Thomaston Manufacturing Company, just down the street from his home at 19 Electric Avenue, for many years, in addition to his town service. The Robinson Family Collection in the Thomaston Historical Society is a lasting tribute and memorial to him and to his wife, Ethel, to his son Robert Jr. and his daughter-in-law Ann, to his younger son, Walter, and his daughter-in-law Phyllis.

IMAGES
of America

THOMASTON

Joseph F. Wassong Jr.

ARCADIA
PUBLISHING

ISBN 978-0-7385-1334-8

Published by Arcadia Publishing
Charleston, South Carolina

Printed in the United States of America

Library of Congress Catalog Card Number: 2003109931

For all general information contact Arcadia Publishing at:
Telephone 843-853-2070
Fax 843-853-0044
E-mail sales@arcadiapublishing.com
For customer service and orders:
Toll-Free 1-888-313-2665

Visit us on the Internet at www.arcadiapublishing.com

To Rebecca Skinner and Shirley G. Wassong.

Contents

ACKNOWLEDGMENTS

Several people have helped in numerous ways to make this book possible. The Thomaston Historical Society allowed me to use its collection, which was indispensable, especially the Robinson Family Collection. My Thomaston High School classmate Myron Roman and Bob Magdziarz gave me permission to use their postcard collections, and another high school classmate, Bill Polowy, helped me to grapple with the mysteries of the computer. Clifford "Kip" Brammer enabled me to photograph the clock seen on page 38.

Others who answered questions, provided images, and helped with identifications of people and places include the following: William Berg, Adeline Dilger Bolton, Joseph Bystry, Marion Wight Conklin, Mario DePecol, Marion Innes DePecol, Helen Monahan Dupont, Dale and Roger Gangloff, Gerda Wehrle Grosso, Patricia Adam Izzo, Kenneth Johnson, Marlene Johnston Hall, Richard Kramer Jr., Gene Martin, Rosemary Lyons Martin, Barbara Moskaluk-Hunter, Frank Noack, Richard O'Connell, Caroline and Henry Osowiecki Jr., Robert Pingpank, Joan Flynn Raccio, Ian Roome, Evelyn Samson, Christine Shearer St. Denis, Dorothy and Frank Vigeant, John Torrence, and Thelma Kramer Snyder. My late cousin and longtime Thomaston teacher, Rosa Gangloff, deserves our praise and gratitude for collecting and preserving much of Thomaston's past. Walter Robinson, who has passed along so much of his father's collection to the Thomaston Historical Society, deserves special mention. The following is, therefore, a collaborative effort.

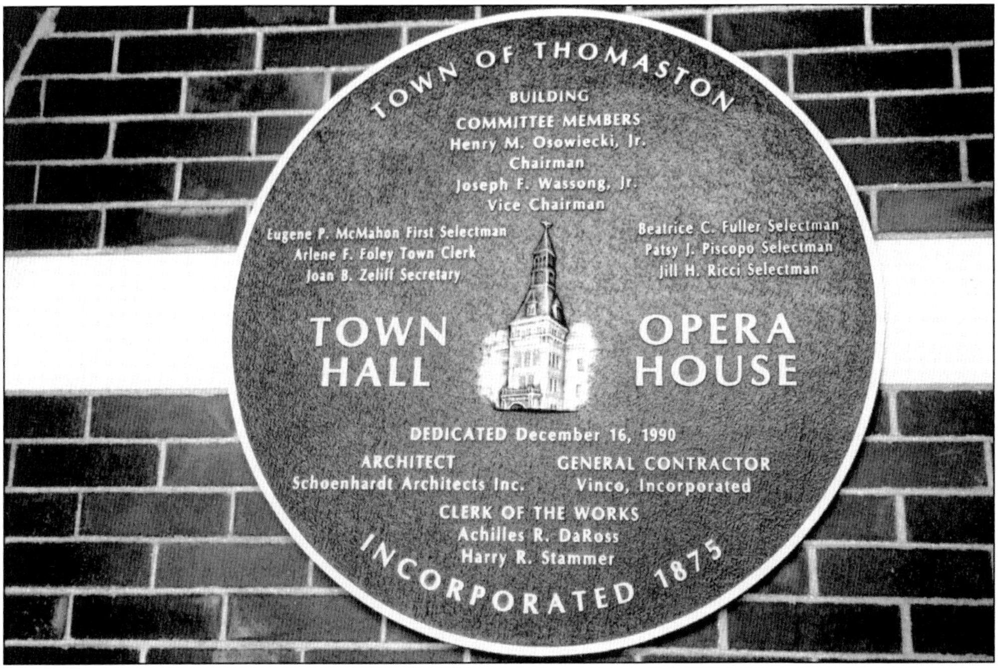

This plaque was erected to commemorate the addition and renovation of the town hall.

INTRODUCTION

The early history of Thomaston revolves around the life of the successful entrepreneur Seth Thomas. A Wolcott native, Thomas came to Thomaston (then called Plymouth Hollow) in 1813. Purchasing a factory from Heman Clark on the site of a later masonry complex, the 28-year-old began the manufacture of clocks. He was not the first settler but perhaps the most important.

This book is a pictorial history of Thomaston from the mid-19th century to 1975. In the period prior to 1875, Thomaston was a part of Plymouth. Neighboring towns included Harwinton, Morris, Bethlehem, Watertown, Litchfield, Torrington, and the brass center of Waterbury, the largest. The town was initially part of Northbury, then Plymouth Hollow, then Thomastown, and, finally, Thomaston. Incorporated by an act of the Connecticut General Assembly in July 1875, the town entered a period of change that would establish the nature of the town and, indeed, its appearance for the next 100 years. What was formerly a town of wood became a town of brick. American Hall was the first brick building, constructed in 1866. Then followed the Morse Block (in 1876), the Bradstreet Block (in 1877), and the town hall (in 1883). In a short span of years, Thomaston's appearance was permanently altered. Thus, the concentration is upon the period of 1875 to 1975. The Thomaston Historical Society has been generous with a number of photographs of this century. Its museum is housed in the same building that contains the town hall and opera house.

A town of Victorian charm, Thomaston's growth was attributable originally to industry. An economic dynamo in the first half of the 20th century, it has since come to include a population representing many occupations and nationalities. As such, it is a nice mixture of the urban and the suburban, a New England story in microcosm.

The first part of the book is designed to provide readers with a guide to a walking tour of the downtown area. Its scope encompasses Victorian portraits, wars and their impact, street scenes of homes, stores, and factories that are now gone, sports, leisure, and recreation, education, culture, and the personalities that have contributed much to the enrichment of life in Thomaston. *Thomaston* does not pretend to be comprehensive; instead, it is a series of vignettes designed to illustrate episodes in the past.

A recent candidate for sainthood in the Roman Catholic Church was Fr. Michael McGivney, founder of the Knights of Columbus. McGivney's only pastorate was at St. Thomas Church in Thomaston, where he died of consumption in 1890, two days after his 38th birthday.

The book includes the heroic Medal of Honor winner Thomas Reeves, who died aboard the battleship *California* at Pearl Harbor. We have an official U.S. Navy photograph of him.

We have images of the Thomaston Ponies football teams (state semiprofessional champions in the 1920s), the fire department, individual portraits of soldiers and politicians, group photographs of charitable activities, schools that have disappeared, and bridges whose appearances have been absolutely altered. In short, we can offer the reader a collection of images that will give the observer a good sampling of Thomaston life, presented in vignette form.

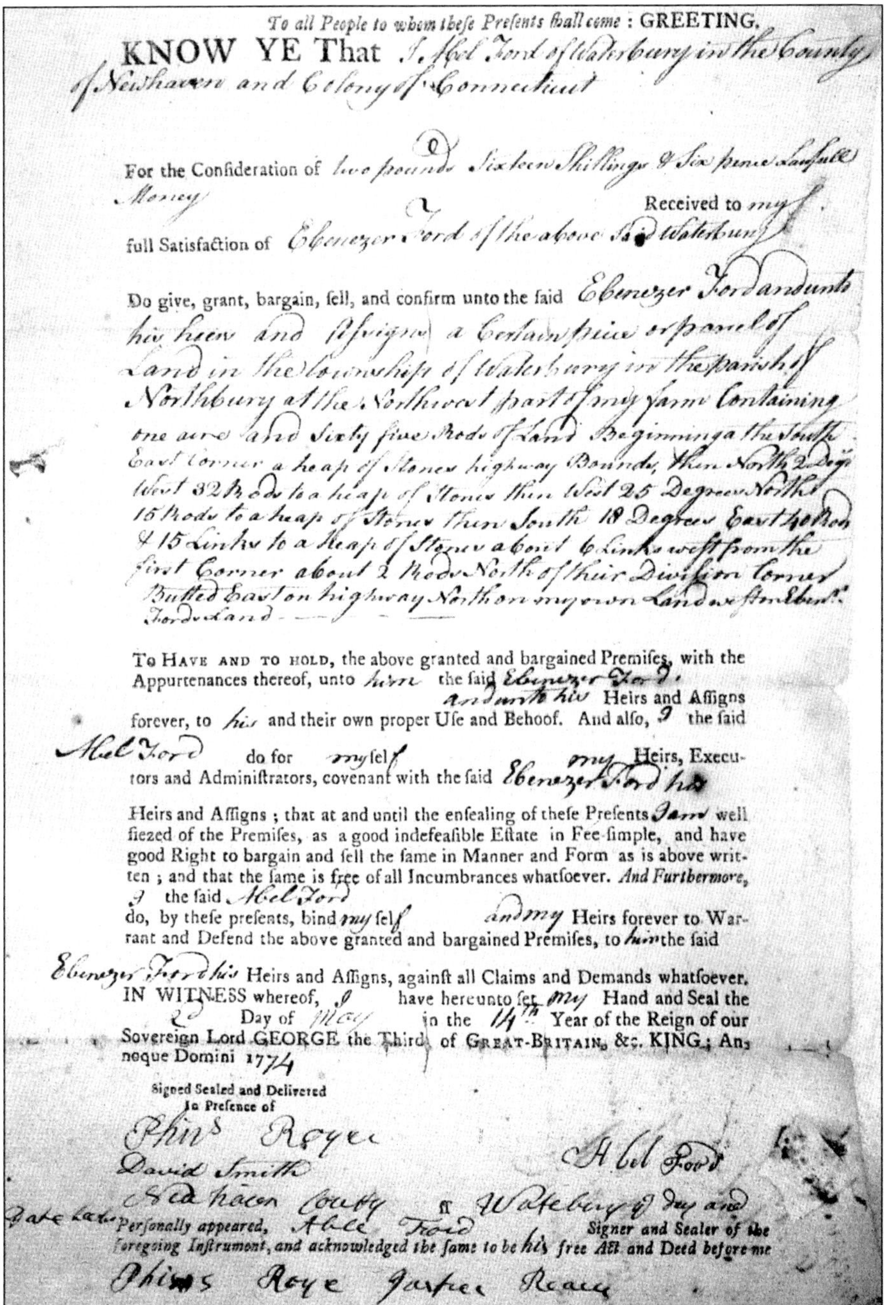

To all People to whom these Presents shall come : GREETING.

KNOW YE That I, Abel Ford of Waterbury in the County of Newhaven and Colony of Connecticut

For the Consideration of two pounds Sixteen Shillings & Six pence Lawfull Money Received to my full Satisfaction of Ebenezer Ford of the above said Waterbury

Do give, grant, bargain, sell, and confirm unto the said Ebenezer Ford and unto his heirs and Assigns a Certain piece or parcel of Land in the township of Waterbury in the parish of Northbury at the Northwest part of my farm Containing one acre and Sixty five Rods of Land Beginning at the South East Corner a heap of Stones highway Bounds, then North 2 Degr West 32 Rods to a heap of Stones then West 25 Degrees North 15 Rods to a heap of Stones then South 18 Degrees East 40 Rods & 15 Links to a heap of Stones about 6 Links west from the first Corner about 2 Rods North of their Division Corner Butted East on highway North on my own Land west on Ebenr Fords Land

To Have and to hold, the above granted and bargained Premises, with the Appurtenances thereof, unto him the said Ebenezer Ford and unto his Heirs and Assigns forever, to his and their own proper Use and Behoof. And also, I the said Abel Ford do for myself my Heirs, Executors and Administrators, covenant with the said Ebenezer Ford his Heirs and Assigns ; that at and until the ensealing of these Presents I am well siezed of the Premises, as a good indefeasible Estate in Fee-simple, and have good Right to bargain and sell the same in Manner and Form as is above written ; and that the same is free of all Incumbrances whatsoever. *And Furthermore*, I the said Abel Ford do, by these presents, bind myself and my Heirs forever to Warrant and Defend the above granted and bargained Premises, to him the said Ebenezer Ford his Heirs and Assigns, against all Claims and Demands whatsoever.

IN WITNESS whereof, I have hereunto set my Hand and Seal the 2 Day of May in the 14th Year of the Reign of our Sovereign Lord GEORGE the Third of Great-Britain, &c. KING ; Annoque Domini 1774

Signed Sealed and Delivered
In Presence of

Phins Royce

David Smith

Abel Ford

New haven County ss Waterbury 2 day and date Personally appeared, Abel Ford Signer and Sealer of the foregoing Instrument, and acknowledged the same to be his free Act and Deed before me

Phins Royce Justice Peace

This document is a deed for a parcel of land that Abel Ford sold to his brother Ebenezer for "two pounds Sixteen Shillings & Six pence Lawfull Money" on May 2, 1774. It was "the 14th Year of the Reign of our Sovereign Lord GEORGE the Third of Great-Britain &c. KING." It involved a section of Abel's farm in the parish of Northbury, "Colony of Connecticut." The Ford brothers and their father, Barnabas, were large landowners in the parish, which was reportedly referred to as "Fordton." (Courtesy of the Robinson Family Collection, Thomaston Historical Society.)

One

A Stroll through Victorian Thomaston

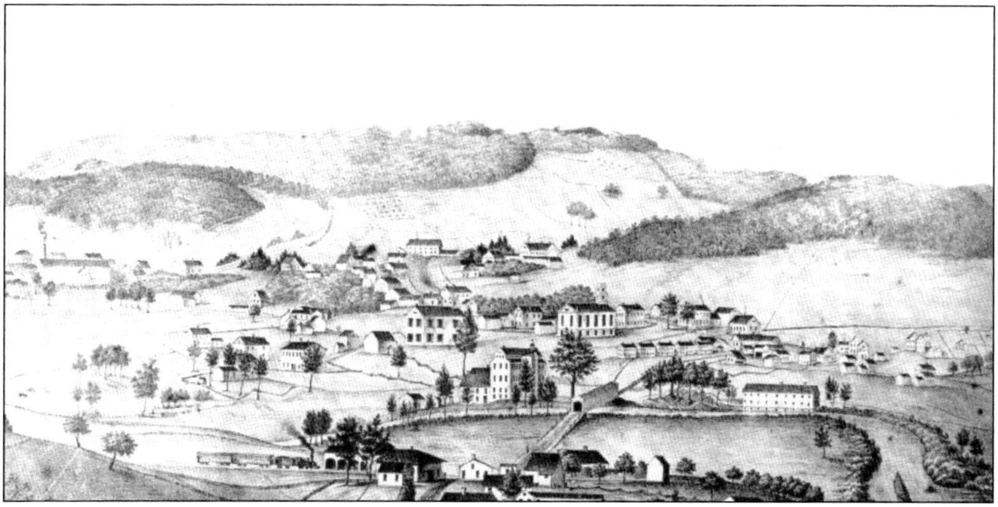

Thomaston was a part of Plymouth until its incorporation as a municipality in 1875. This lithograph shows what the village was like at the time of the Civil War, still nine years away. The Seth Thomas Clock Company was already nearly 40 years old. The Seth Thomas movement shop is just west of the river, to the left of the covered bridge. To its right in the image and just beyond is the First Congregational Church, which still looks much as it did in 1852. At the extreme left is another factory of the Seth Thomas Company.

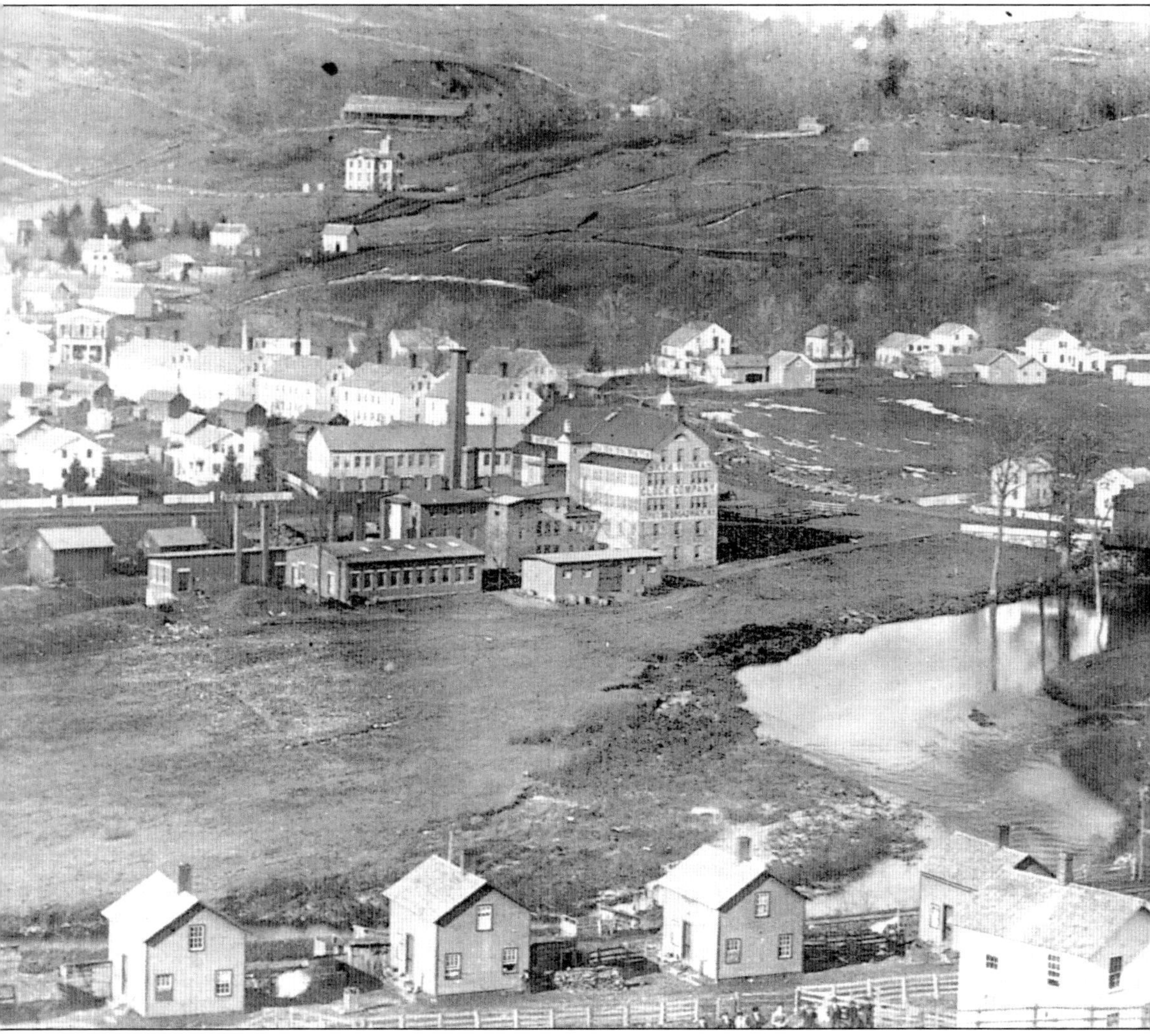

As we see the Naugatuck River wind southward, the covered bridge appears at the right in this *c.* 1880 photograph. Other recognizable features are, from left to right, the Methodist church, American Hall, the five identical houses of Cotton Row, the Seth Thomas Clock Company movement shop, the Hillside Academy School, and North Main Street. Chapel Street, in the foreground, disappeared with the construction of Route 8. The church remains as it was; the hall and houses are much altered but still exist.

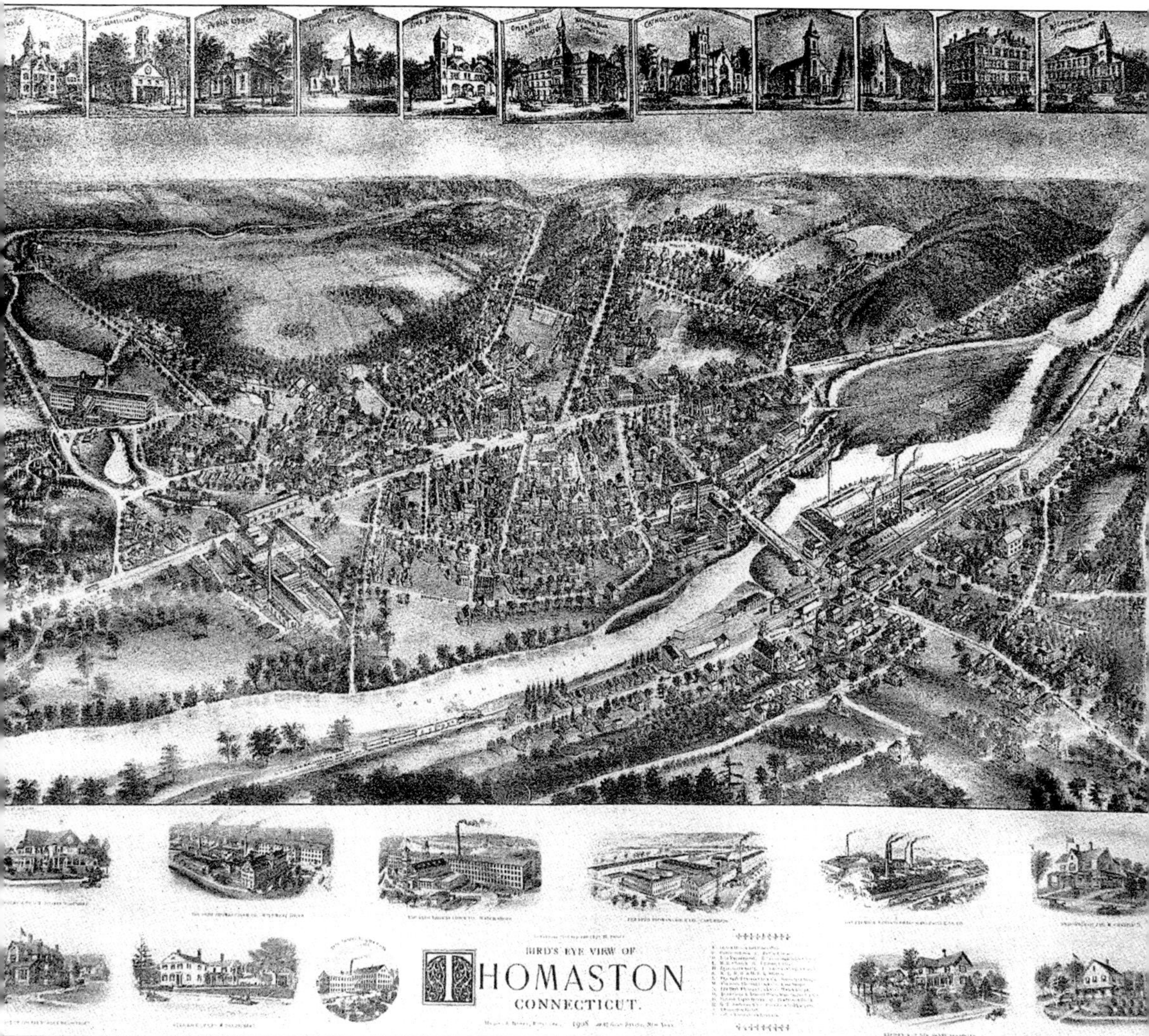

As we look west across the river, we see a useful view of Thomaston in 1908. The rail line is on the near side of the river, as is the Plume & Atwood brass factory. Just across the bridge is the Seth Thomas movement shop, while on South Main Street sits the case shop. To complete the Seth Thomas complex, the marine and watch shop is to the upper left of the image.

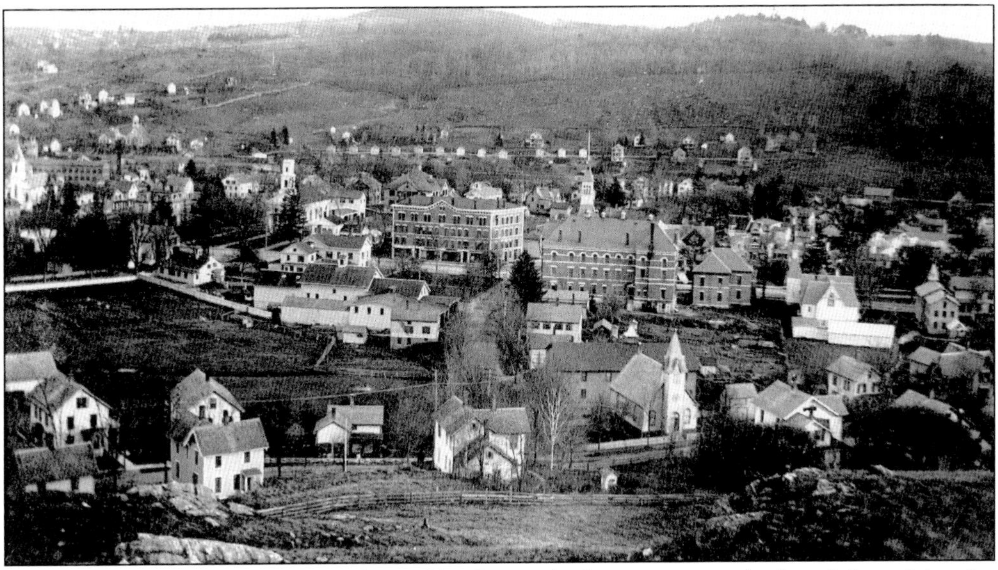

This rare view of the center from above Clay Street, looking east, reveals, from left to right, the Methodist church, the First Congregational Church, the Seth Thomas house, the complex of barns that would become the site of the new Center School, Bradstreet Block, the town hall, the Mission Covenant Church, the Trinity Episcopal Church, and the Episcopal chapel. The photograph was taken c. 1900.

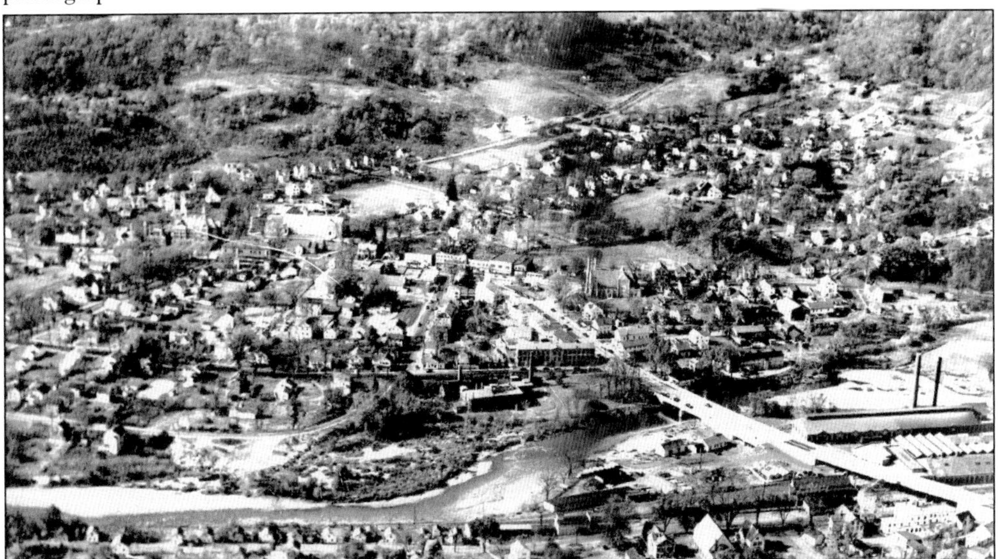

An aerial view of the town taken c. 1940 provides the same perspective as that of 1908. The old St. Thomas Church building is at the near right center, while the Thomaston House hotel is to its right. The concrete bridge is new, and so is the Thomaston High School, the large brick building in the left background.

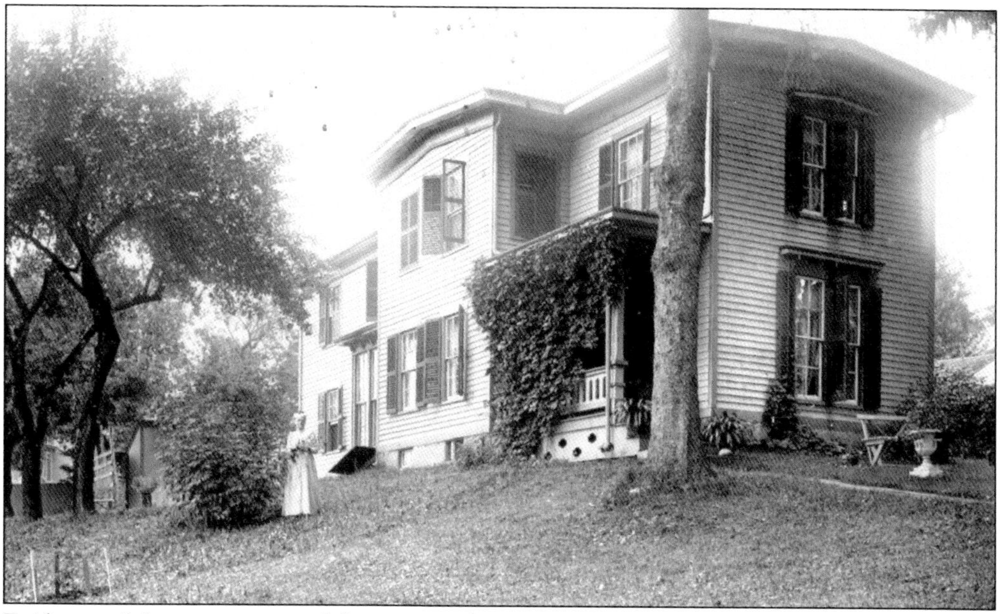

Evidence of the importance of the center of town is reflected in the multitude of images that people have taken over the years. In photographs and postcards, Main Street has been a focal point. This was the residence of George and Mary Stoughton. An East Main Street address, the house was on the slope of Route 6 known as Plymouth Hill. A Dunkin' Donuts is now on the site. Stoughton's Store was below the house, next to the Plume & Atwood factory. Stoughton Street is named for George, a civic and business leader. The photograph was taken c. 1910 by F.J. Taylor of Tremont Street in Boston.

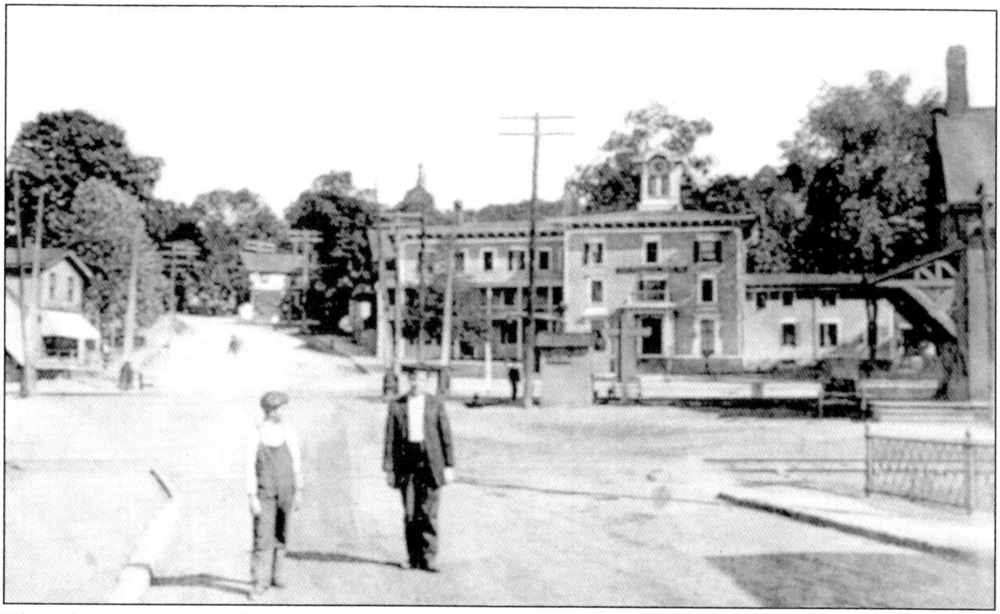

These boys stroll toward the downtown area from the east side. Behind them is one of Thomaston's two hotels, the Thomaston House. Situated right across the tracks from the railroad station, this hotel welcomed guests from around the country. It was demolished in 1964 to allow for the construction of Route 8. This is a postcard from c. 1906. (Courtesy of Robert Magdziarz.)

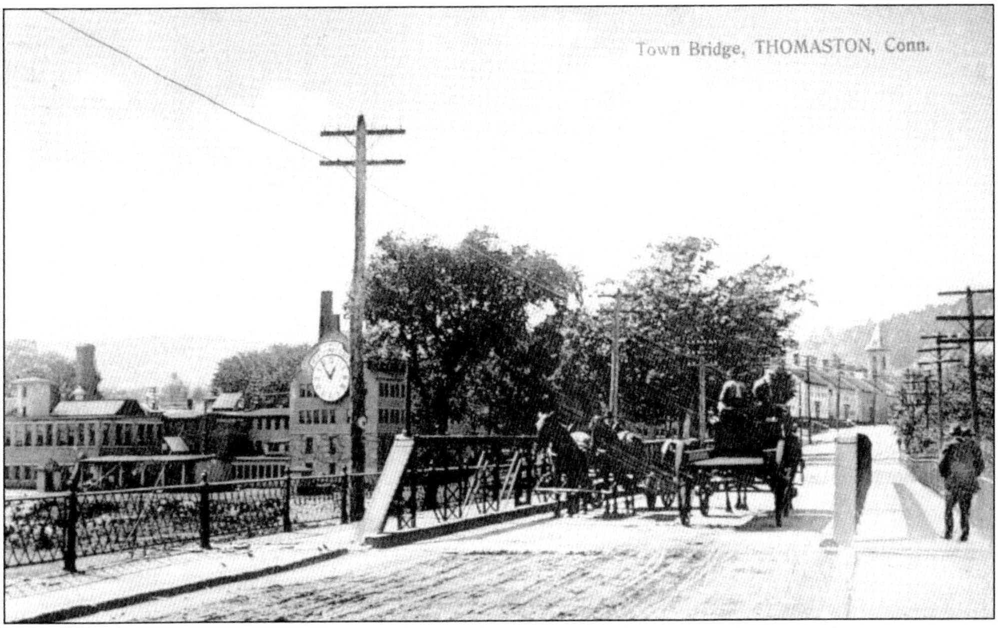

The Town Bridge was an extension of East Main Street. The Seth Thomas Clock movement shop is at the left. The Thomaston Historical Society has the two-page contract that Aaron Thomas, son of Seth, signed along with four other town officials for the construction of the wrought-iron truss bridge. The cost was $9,650. (Courtesy of Myron Roman.)

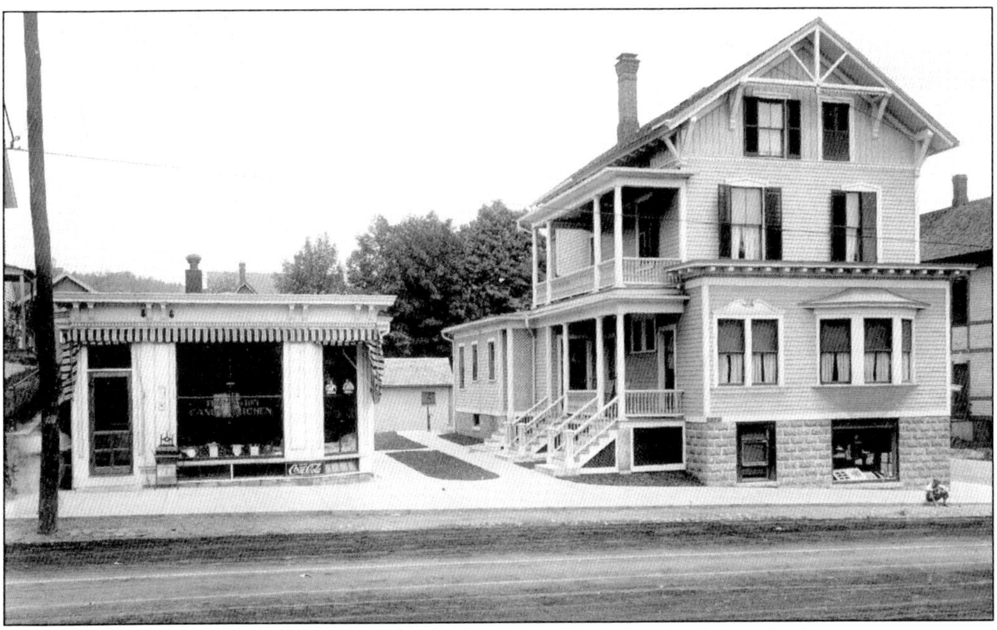

The Candy Kitchen was housed in the building at the left, which has had many tenants in its history. The tall structure at the right, at 97 East Main Street, has been the home of the Thomaston Savings Bank, Patrick Feeley's Market, and Patricia Adam Izzo's Flower Shop. The location is the northwest corner of Electric Avenue and Main Street.

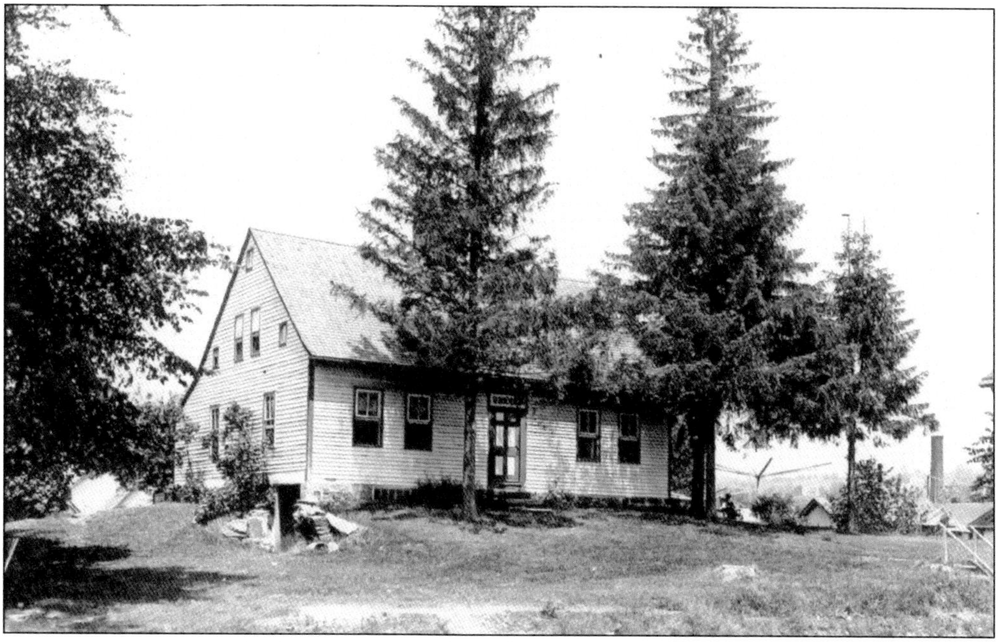

Named the Isaac Castle House or the Wood House, this building would later become the Madden House. The chimney at the right identifies a Plume & Atwood plant. The house, seen here in 1904, still exists in an altered state at 81 East Main Street as Buell's Florist Shop.

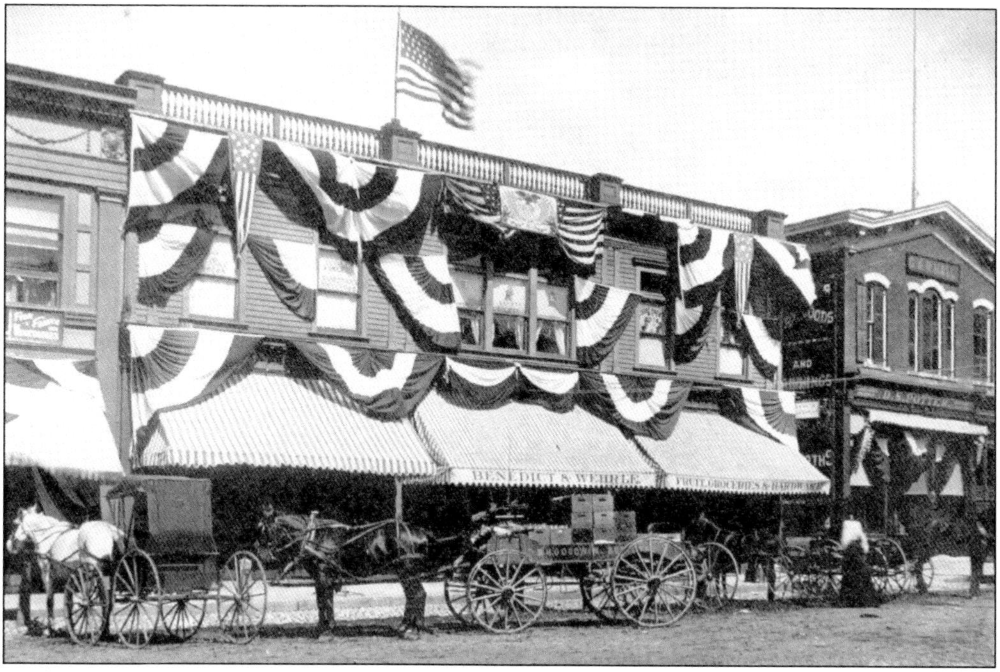

In this Main Street store, Chauncy Benedict and August Wehrle sold fruit, groceries, and hardware. The buggy and wagon indicate that automobiles were still a rarity c. 1910. The wagon was owned by the B.H. Goodwin Bottle Company. Known as Webster's Block, the building is now the site of Fuller's Store. The photographer was Harold DeWolfe Hotchkiss, president of the Thomaston High School class of 1906.

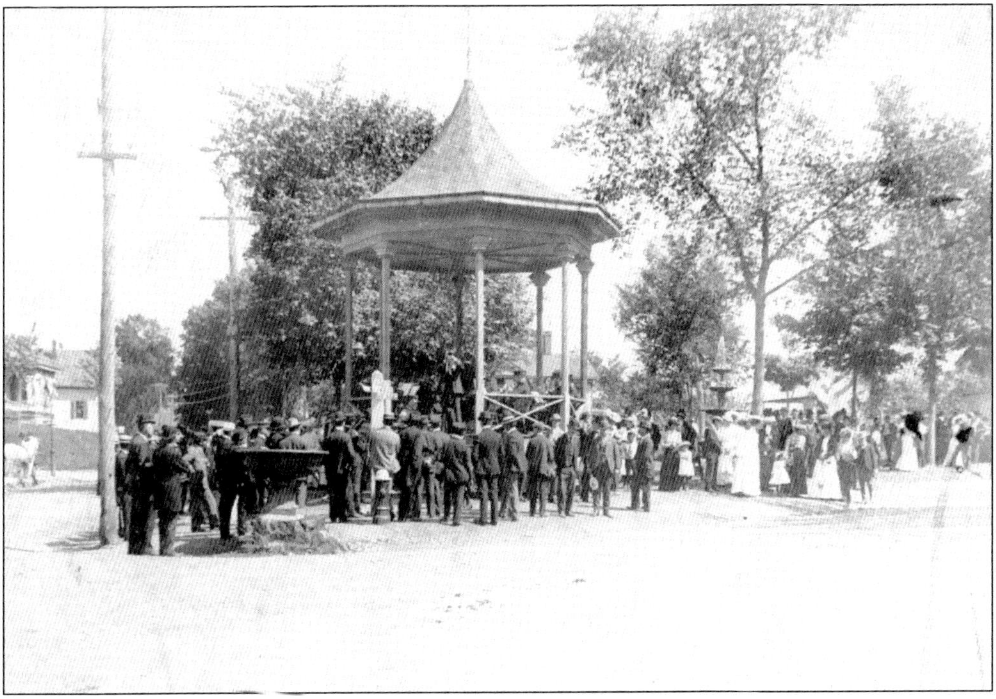

In this c. 1902 image, a well-dressed audience has gathered around the old bandstand to hear a morning concert in what is now Kenea Park. The men are clothed in bowlers. Looking north, we see McGrath's house at the far left, a directions post, and the three-tiered fountain. St. Thomas Church has not yet been built.

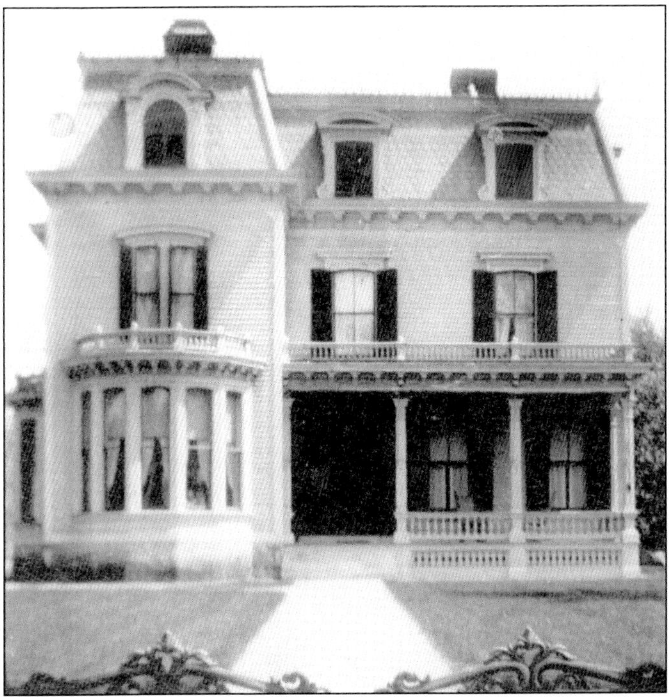

The house that Miles Morse (1816–1886) built on Main Street was a landmark for many years. He married Laura Thomas (1839–1899), the youngest child of Seth Thomas, the clock company's founder. A clock manufacturer himself, Morse built the Morse Block across the street. The Morse property included everything north of the Congregational church to Park Street. In the foreground is the top of the wrought-iron fence that surrounded the property.

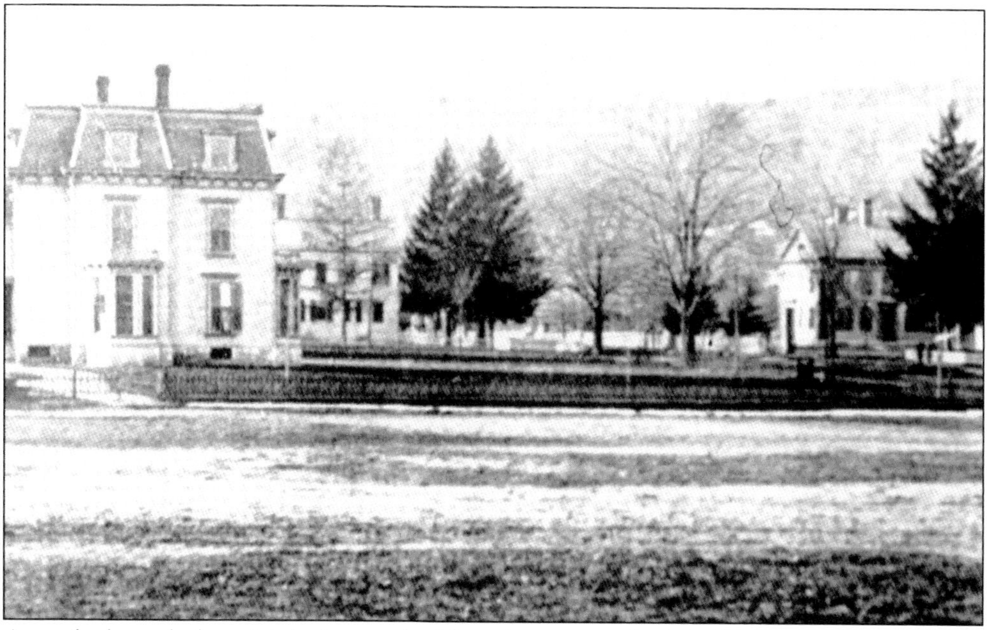

As we look south down Main Street, the Morse house is at the left. Surrounded by a wrought-iron fence, it would later be bought by Frank Etheridge (1858–1914). It was torn down and replaced by stores on Park and Main Streets. The house in the background is the Canfield house, later Talley's House and Restaurant and, at present, the site of a number of stores and offices immediately south of the First Congregational Church. Across Main Street is the Seth Thomas house.

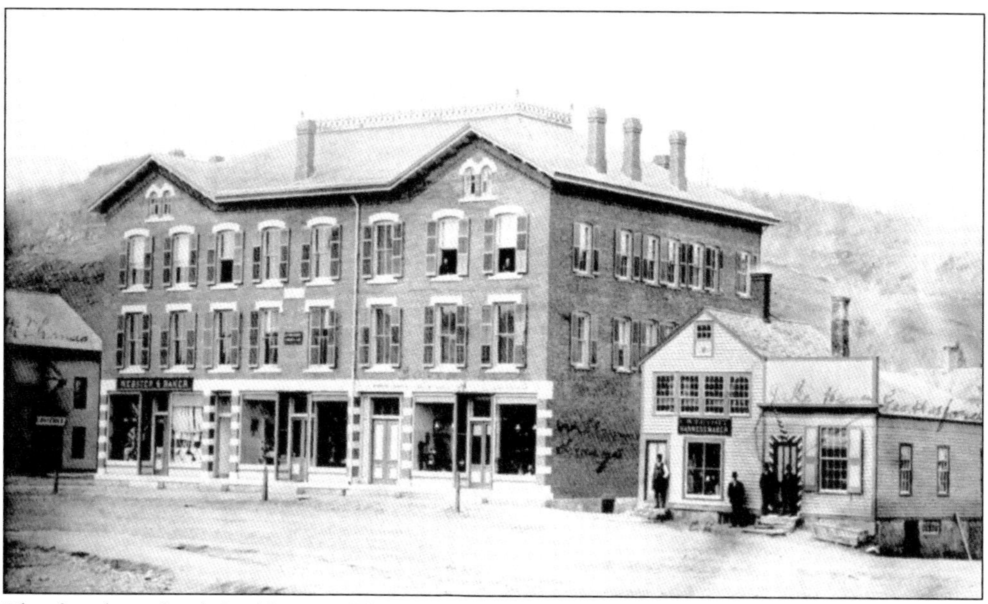

The first large brick building in Thomaston was the Morse Block, on the west side of Main Street. It was built in 1876, burned down the next year, and was rebuilt in 1878. The Seth Thomas Clock Company store appears at the left. Among Morse's tenants were the Webster & Baker Store, attorney Albert P. Bradstreet, and the Thomaston Savings Bank. In the next building to the north, C.W. Talcott stands in front of his harness maker's shop.

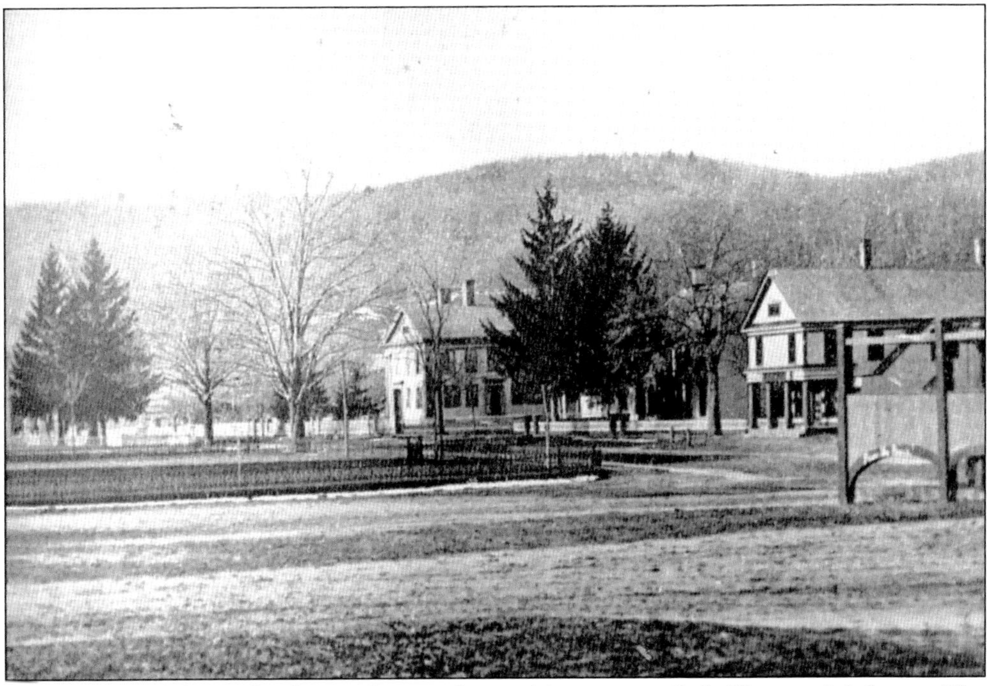

To the right of the Seth Thomas house, obscured by trees, is Seth Thomas Jr.'s house. The building at the right is Seth Thomas's store, which burned down in 1877. We know it as the site of the Country Grocer today. Seth Thomas's house was replaced in the 1930s by the post office and the Thomaston Savings Bank. At the time of the photograph (*c.* 1870), Seth's son Aaron was the owner of his father's house. South of this house is the Old Cemetery.

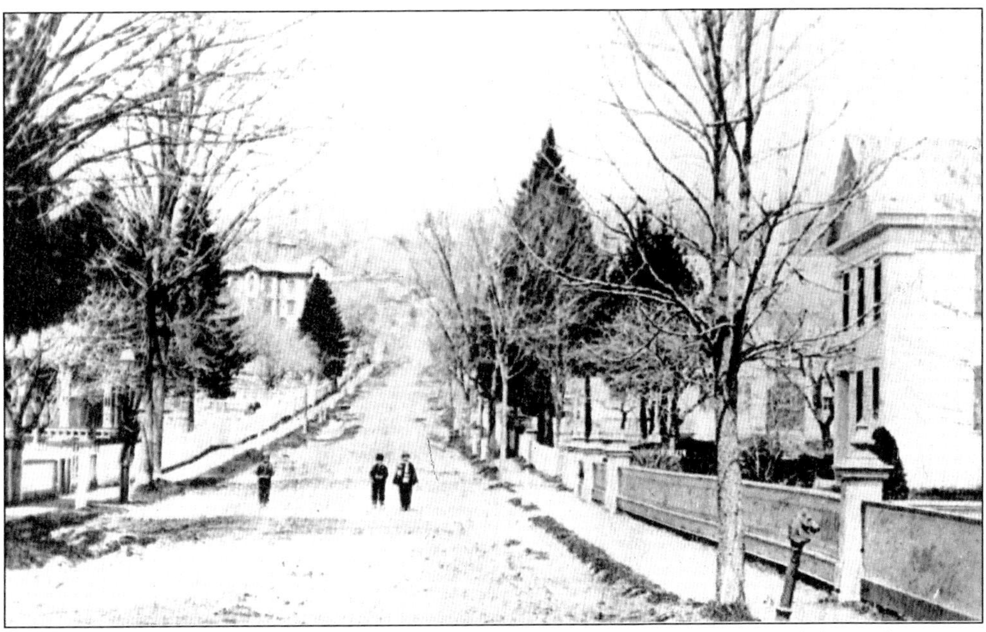

Three boys stroll down High Street *c.* 1890. Neat picket fences line one of the earlier, nicer dirt streets. Note the metal hitching post with a horse's head design. In the left background is the Academy School, which was used as a high school.

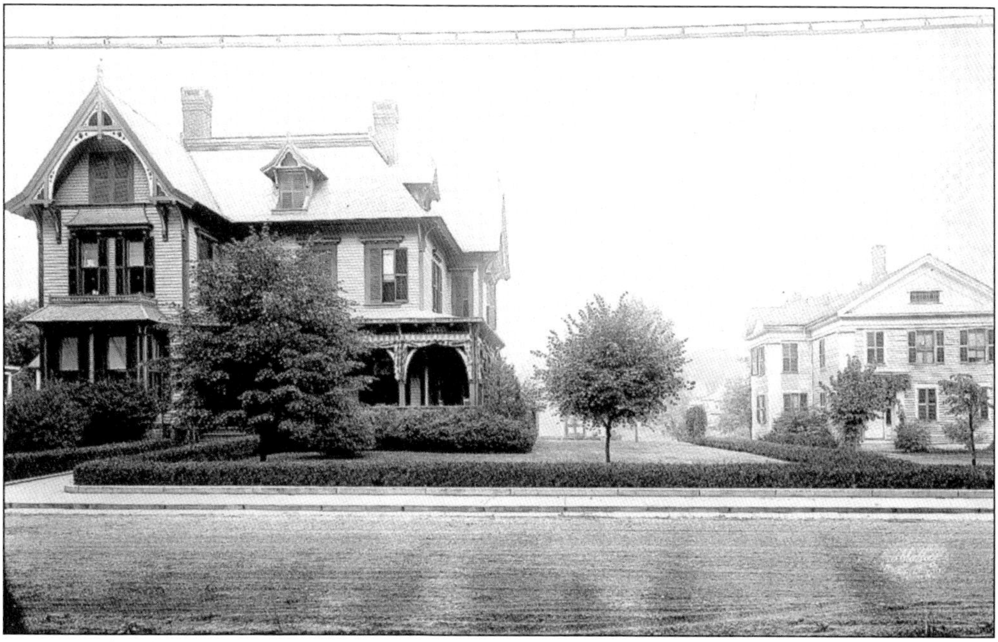

In 1905, this handsome house at 46 High Street was home to the Pierponts. Later, the Innes family lived here, and the Lyons Funeral Home occupies the house now.

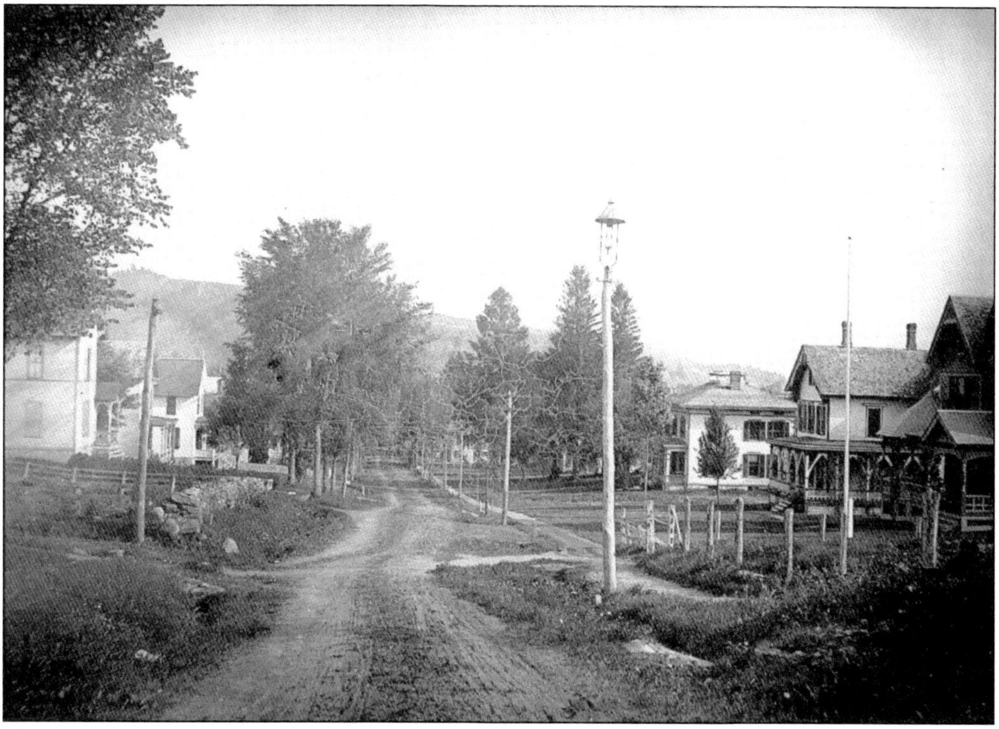

The view looking down High Street *c.* 1900 from a point near Randolph Avenue includes a utility pole in the foreground. The three houses to the right still exist, although the street is wider.

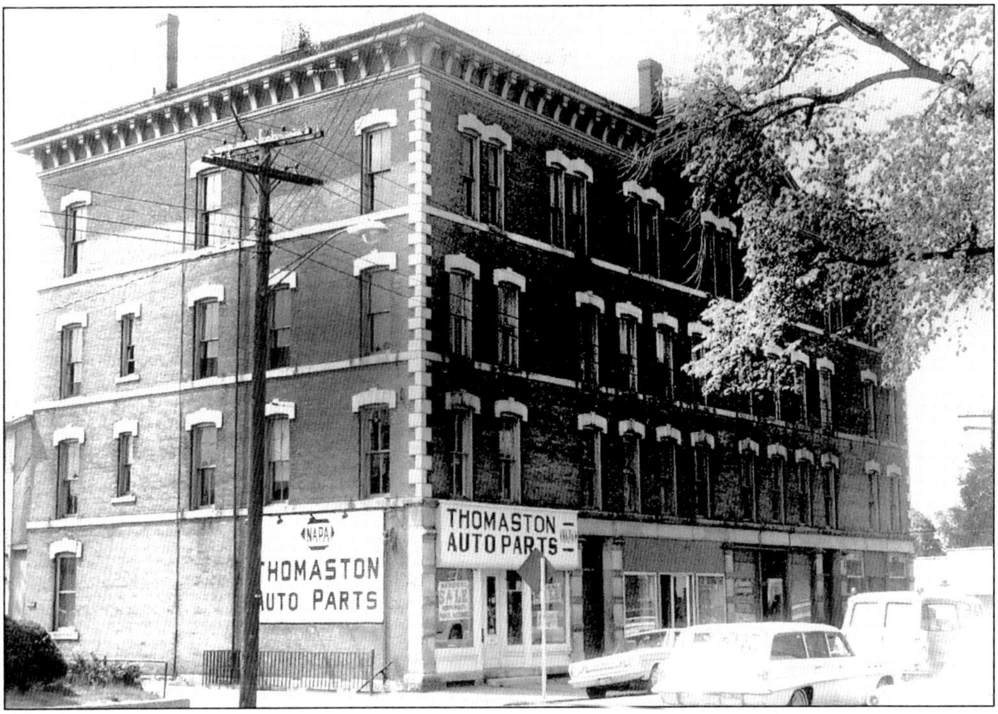

The Bradstreet Block was part of the transformation of the center area from smaller, wooden structures to larger, brick structures. Built in 1877, it had stores, offices, apartments, and a ballroom on the top floor. Pictured here *c.* 1967, the building was demolished soon after. The present occupant of the site is the Webster Bank.

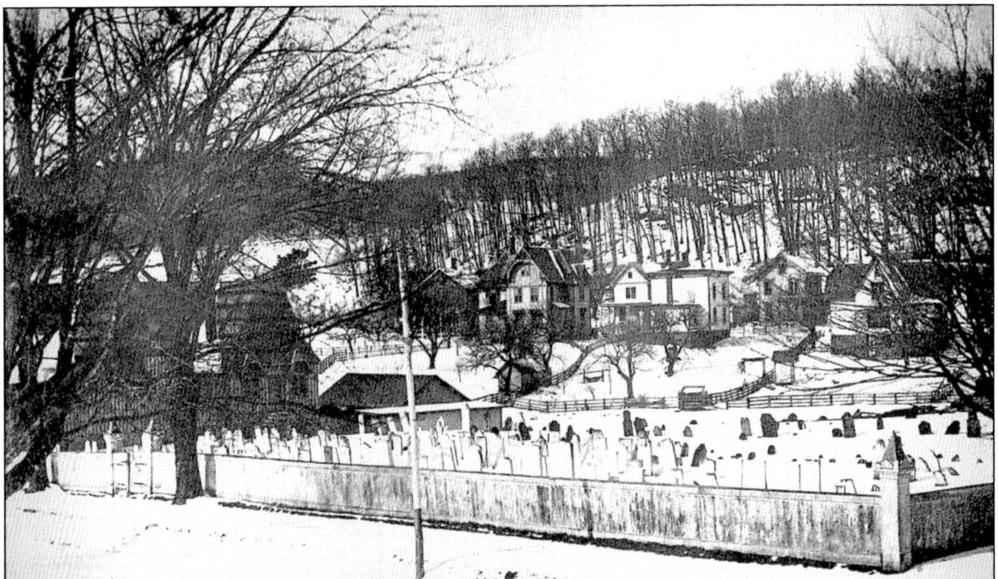

This is the unlikely site of the Thomaston Town Hall, the opera house, and the old firehouse before the Old Cemetery was removed to Hillside Cemetery. The gravestones were taken to Hillside in 1882, and the new town hall was built the next year. Trinity St. Peter's Episcopal Church is at the left; in the background are houses along Clay Street.

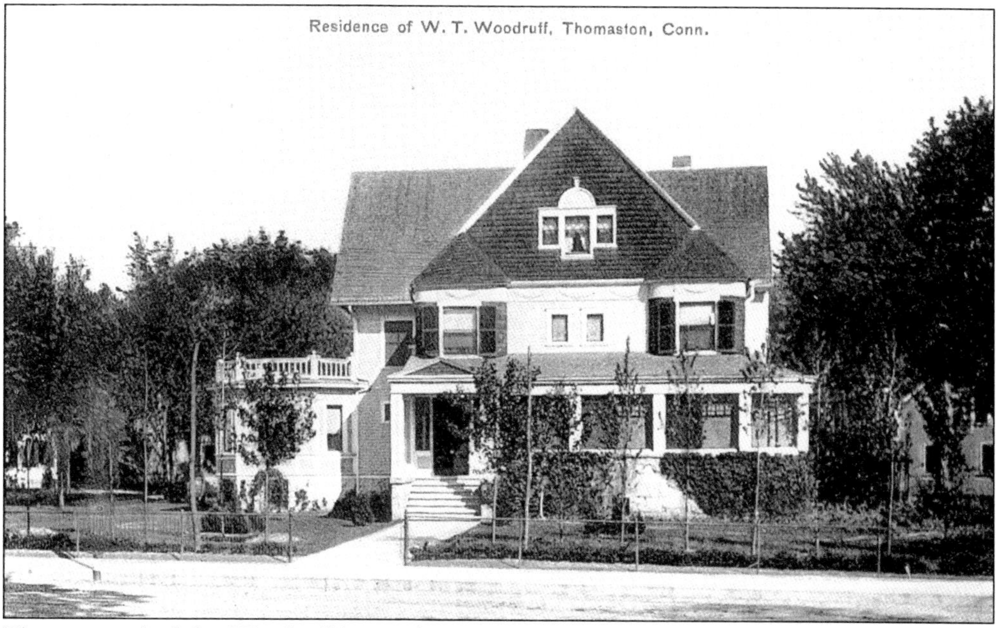

This postcard of the Woodruff house shows one of the properties across from the town hall. Dr. William T. Woodruff married Martha Thomas, a daughter of Seth Thomas. This magnificent house stood on the corner of Main and Union Streets. It was later owned by the Upsons and then demolished *c.* 1951 to make room for a number of stores. Now it is the site of Thomaston Savings Bank's main office. (Courtesy of Myron Roman.)

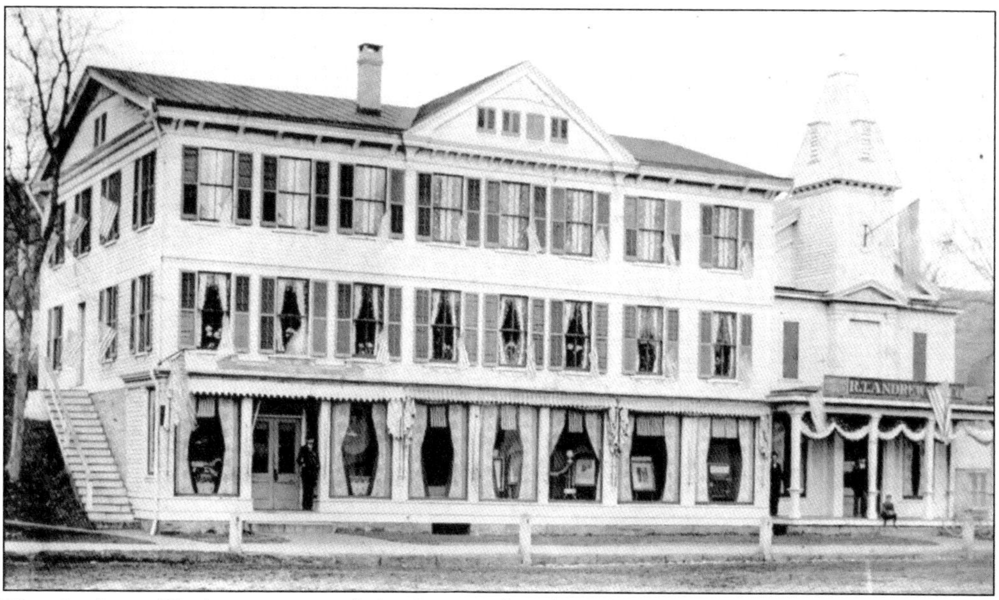

The Andrews Block incorporated the former chapel of the Trinity Episcopal Church into its design. Displaced when the Trinity Episcopal Church was built, the chapel came to rest on top of the Andrews Block next door. Situated prominently at the north end of the building, it was used as the Masonic hall for many years. Stores occupied the first floor, while the Trinity Episcopal Church used the upper level as a church hall. The picture, taken by Rice (the photographer in Thomaston), dates from *c.* 1910. The site is now occupied by the public library.

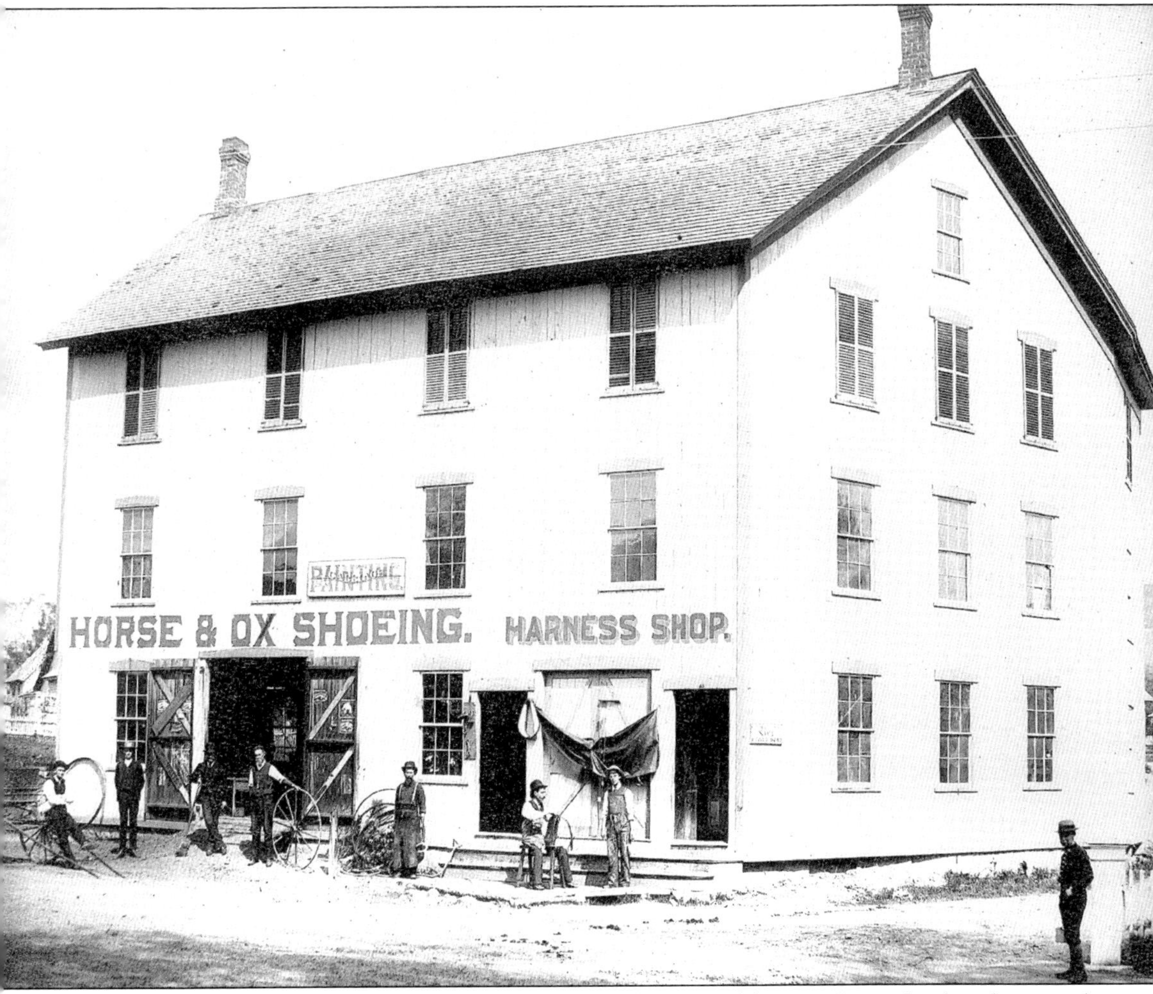

Eight men in different postures, posing with the implements of their trades, make this photograph appealing. Carriage painting, horse and ox shoeing, and harness making must have kept them busy. A wagon wheel, a horseshoe, and a horse collar are seen in this *c.* 1890 photograph of C.L. Bever's shop. Much altered, the building still stands at 13 South Main Street.

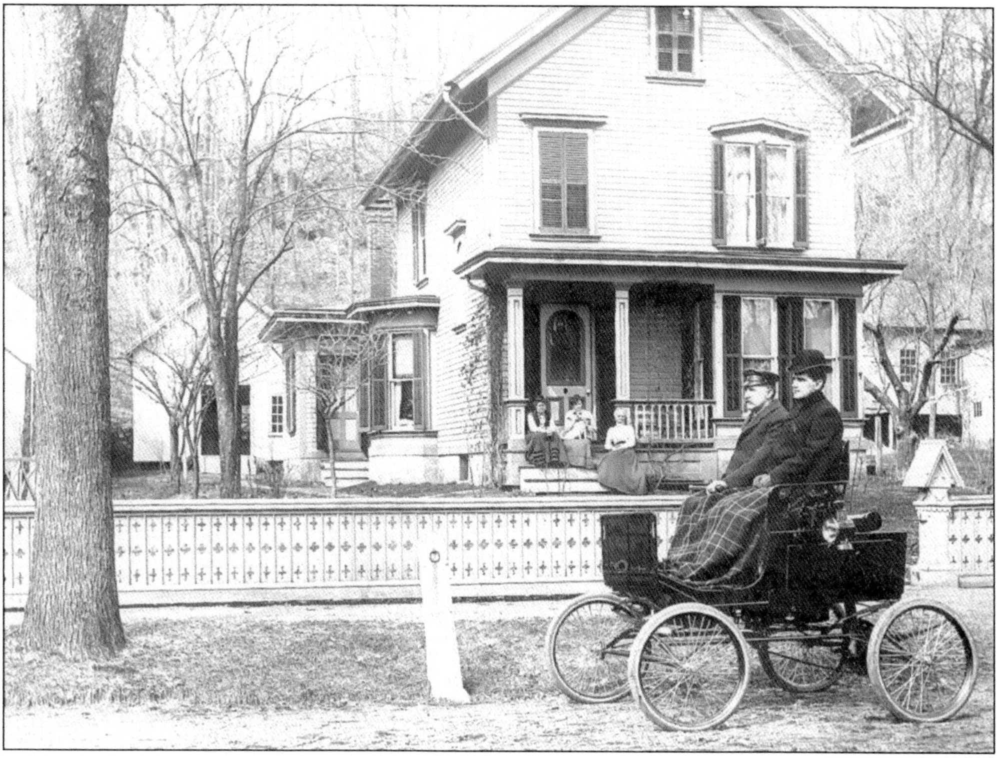

Joseph Stubbs and his son Perly sit in a locomobile steamer in 1902. The Stubbs family lived at 45–47 Grove Street, and the three female members appear on the building's steps. The locomobile was reportedly the second auto in town. Note the hitching post, soon to become obsolete, the ornate fence design, and the dog held by one of the women. Stubbs moved to Waterbury *c.* 1910.

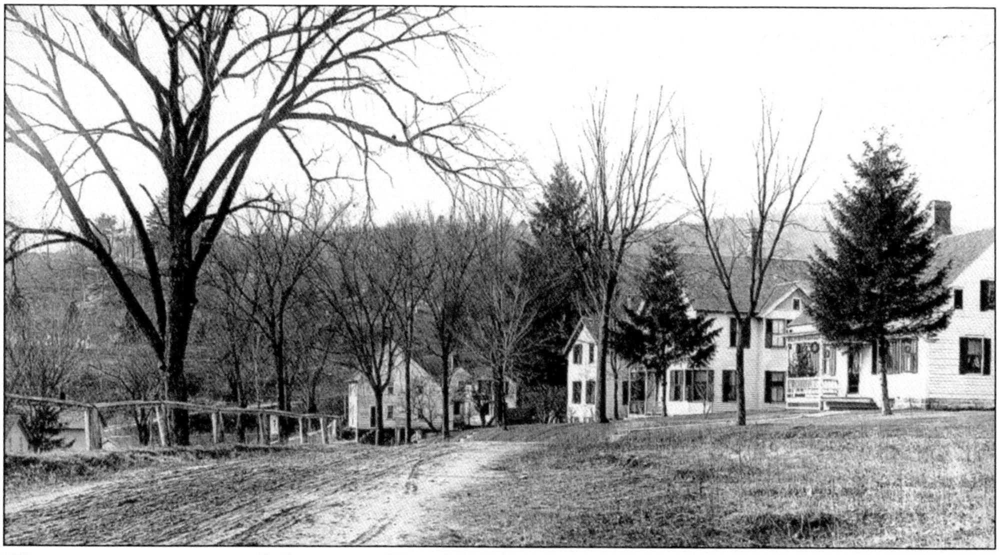

The quiet intersection of Center and Litchfield Streets is shown here. Note the frail rail fence at the left and the gravestones of the Hillside Cemetery in the background. The trees are barren, and the dirt streets are rutted. This picture was taken *c.* 1900.

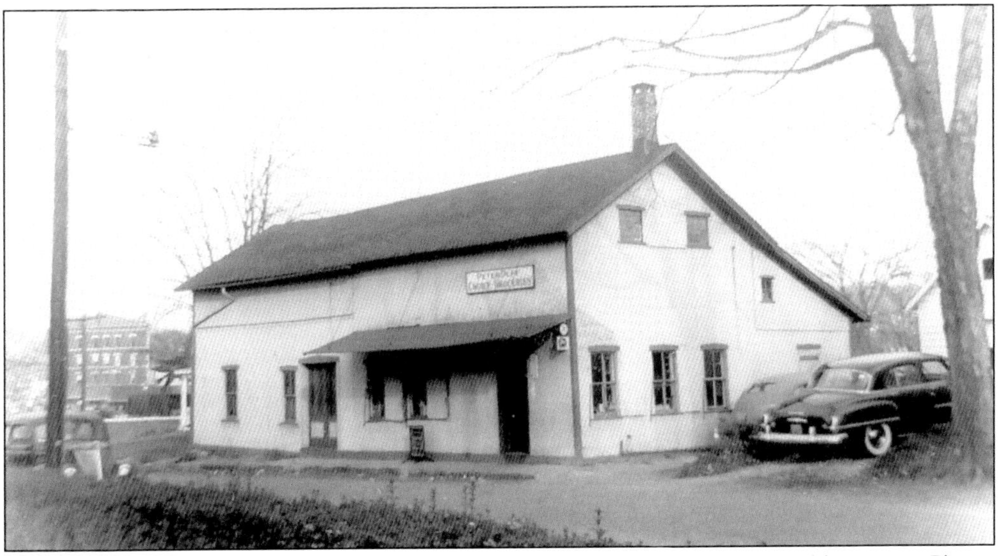

Duff's Store, seen here *c.* 1948, was located on Center Street across from Neddermann's Florist Shop. Opening *c.* 1874, it thrived for more than 70 years. It was the second building on the east side of the street. Later the home of the Knights of Columbus and still later the Veterans of Foreign Wars, it is now the site of a vending machine company.

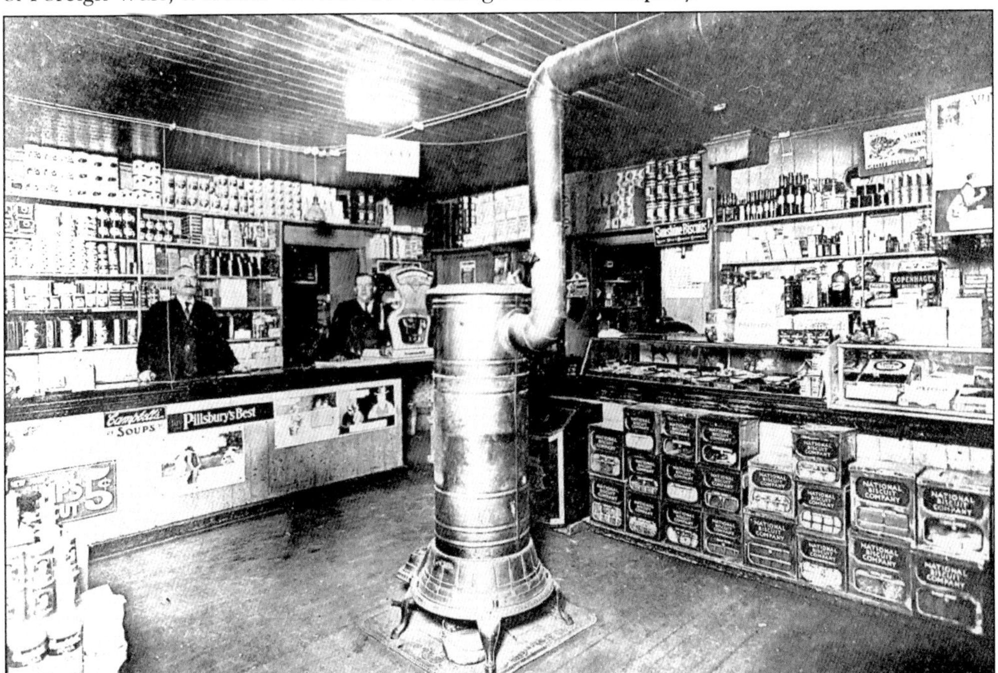

Inside the store, Peter Duff (left) awaits customers. The man at the right may be Peter's son George. The store is well stocked with a variety of goods that residents would need *c.* 1900. Among these are Pillsbury's Best, Campbell soups, potato chips, and Copenhagen chewing tobacco. Born in Scotland, Margaret Band and Peter Duff lived at 39 Grove Street. Peter (1852–1935) served on the board of selectmen from 1897 through 1909. His daughter Elizabeth (1878–1954) ran the store after her father's death.

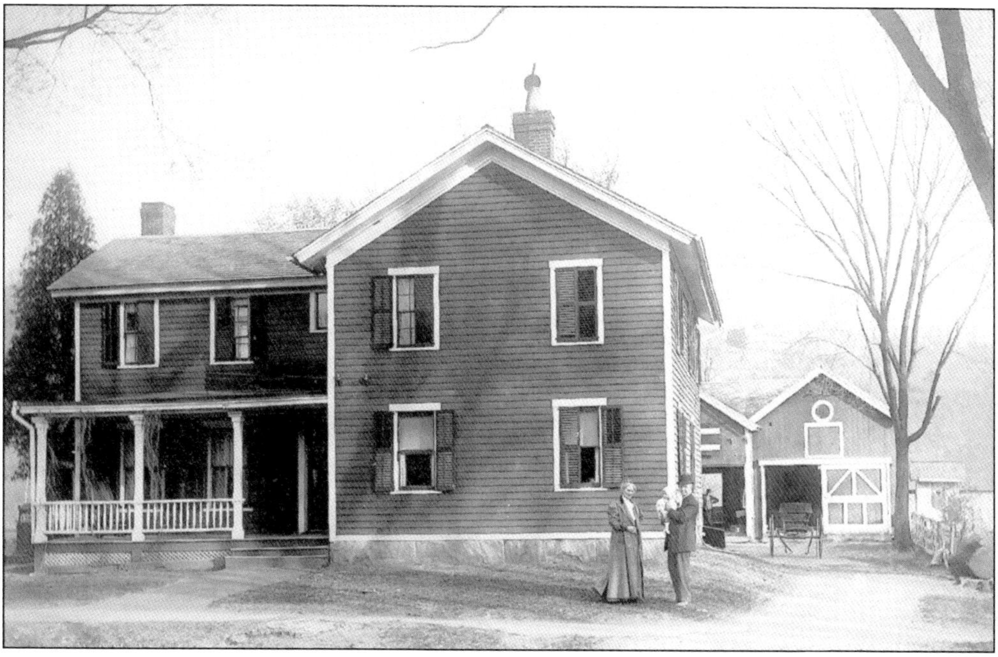

Mr. and Mrs. Edward C. Root proudly pose with an infant at their home at 80 Elm Street. A buggy and a young man are in the background of this *c.* 1900 photograph. Elm Street is dirt, and four windows are curiously half-shuttered.

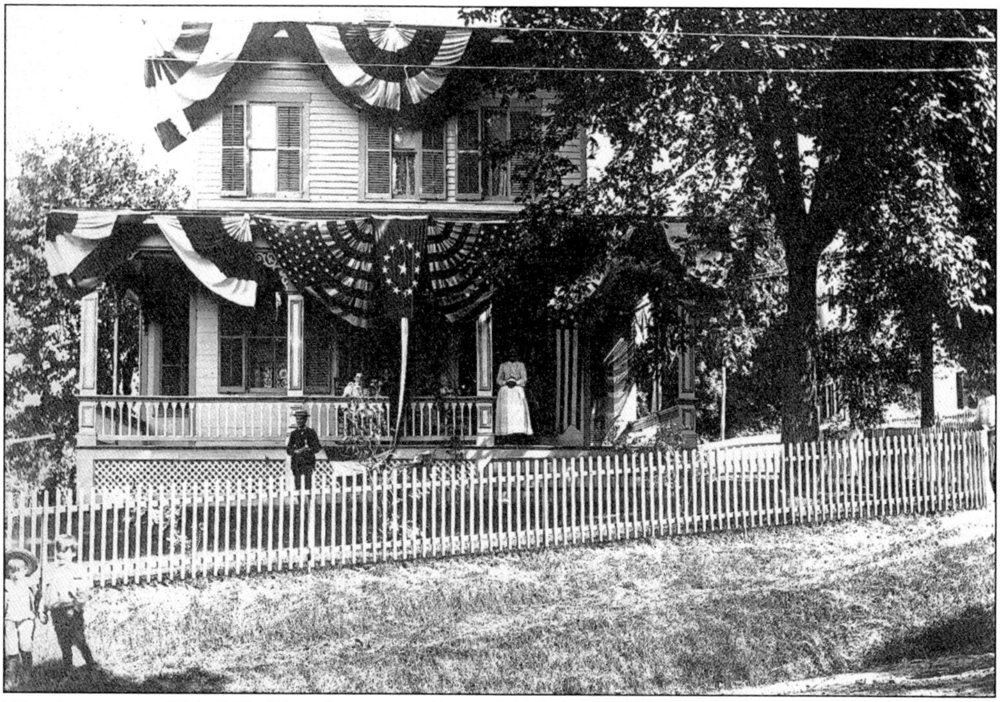

The house at 186–188 Elm Street is dressed up in patriotic bunting in this summertime photograph. The children are dressed up too in this scene at the corner of Elm and River Streets *c.* 1900.

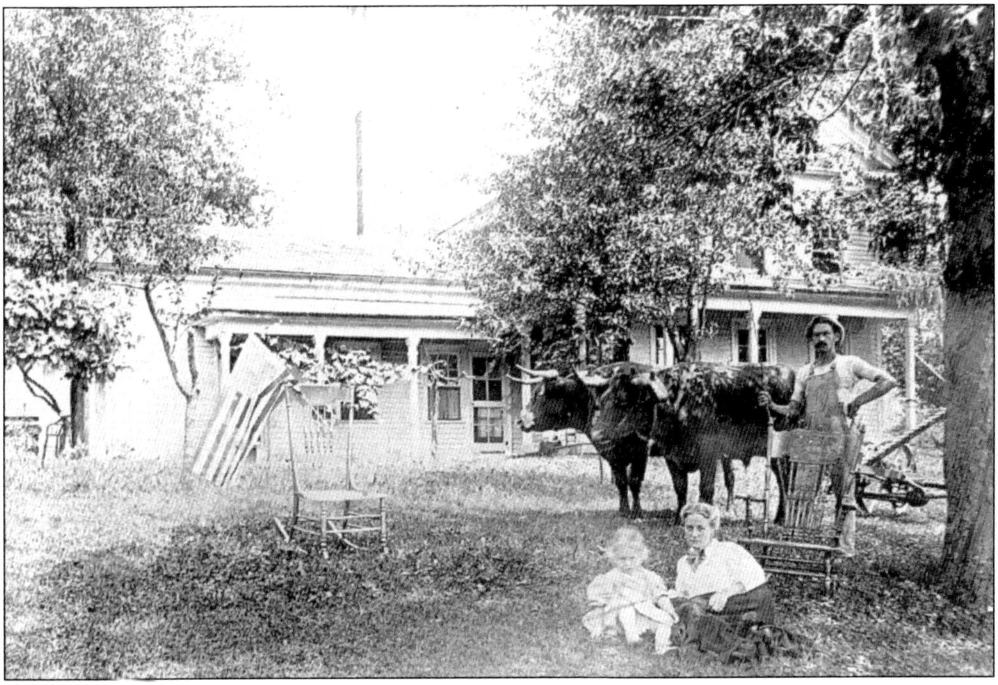

The Egbert Johnson family stands in front of the home at 882 Hickory Hill Road. The flag, rocking chair, and oxen in the front yard present an interesting scene. The house was sold in 1907 to Joseph Wassong.

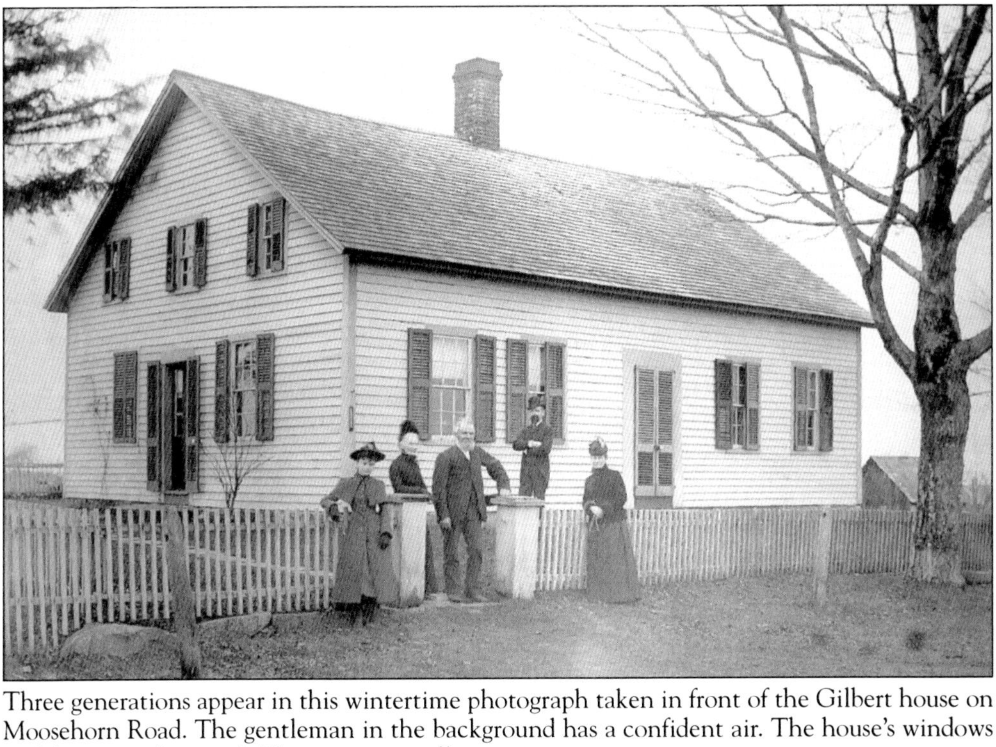

Three generations appear in this wintertime photograph taken in front of the Gilbert house on Moosehorn Road. The gentleman in the background has a confident air. The house's windows and doors are shuttered. This structure still exists.

The Victorian age ended with the death of the queen in 1901, and the Edwardian age ended with the death of Edward VII in 1910. However, there was no visible change in dress, manners, or customs until World War I. This portrait of Dr. Ralph Schuyler Goodwin is that of a very successful gentleman. Born in Morris, Connecticut, in 1839, he died in his home at 55 Elm Street in 1904.

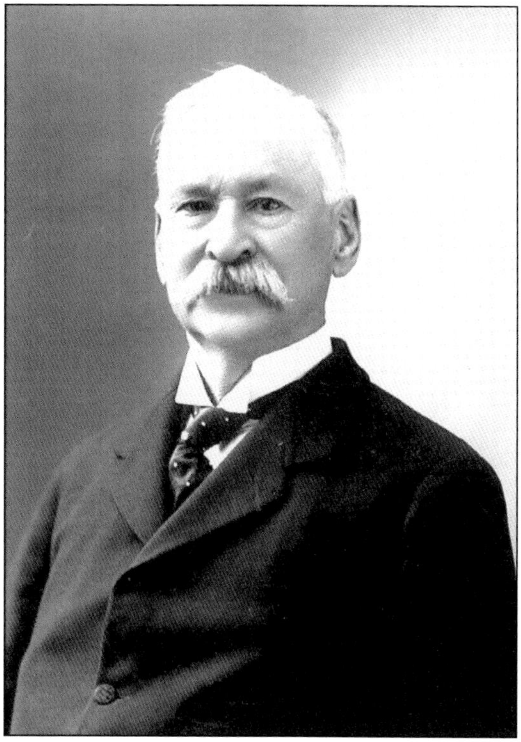

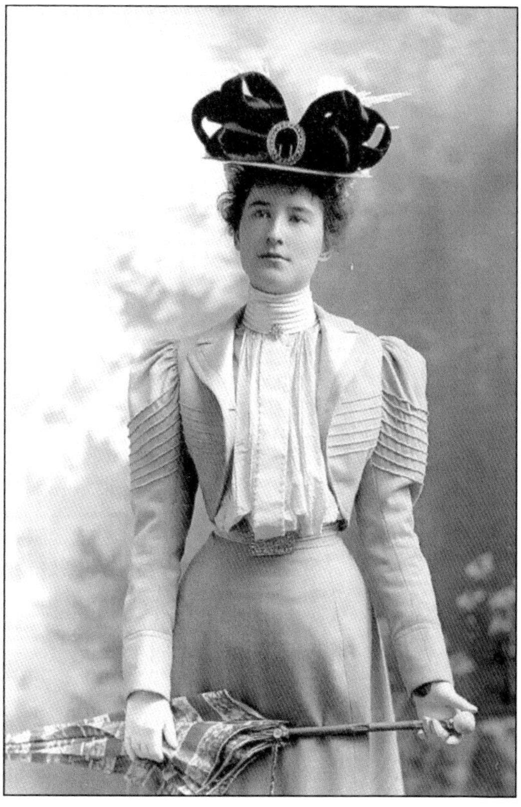

The only daughter of Dr. Ralph Goodwin and his wife, Jeanie (Irvine), Grace Goodwin was as bright as she was beautiful, graduating from Thomaston High School at 15. This c. 1895 portrait is a splendid study. In 1899, she married Francis Wolfe of Albany, New York, in a ceremony celebrated by the Reverend John Sheridan Zelie of Cleveland. A year later, she died. When Grace was buried in Hillside Cemetery, she was the first of her family to be interred in the Goodwin plot.

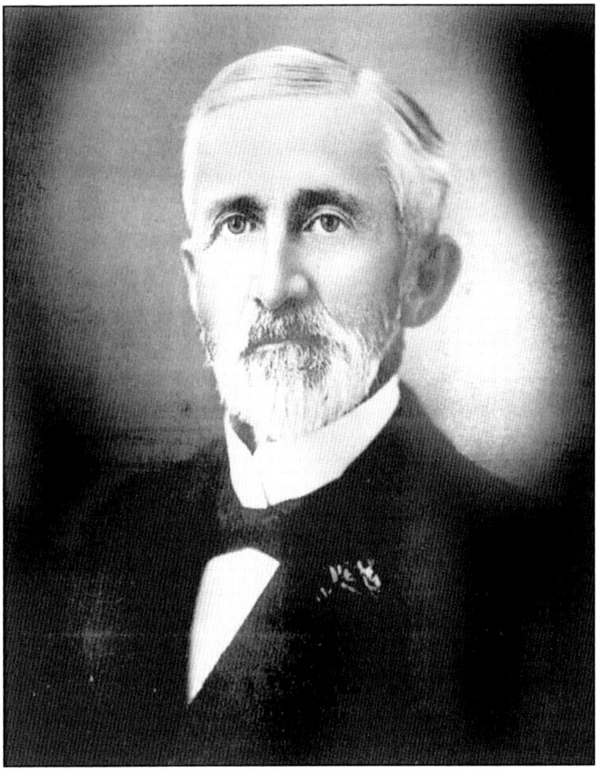

George A. Stoughton (1834–1914) was a 19th-century entrepreneur. Owner of a large store on the east side near Plume & Atwood, he was the founder of the Thomaston Savings Bank. The first deposit was made in his store in September 1874. The bank is the oldest Thomaston business in continuous service. He and his wife, Mary A. Hemingway (1837–1921), are buried in Plymouth's West Cemetery.

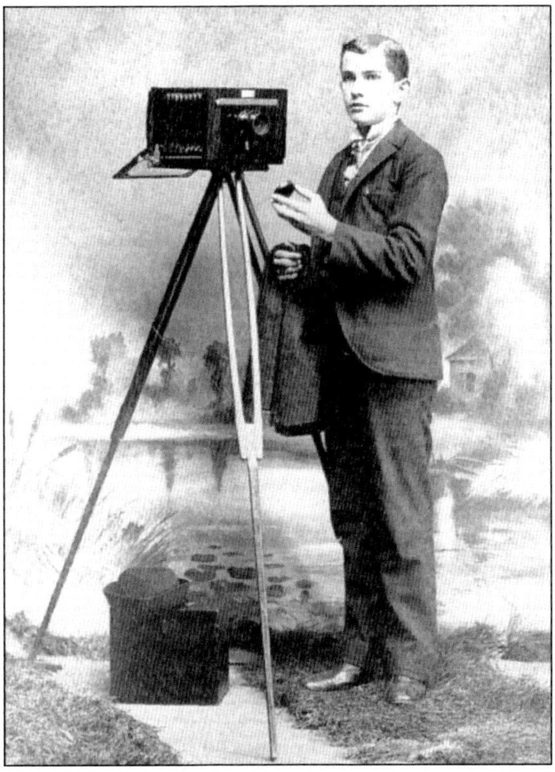

This studio photograph was taken by Allderige of Thomaston in 1888. The address of the studio was "near depot." This handsome young man is Perly J. Stubbs, whom we saw on page 23. His interest in photography is evident in the pose, as he holds a lens cap in his hand, his hat at his feet.

Teresa Tucker (Johnson), at the left, is joined by two females who are reportedly her sisters. This well-dressed trio had their photograph taken at Farrell Brothers in Waterbury.

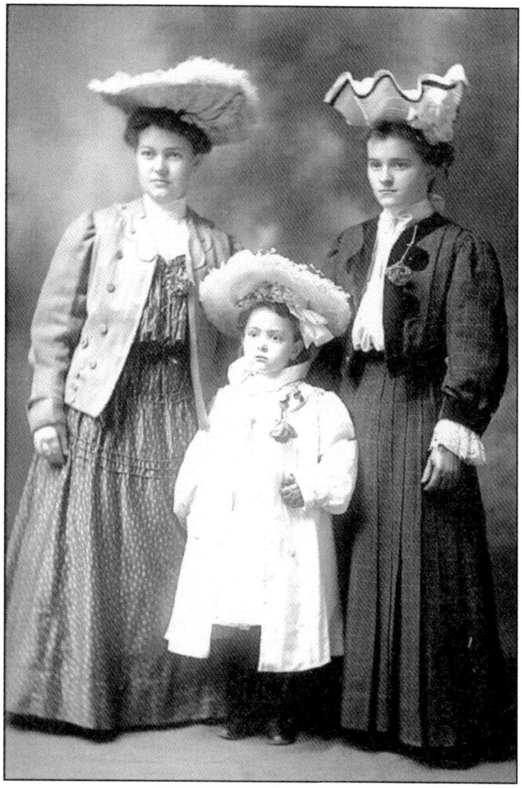

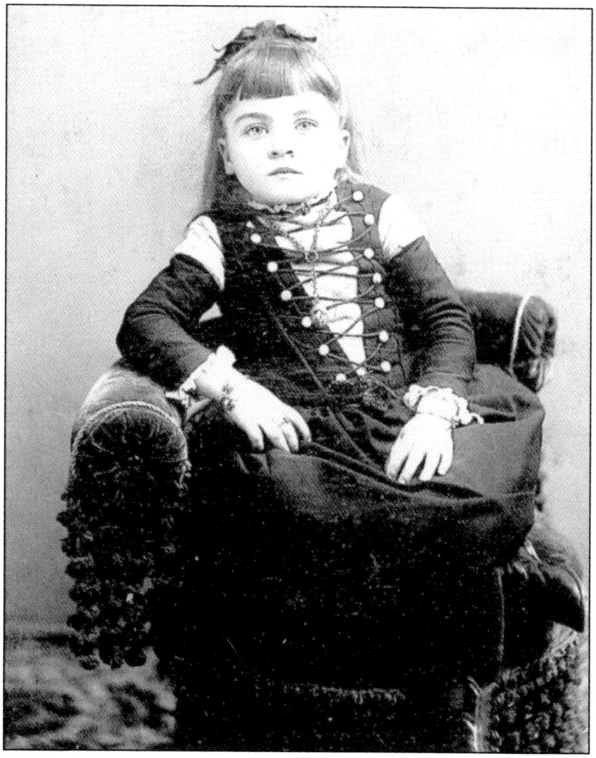

The charming child's high-button shoes and the stuffed velvet chair help to date this picture at c. 1885. Jennie Dick's casual pose, serious manner, and abundant jewelry add to the quality of the photograph by W.F. Page of Thomaston. Jennie Dick was Rosa Gangloff's second-grade teacher at the Center School in 1905.

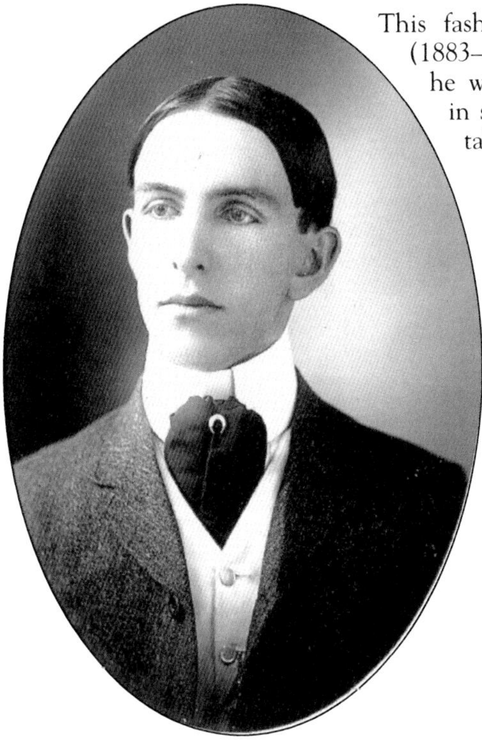

This fashionable young man is John "Jack" Waters (1883–1963). A longtime employee of Seth Thomas, he was well known in Thomaston for his interest in sports and entertainment. The photograph was taken *c.* 1904.

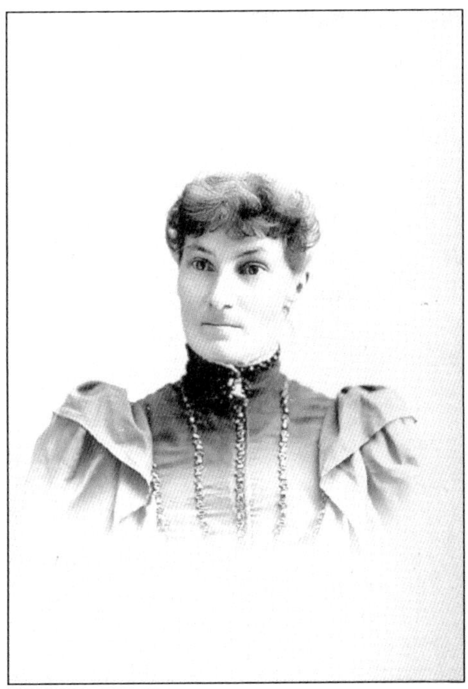

This marvelous image of an unidentified well-dressed Victorian woman was done by the White Photography Company of Thomaston.

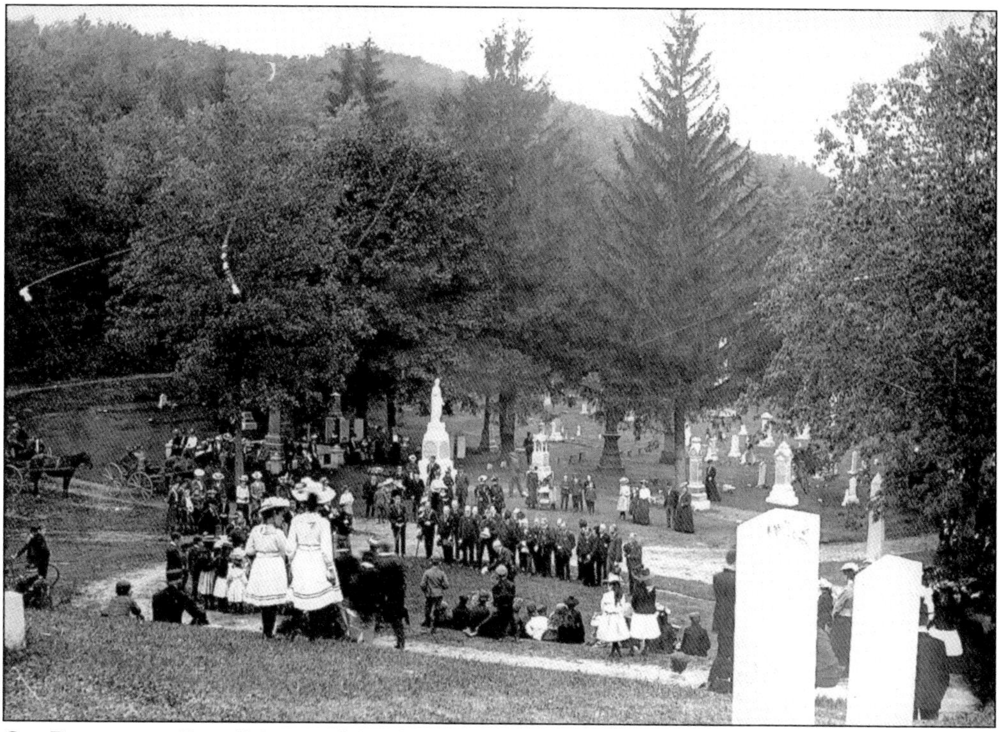

On Decoration Day (Memorial Day) in 1902, residents gathered at Hillside Cemetery to observe and remember. They came in their Sunday best, the men standing bareheaded in honor of those who had given the last full measure of devotion.

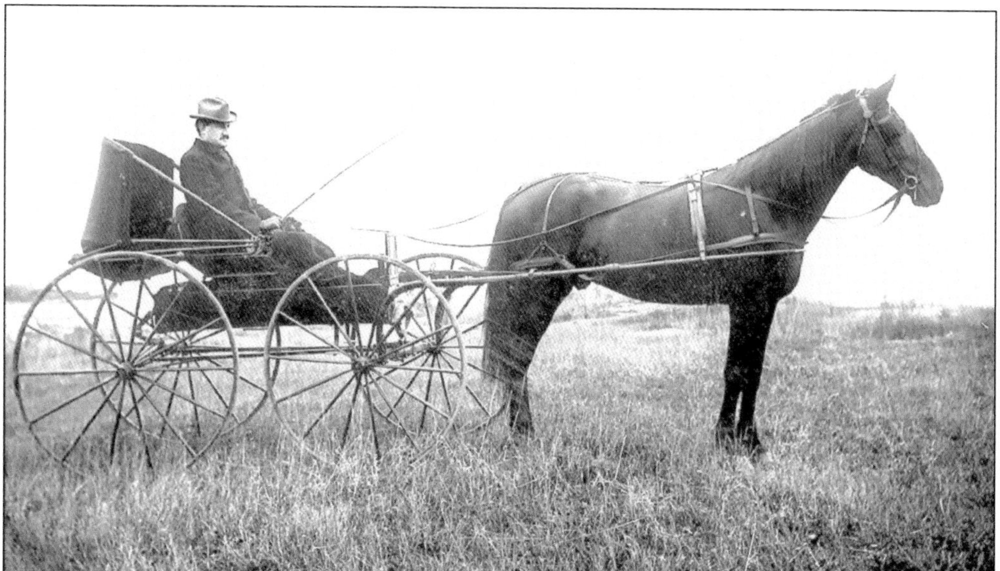

The second Dr. Goodwin was Ralph Schuyler Goodwin Jr. (1868–1924). He sold the large house at 55 Elm Street to Dr. Winfield E. Wight. In this rather stark c. 1906 photograph, we see the doctor bundled up in blanket and gloves, outlined against a bleak landscape.

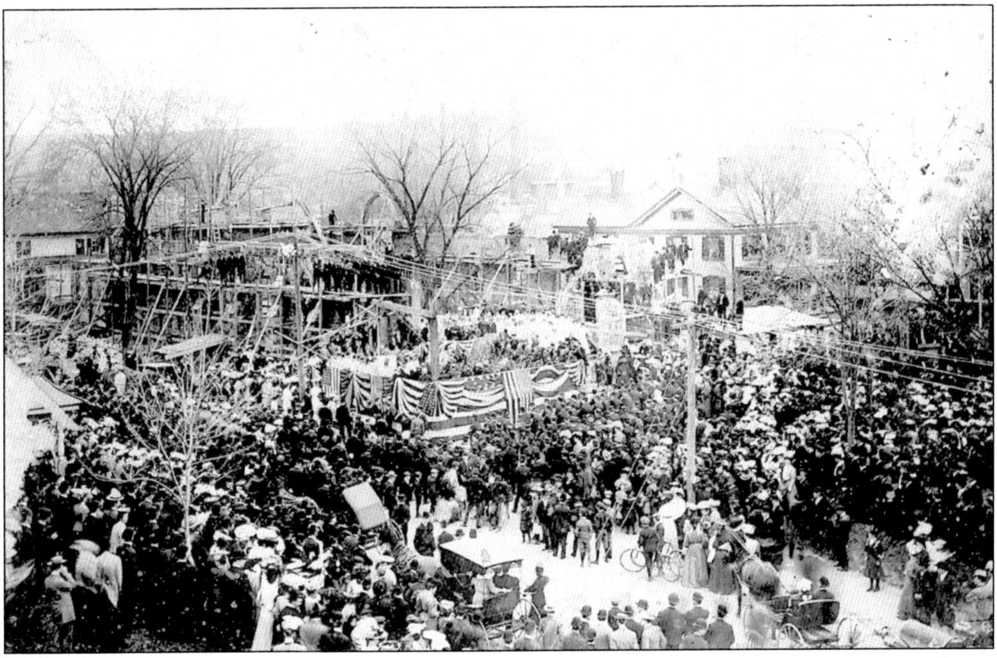

This day in 1906 was glorious for the town's Roman Catholics. The ceremony to celebrate the laying of the cornerstone for their new St. Thomas Church was attended by hundreds of well-dressed people. The women's hats are the most striking feature. Buggies and bicycles brought the crowd. The houses in the photograph have since disappeared, but the church still stands.

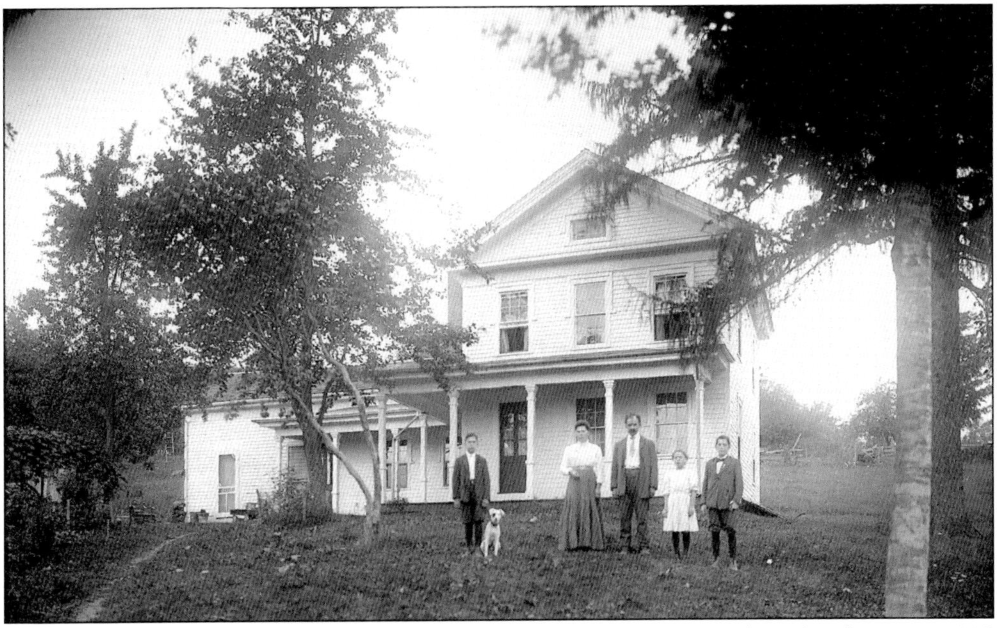

In 1907, Joseph and Mary Wassong and their family moved into their farmhouse, at 882 Hickory Hill Road. Here we see them in their Sunday best on a warm summer's day. The Wassongs are, from left to right, Joseph Jr. (1896–1973), Mary (Gangloff) (1874–1956), Joseph (1866–1942), Mary (Adam) (1899–1981), and Louis (1898–1963). They owned this property for 37 years.

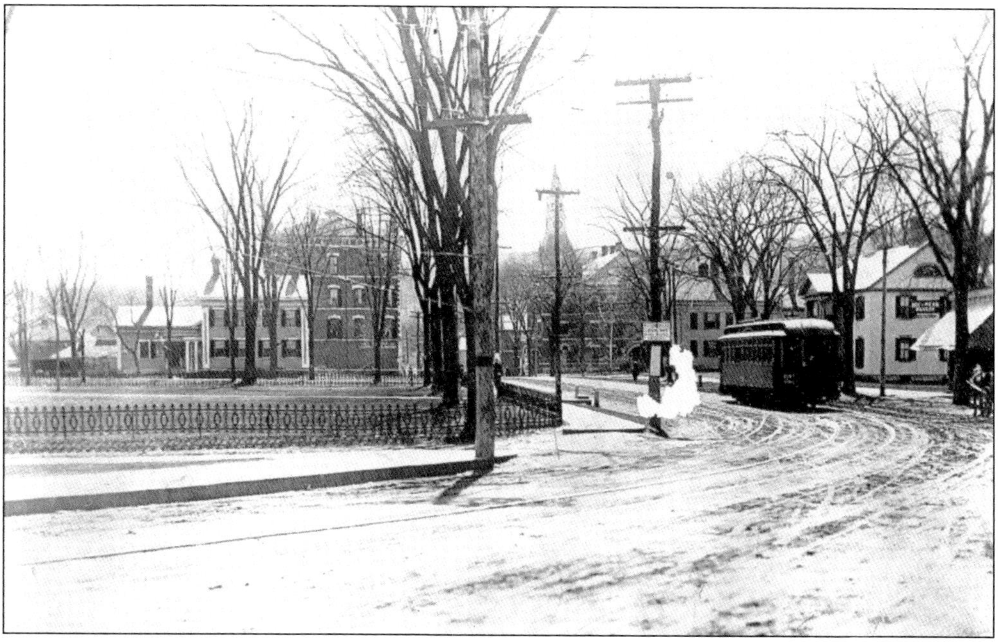

The trolley came to town in 1908. The greater mobility that it brought was welcome. The days of the horse and wagon, pictured at the right, were numbered. Here, the trolley car heads south on Main Street past an ice-cream parlor. The house on the right was owned by Seth Thomas Jr., currently the site of the Country Grocer. The house to the south was the Seth Thomas house, now the post office. Opposite the Seth Thomas house was the Bradstreet Block.

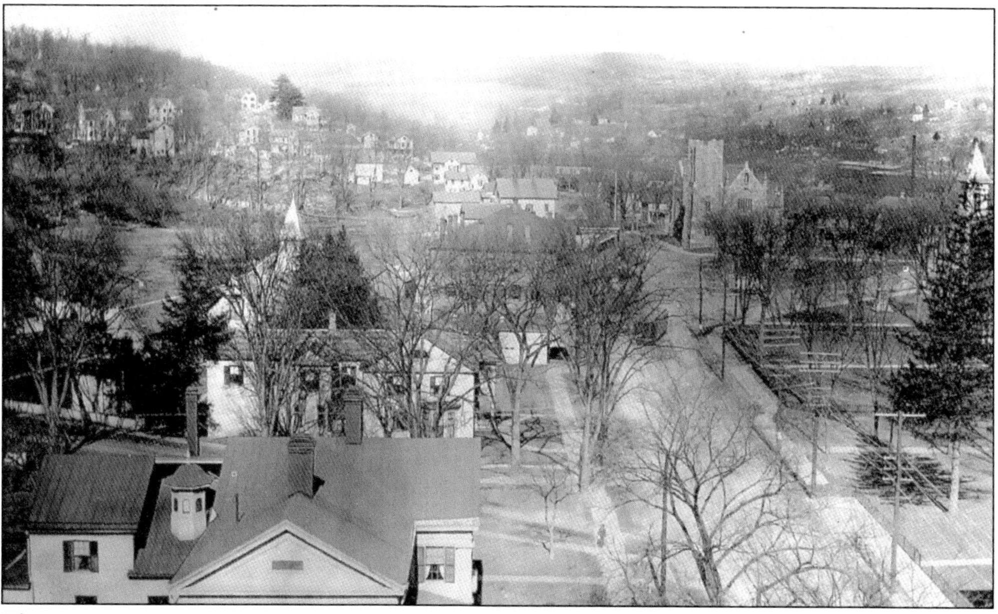

This *c.* 1909 view points north from the top of the opera house, above the clock. We see the Seth Thomas house in the left foreground (now the site of the post office and Thomaston Savings Bank), the Seth Thomas Jr. house just beyond (now the Country Grocer), and across on the east side of Main Street, the Morse-Etheridge house and the Canfield house. To make it more interesting, a trolley car is turning into the scene.

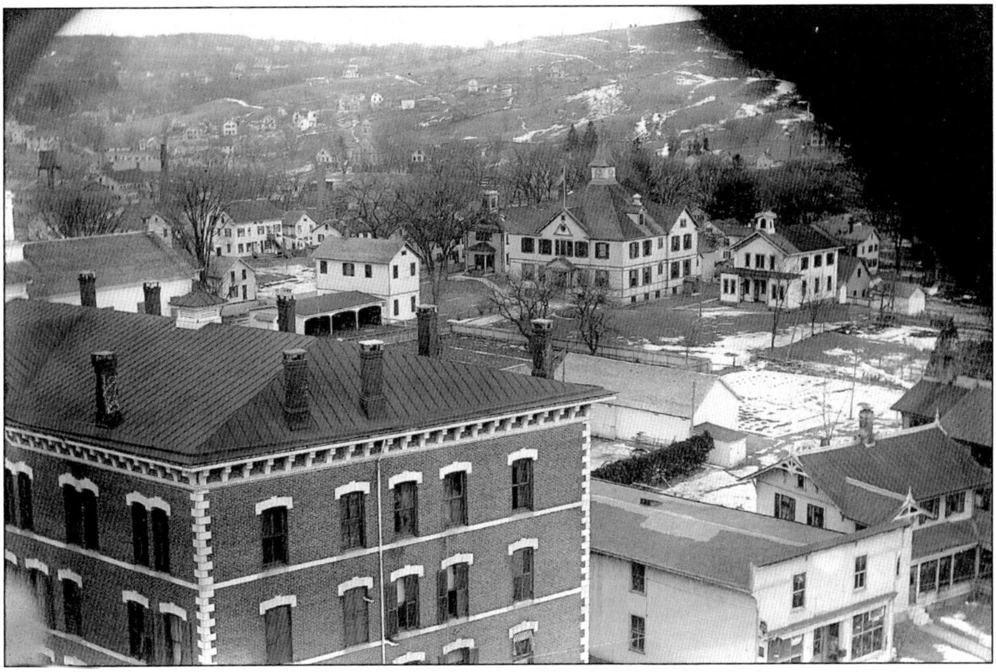

From the same location as the previous image, the photographer now looks east. The Bradstreet Block is easily identified, but in the background is the former St. Thomas Church building. The three schools (now the site of Green Manor) stand out, and in the right foreground, the former Great Atlantic & Pacific Tea Company (A & P) and Stephen's Markets and the Harkness House have all been demolished for the construction of the Colonial Bank and Trust (now the Webster Bank).

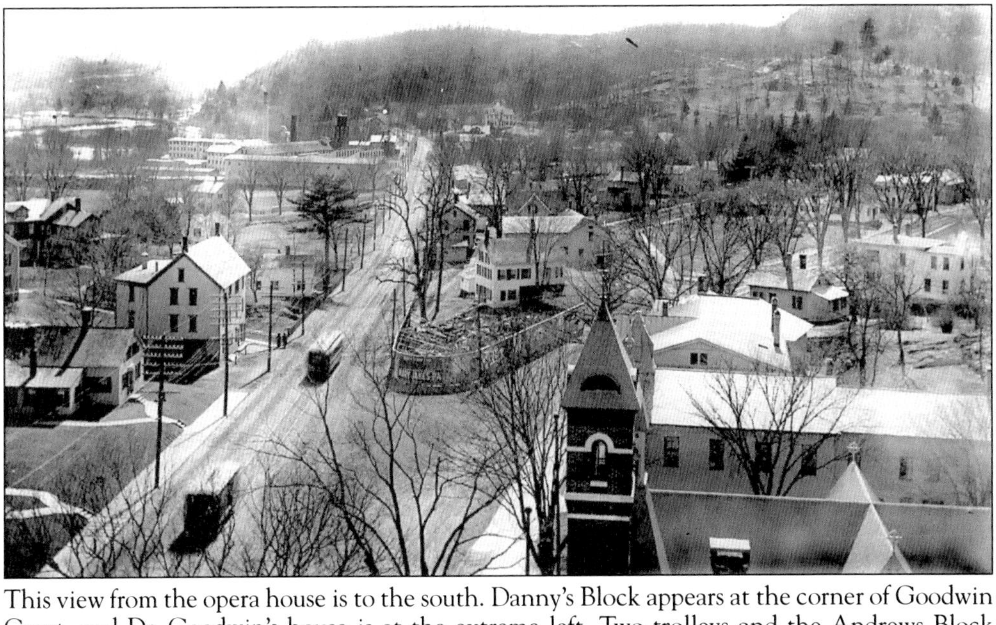

This view from the opera house is to the south. Danny's Block appears at the corner of Goodwin Court, and Dr. Goodwin's house is at the extreme left. Two trolleys and the Andrews Block almost complete the scene. Unfortunately, the trash hidden behind the billboards is visible to the camera.

Two

An Economic Dynamo

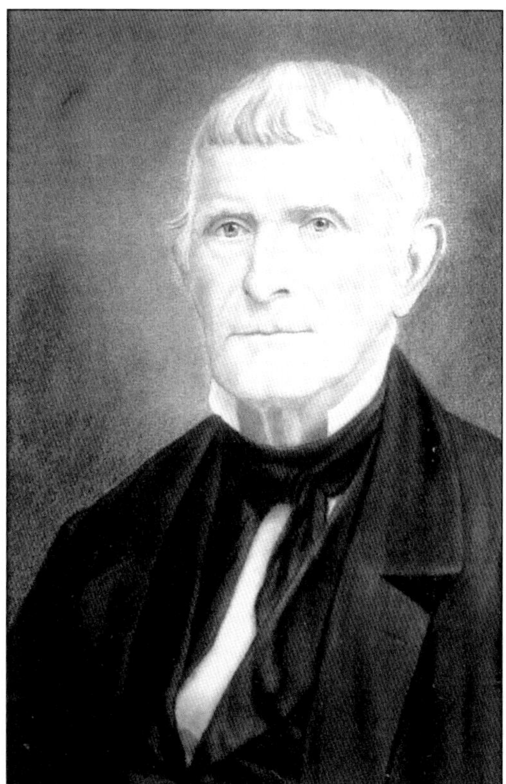

This portrait of Seth Thomas, the founder of the clock company that bears his name, is evidently the only image of the man. Born in Wolcott in 1785, he worked for Eli Terry as a young man. A joiner by trade, Thomas saw an opportunity to go into business for himself, so he bought a factory from Heman Clark in Plymouth Hollow in 1813. Who would have imagined that the company would become internationally known and would last for 188 years?

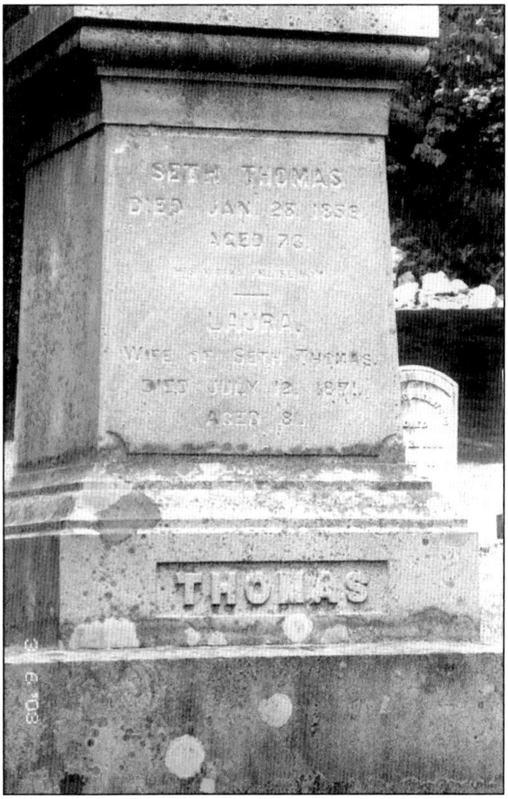

Seth Thomas died on January 28, 1859, seven months before his 74th birthday. Shown here is his monument in Hillside Cemetery. He had much to be proud of—a growing business, a family, and a town that had grown up around his company and that would soon bear his name. By an act of the General Assembly, Thomaston was created in 1875.

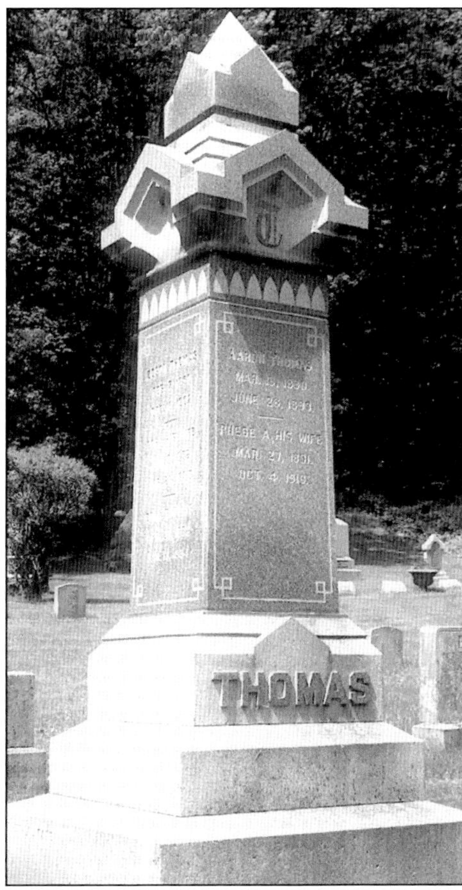

Aaron Thomas (1830–1899), whose grave site in Hillside Cemetery we see here, inherited much of his father's sense of vision. A man of great civic pride, he was active in business and political affairs throughout his adult life, dying as Thomaston's first selectman, a post he held for 13 years. He was the last surviving child of the founder.

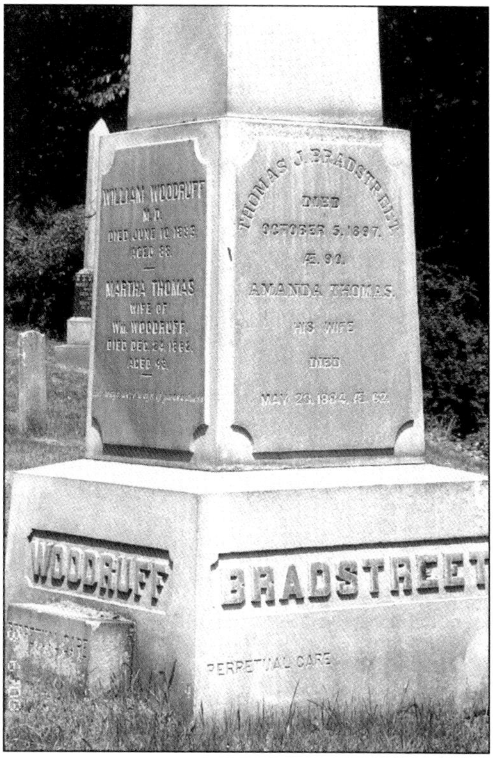

Two of the founder's daughters are buried beneath this monument in Hillside Cemetery. Martha (1819–1862) had married Dr. William Woodruff (*c.* 1804–1893) and Amanda (*c.* 1822–1884) had married Thomas Jefferson Bradstreet (*c.* 1807–1897). Other family members' graves are nearby. Woodruff and Bradstreet Avenues, named for these men, serve as reminders of their former prominence.

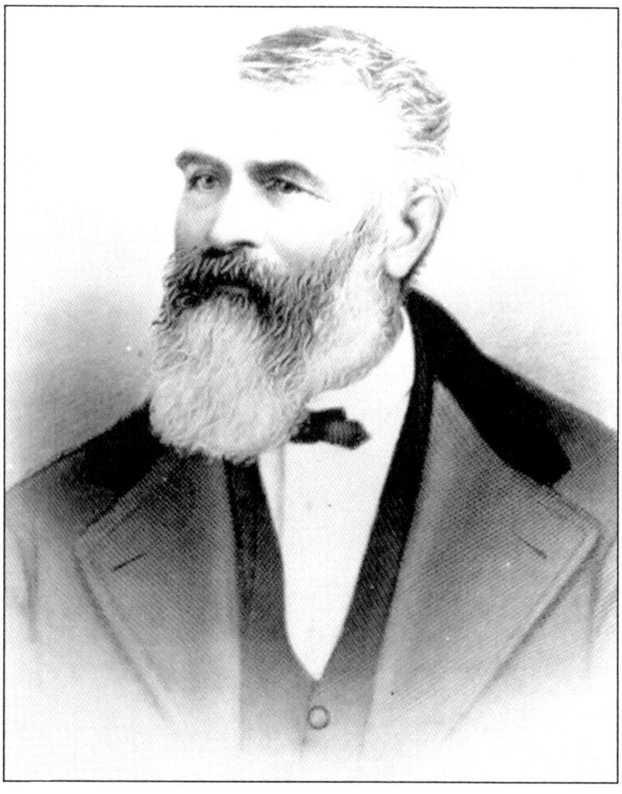

The eldest son of Seth Thomas bore the same biblical names. Born on New Year's Eve in 1816, Seth Jr. was active in the family business, as well as public affairs in Thomaston. He lived in a fine house on Main Street. The notorious blizzard struck New England in March 1888; Seth Jr. died a month later.

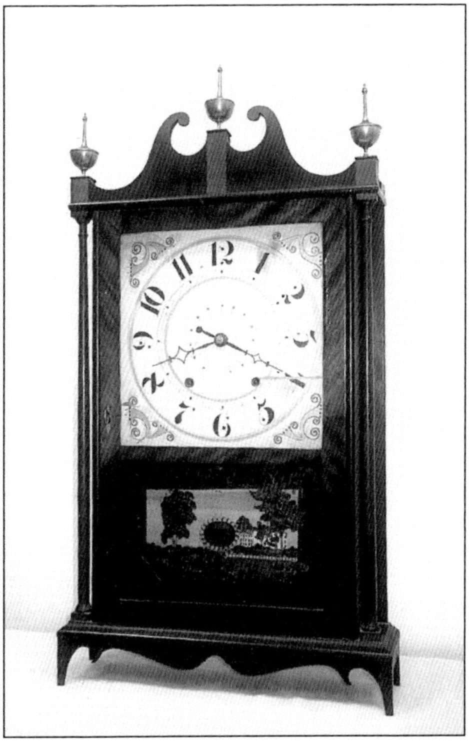

The earliest type of shelf clock was this pillar and scroll. Named for the pillars at both sides and the ornate scrollwork at the top, this fine example was made in the original factory on South Main Street *c.* 1825. The hands, face, glass, and tablet are original, and it is still in working order. The clock is in the collection of the Thomaston Historical Society.

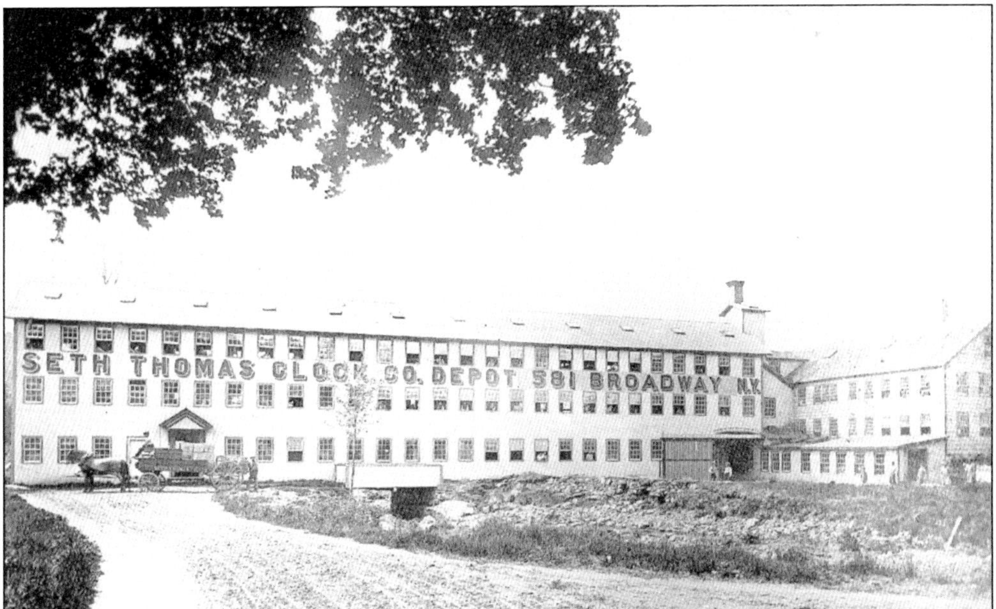

Seen at the right is the original factory building that Seth Thomas bought from Heman Clark. It is the smaller of the two and forms an L shape. The long building parallels South Main Street. The wagon at the left bears the name Seth Thomas, while the sign over the entry at the right warns that "smoking on these premises [is] prohibited." The clock company had an office on Broadway for sales and distribution. The brook in the center of the photograph flows from Northfield, under Route 254 and past the Pizza Pal, before emptying in the Naugatuck.

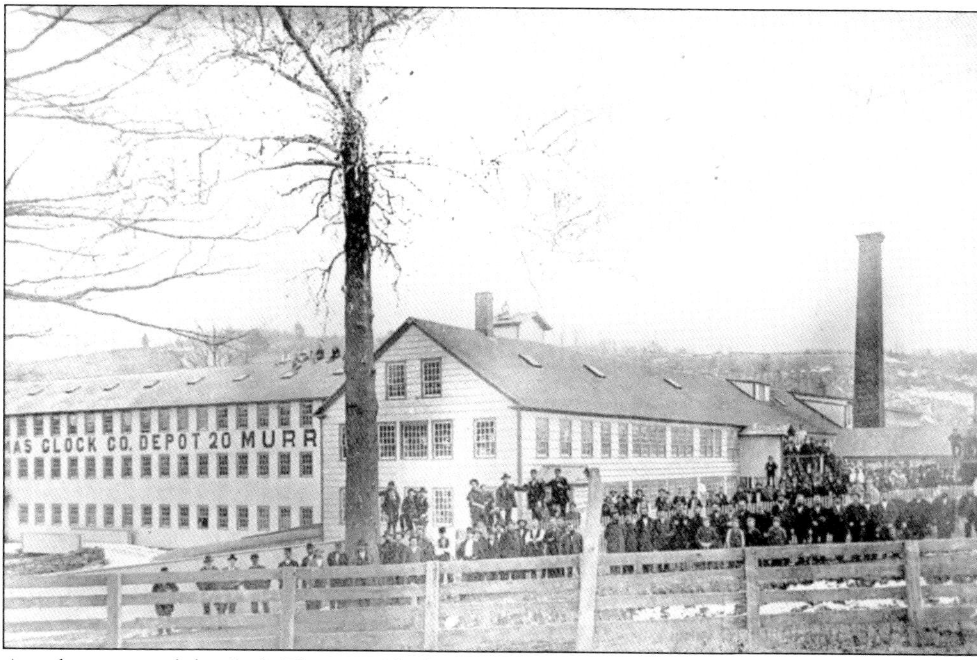

Another view of the Seth Thomas Clock buildings shows the original Heman Clark building on the right, while the New York City address has changed. These buildings housed the case shop. Note the men on the roof for the picture taking.

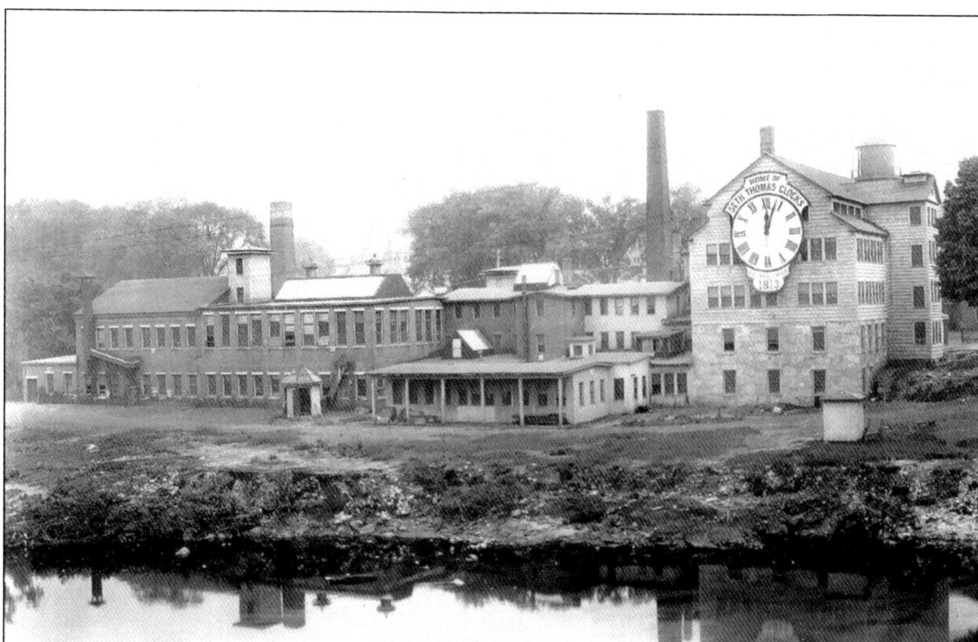

In 1834, Seth Thomas built this new plant on the corner of Elm and Main Streets. It was used as a cotton mill, the movement shop, and the tower clock factory. The Naugatuck River is in the foreground. Seth Thomas tower clocks were sold worldwide. The company made the Centennial Tower Clock for Independence Hall in Philadelphia in 1875.

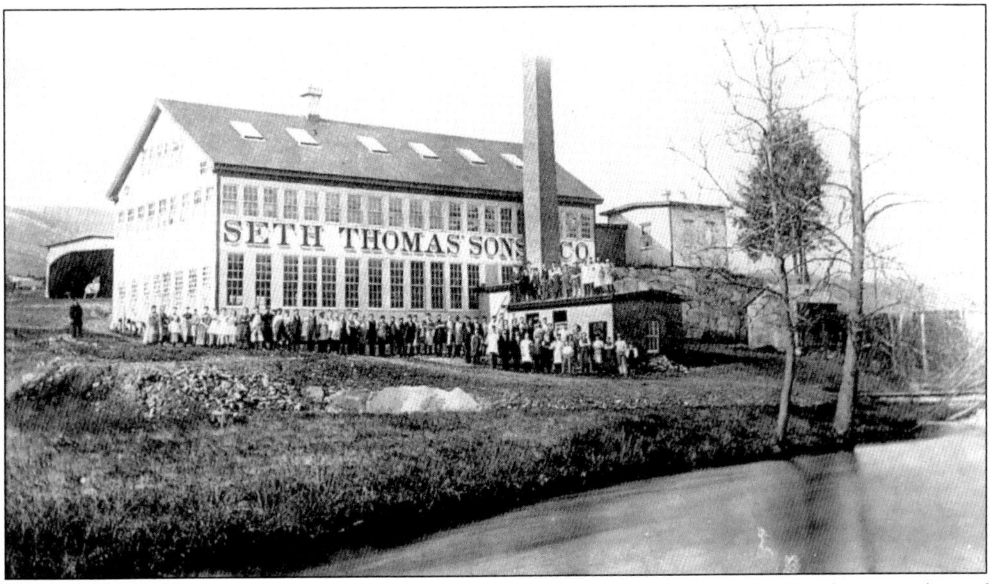

As the company grew, a sawmill owned by Aaron Thomas was added to the complex of buildings. It was modified and became the company's marine shop. The corporate name of Seth Thomas' Sons & Company was the legal name for the period from 1864 to 1879. Northfield Brook is in the right foreground.

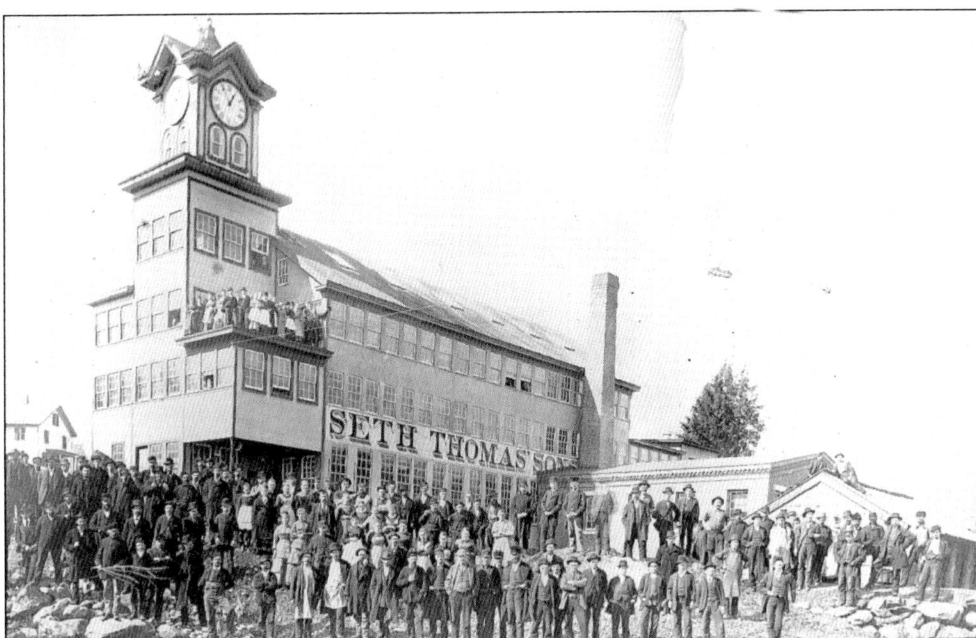

Seth Thomas' Sons & Company added a tower to the east end of the building. Enthusiastic employees climbed onto roofs and looked out of windows for this photograph. In the post–Civil War period, many male employees sported facial hair. No president before Lincoln had a beard or moustache; all of his successors except Andrew Johnson and William McKinley, until the inauguration of Woodrow Wilson in 1913, had a beard, extraordinary sideburns, or a moustache.

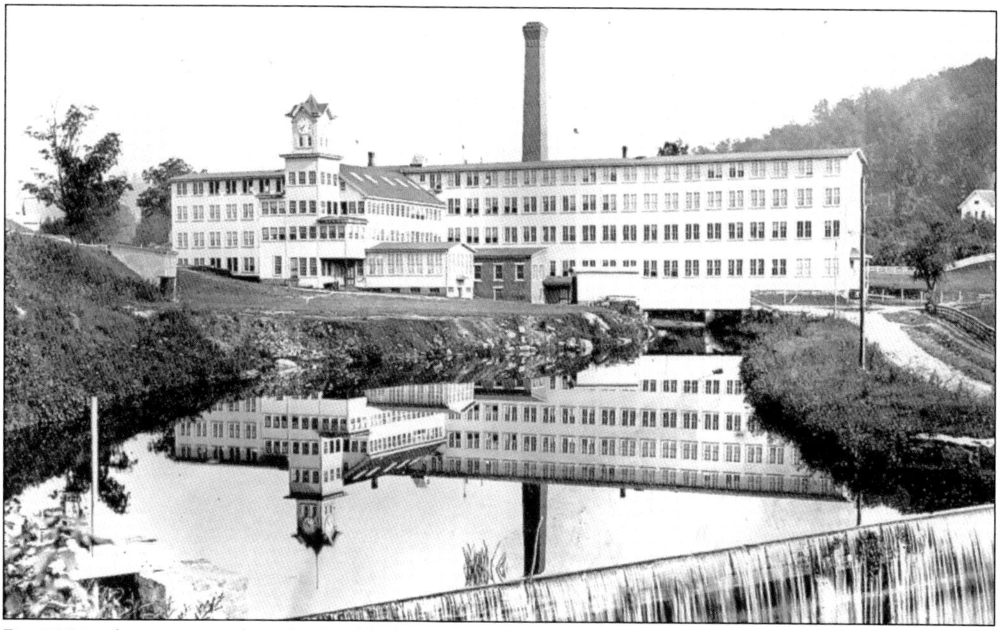

By 1884, the marine shop had added north and south wings and was manufacturing watches too. It was called the marine shop because the movements were spring-driven and could withstand the roll and pitch of a ship, unlike a pendulum. The similarity between movements for ships and for watches led to the company's combining the operations at the Marine Street location. Watches were made by Seth Thomas in this division from 1884 to 1914. At present, Route 254 is located where the brook flows. Hillside Cemetery is beyond the picture at the left, and Marine Street is in the left background.

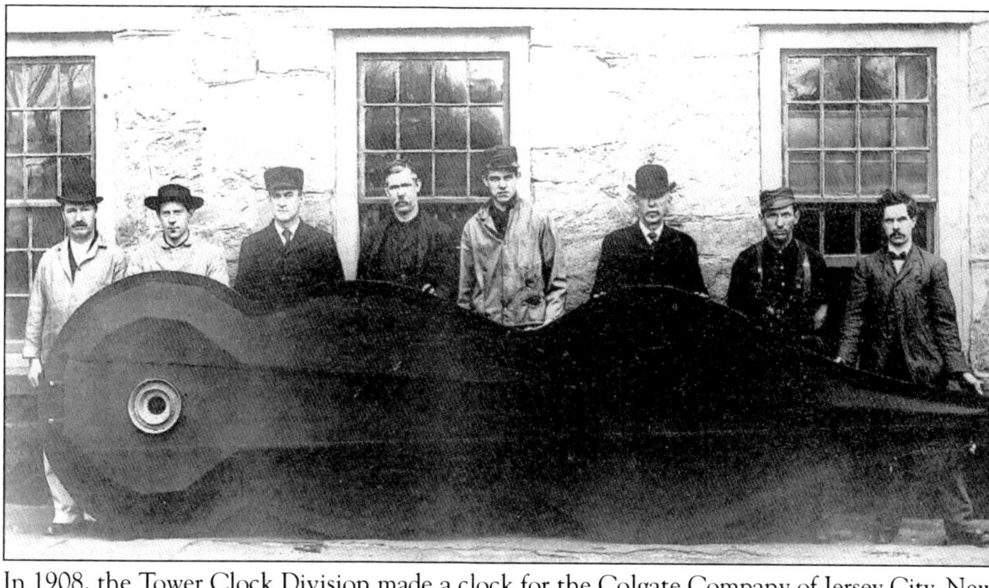

In 1908, the Tower Clock Division made a clock for the Colgate Company of Jersey City, New Jersey. At the time, it was the largest clock in the world. Eight of the men involved in the production of the clock stand behind its 15-foot hour hand. They are, from left to right, Jim Edgerton, Lev Tanner, Charlie Botsford, Pete Martin, Robert Innes Jr., Arthur Gordon, ? Spath, and Nicholas Winn. (Courtesy of John Torrence.)

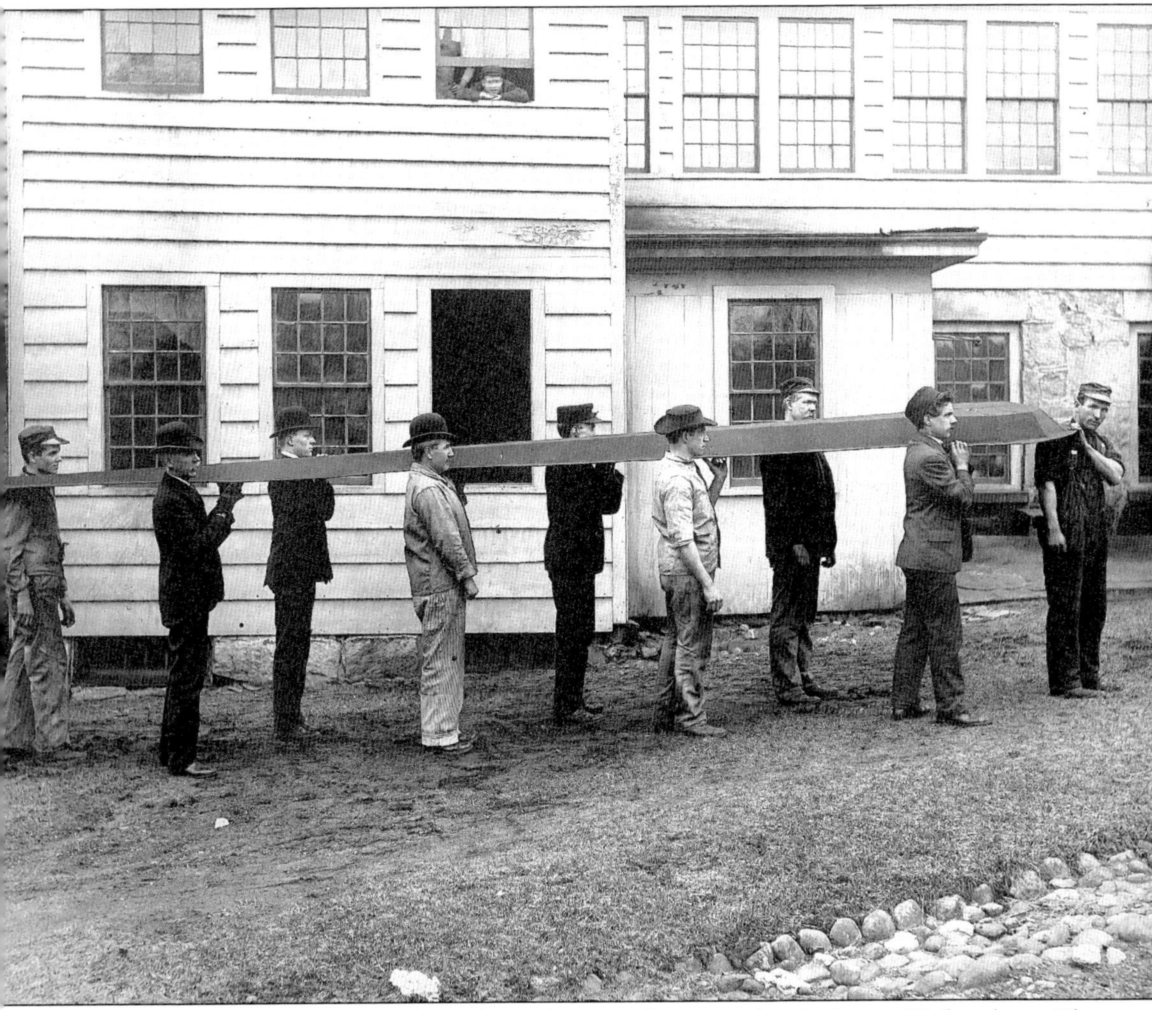

It took nine men to carry the Colgate Company's minute hand. It was 20 feet long. The round clock face was 1,104 square feet. Note the hour hand standing at the right and the boy peering out the second-floor window. In 1924, the clock was taken to another Colgate plant in Jeffersonville, Indiana, and replaced by an even larger Seth Thomas clock. Pictured, from left to right, are Robert Innes Jr., Arthur Gordon, Ed McCool, Jim Edgerton, Charlie Botsford, Lev Tanner, Pete Martin, Nicholas Winn, and ? Spath. Arthur Gordon was the superintendent of the Tower Clock Division. Later a state representative from Plymouth, he was killed in a traffic accident in July 1935. While crossing Main Street (Route 6) in Plymouth, the 76-year-old was struck by a car.

Early in the 20th century, the Seth Thomas Clock Company erected an 85-foot-tall chimney on its Elm Street foundry. It was eight feet square at the bottom and was three bricks thick. Among the daredevils was blacksmith Andrew Anderson (1867–1944), pictured on the left. Park Street is in the immediate background, and in the distance, the tops of the Old Center School and the First Congregational Church appear.

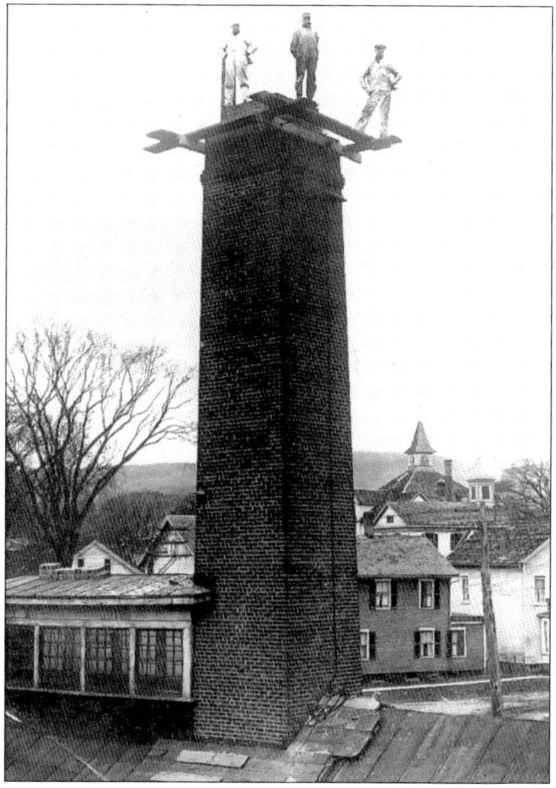

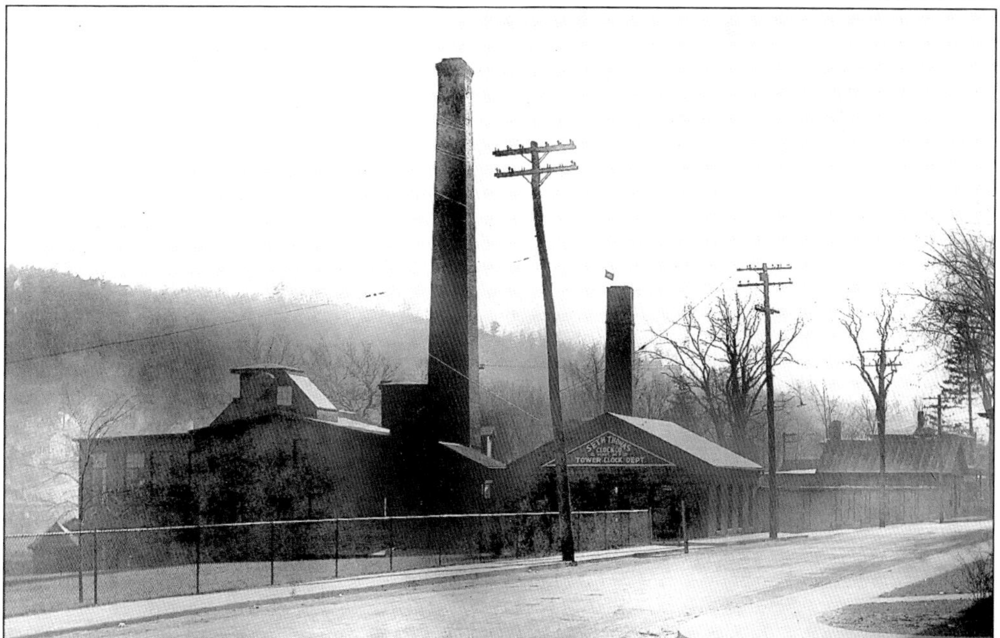

When the chimney was completed, it towered over the other Seth Thomas buildings on the east side of Elm Street. The building with the lettering still exists, as does the structure in the right background.

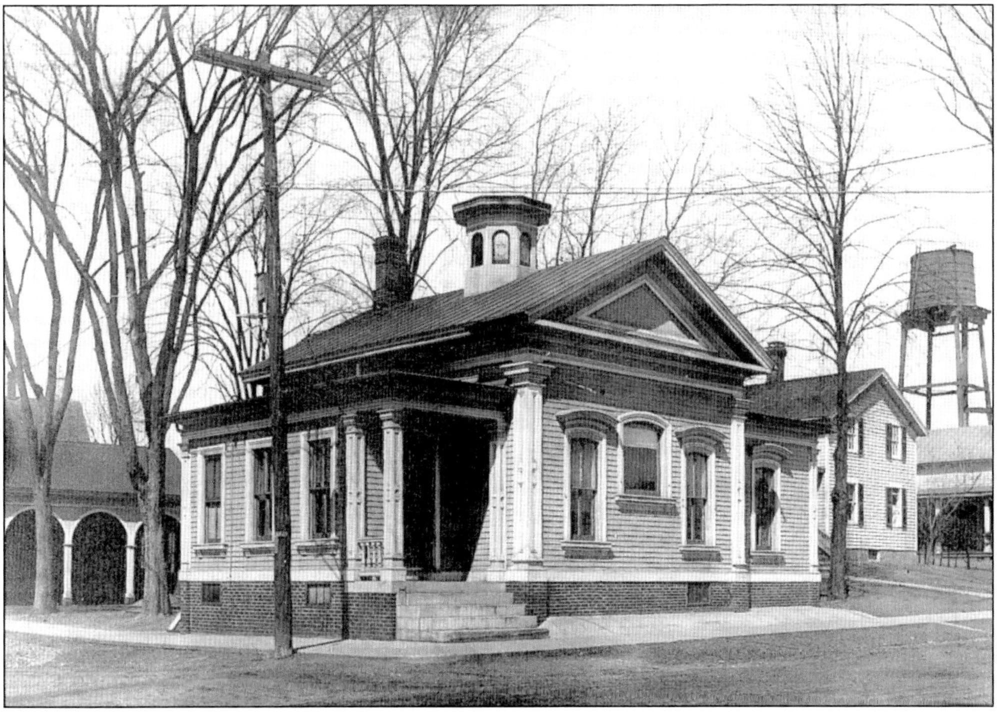

The Seth Thomas building on the northern corner of Park and Elm Streets is easily recognized as today's American Legion Hall, Clifford R. French Post 22. The structures on either side (and the elm trees) are now gone.

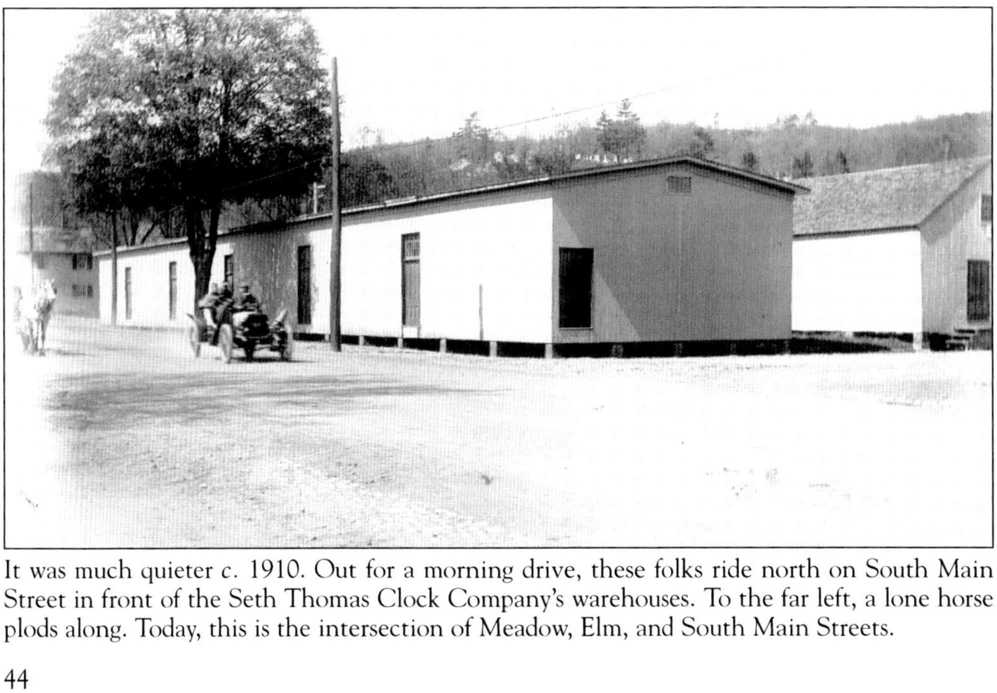

It was much quieter *c.* 1910. Out for a morning drive, these folks ride north on South Main Street in front of the Seth Thomas Clock Company's warehouses. To the far left, a lone horse plods along. Today, this is the intersection of Meadow, Elm, and South Main Streets.

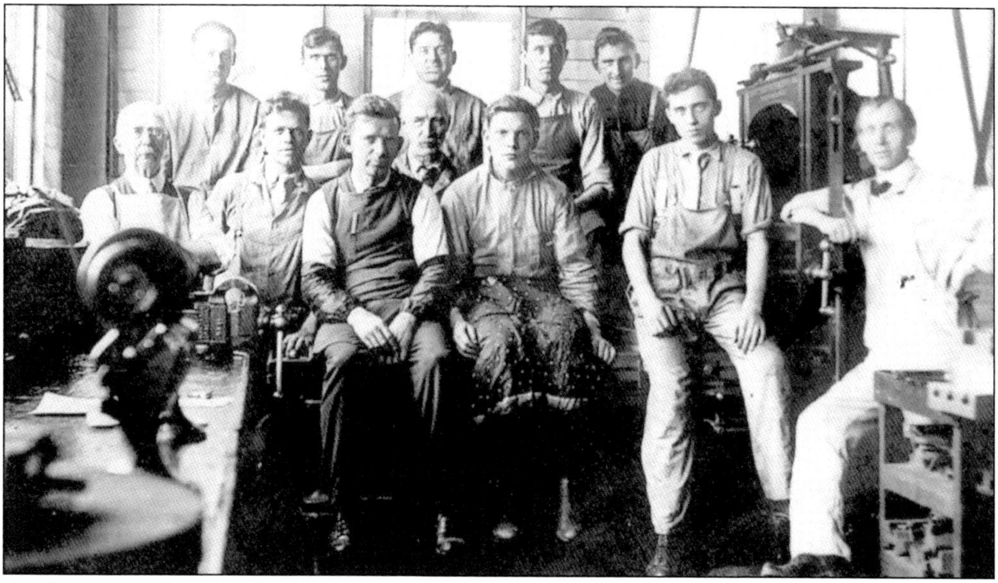

As the company continued to grow, it occupied three major sites: the movement shop and Tower Clock Division on Elm Street, the marine and watch shop on Marine Street, and the case shop on South Main Street. Pictured *c.* 1912 are, from left to right, the following: (front row) H. Canfield, Bill Lundahl, Billy Grey, John Todd, Wes Billings, Aurd Ekstrom, and Carl Johnson; (back row) S. Stoddard, G. Fordyce, Oscar Ebner, G. Ross, and P. Shanahan.

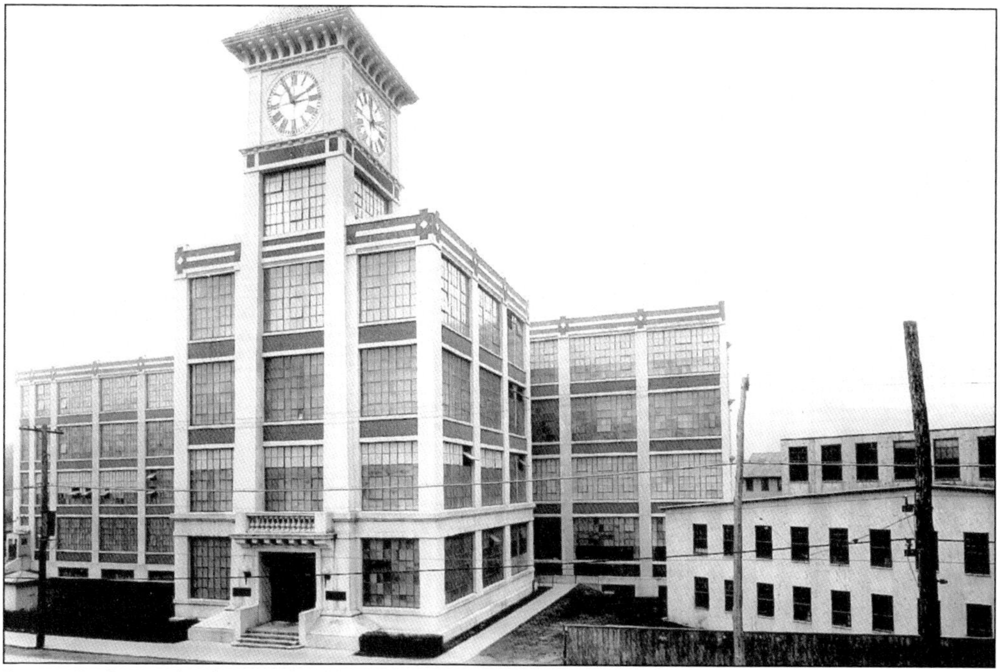

In 1915, the Seth Thomas building was erected on the corner of South Main and Elm Streets. Eventually, the company combined its operation into this plant, shrinking its landholdings substantially. A southern wing was added in 1935. Seth Thomas was moved to Georgia in 1982, and the company was dissolved in 2001. The plant stands today as a successful multiple enterprise structure owned by George Lacapra.

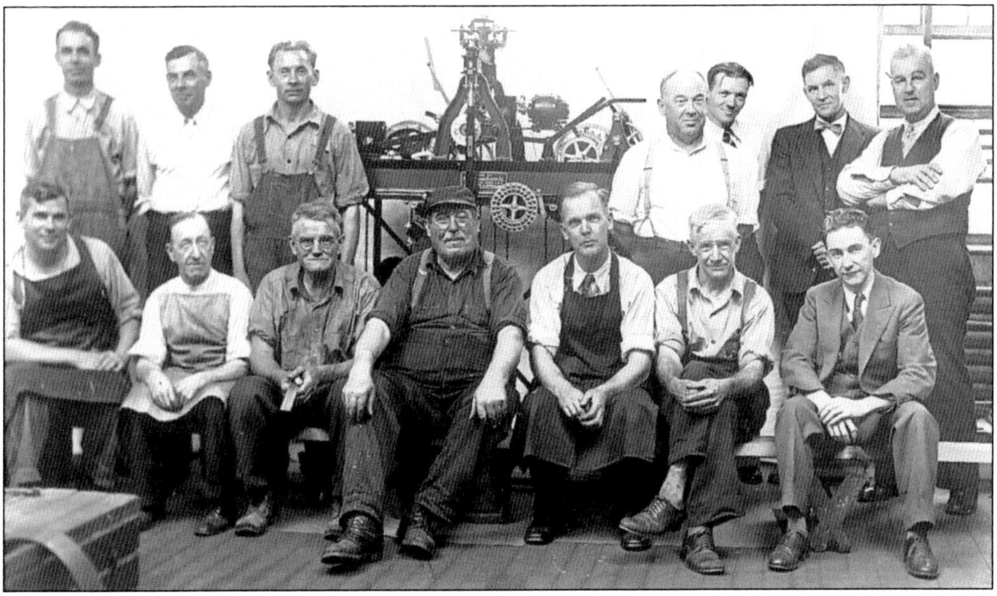

Employees of the Tower Clock Division pose with one of their movements, a No. 15 Westminster Power-Wound Tower Clock, made for the Masonic Home in Cockeysville, Maryland, in 1935. Pictured are, from left to right, the following: (front row) Alfred Bull, Joseph Reichenbach, Mortimer Quinlan, Andrew Anderson, Albert Thulin, William Gill, and Joseph Farrell; (back row) William Nichols, Ralph Stumpf, Algot Olson, Charles E. Smith, Ernest Brown, George Duncan, and Albert Mellor. (Courtesy of Marie Farrell Porzio.)

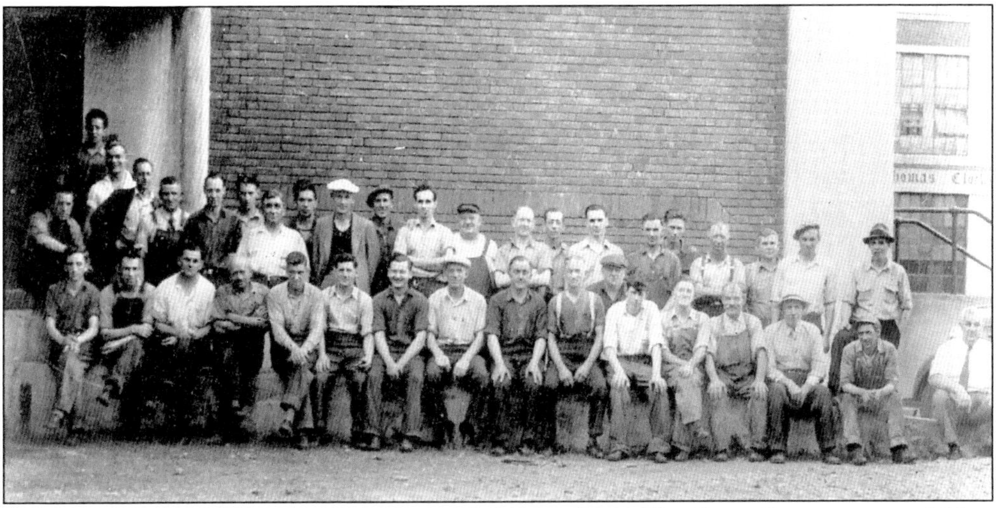

By 1938, the country's economy was in much better shape. The Great Depression would last for another year, but the Seth Thomas maintenance department was still sizeable. Employees of that department are, from left to right, as follows: (front row) Bill Kobryn, Joseph Wassong, Otto Handlowitch, Otto Poit, Roland Cyr, Joseph Sarasin, Paul Ososki, George Smail, Adam Roskoski, Gus Johnson, Ken Potter, Tom Mott, Frank Gangloff, John McGowan, ? Norton, and Albert Mellor; (back row) Pat Ryan, two unidentified men, George Elty, Bob Wardell, Royal Bullock, John Gunn, John Connors, Bill Gruen, Dan Ryan, Dayton Sanford, unidentified, Lawrence Barrett, Ken Stewart, Bob Smail, unidentified, Les Hall, Estine Benedict, Al Bull, Calvin Woods, and William Nichols.

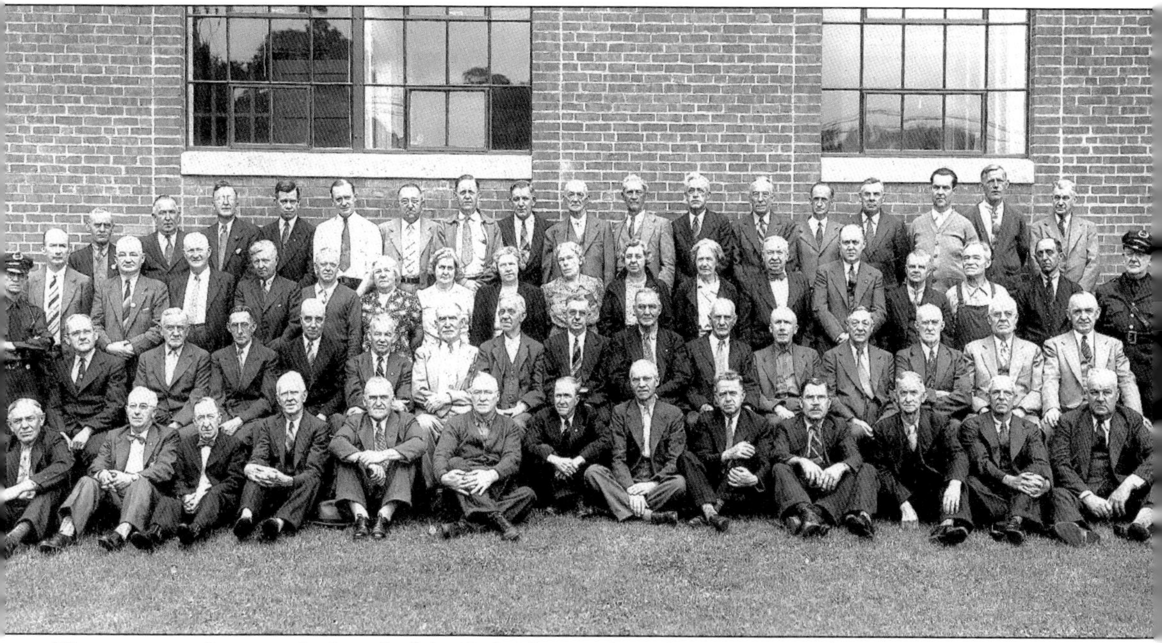

These men and women had worked for Seth Thomas for at least 25 years. This photograph of the 25 Year Club was taken in May 1942, when the factory's efforts turned toward war production. Seen here are, from left to right, the following: (first row) Alexander Konitski, William St. John, Joseph Reichenbach, Michael Barrett, Albert Brown, Albert Olmstead, Leroy DeForrest, Frank Benson, William Lundahl, Jacob Gangloff, Gustaf Johnson, Walter Gilman, and Albert Mellor; (second row) James Scott (in uniform), Oscar Ebner, Julius Kellar, William Doran, Thomas Mageen, Frank Wehrle, Patrick Hamilton, Max VanHorsten, George Stone, Harold Bidwell, Joseph Faller, John McGowan, Ernest Weise, Charles Botsford, Charles Larson, Forbes Gibbs, and Peter Glennon (in uniform); (third row) Dennis Sullivan, Michael Monahan, Frederick Robertson, Michael McMahon, Frederick Coates, Mary Downey, Margaret Dee, Margaret Glennon, Mary Green, Rose Bernatchez, Katherine Rabbitt, Thomas Ryan, Edward Springberg, James Bothroyd, Frank Gangloff, and Adolph Gregor; (fourth row) Salvatore Longo, John Waters, William Watson, Carl Erickson, Howard Hurley, John Braxl, Oscar Gustafson, Robert Warland, Charles Clyne, William Lamontagne, Joseph Simpson, Burton Nase, Charles Brooker, Ralph Stumpf, Harry Mendelson, George Klocker, and William Sanford.

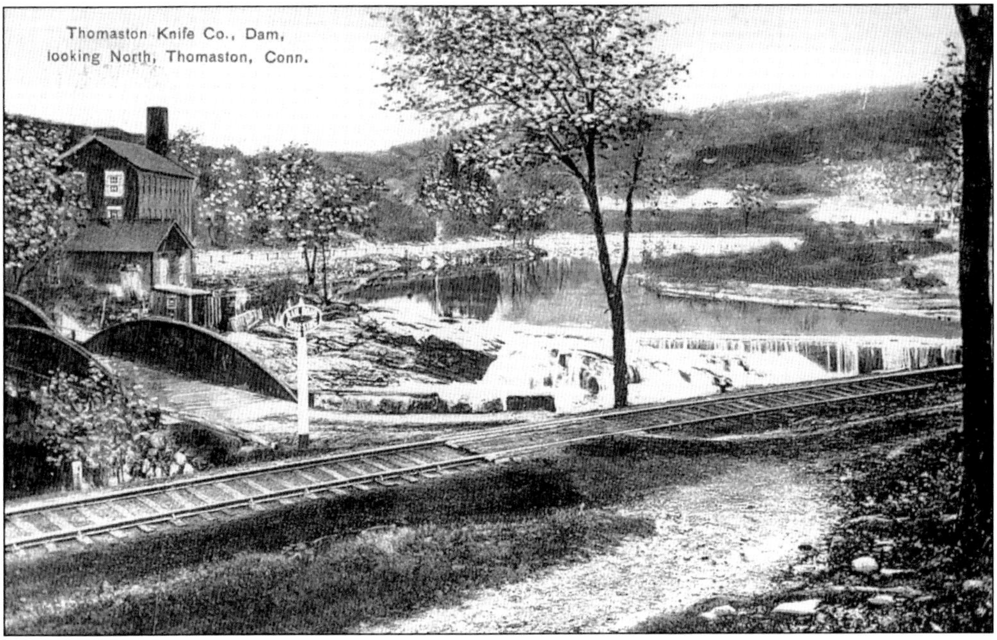

The Seth Thomas Clock Company was preeminent in longevity, in extent, and in impact upon the town but was not the only manufacturing enterprise. Among the older firms was the Thomaston Knife Company, owned by Joseph M. Warner. The company is pictured here on a postcard in 1909. Situated along the Naugatuck River, the company was south of the center at Terry's Bridge. (Courtesy of Myron Roman.)

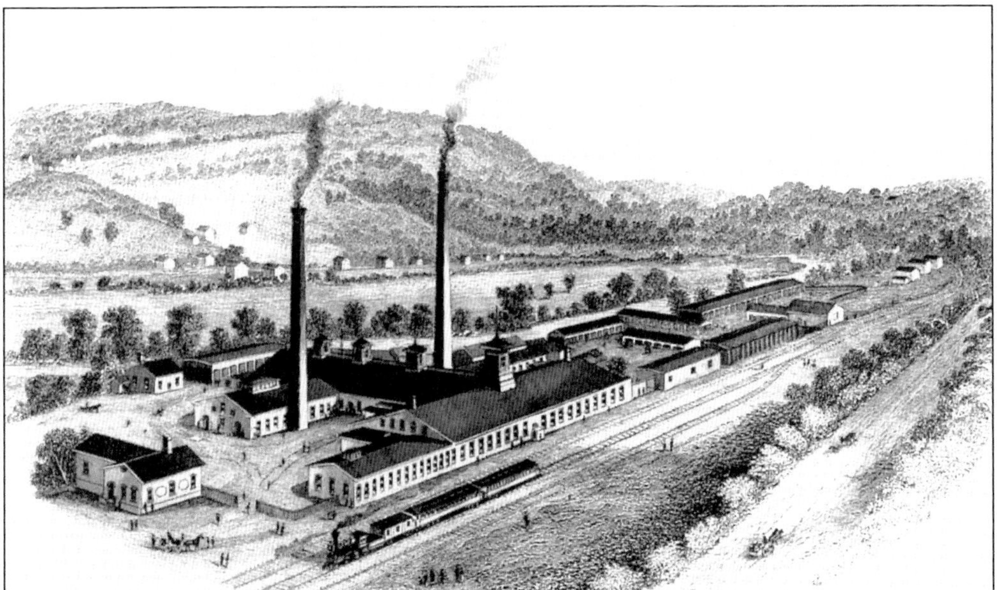

In this engraving, the Plume & Atwood Manufacturing Company is portrayed. Established by Seth Thomas in 1854 as a source of brass for his clock movements, it was sold off to others who organized it as Plume & Atwood in 1870. David Plume (1829–1907) and L.S. Atwood had a Waterbury plant and wire and rolling mills in Thomaston. (Courtesy of Walter Robinson.)

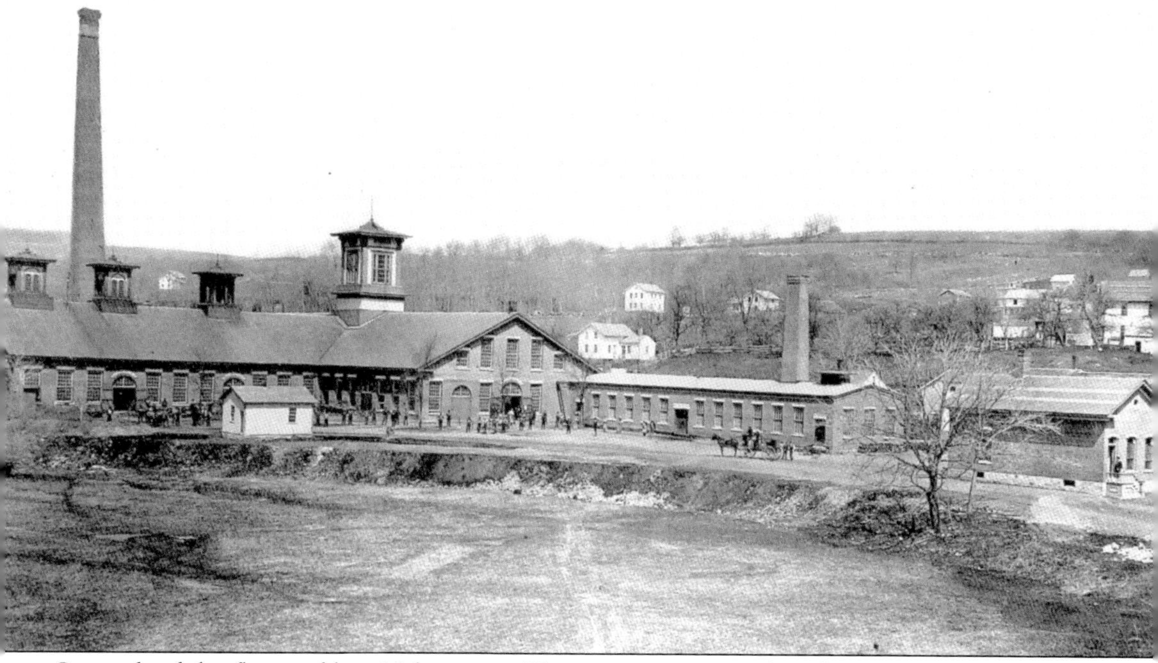

So much of the flavor of late-19th-century Thomaston is captured in this picture of factory, farms, wagons, and fences. Looking east, we see hills that have been denuded by the need for fuel. In this wintry scene of Plume & Atwood, the guard-watchman stands at the right. Beyond him, the Stoughton Store, which supplied necessities to the neighbors, appears.

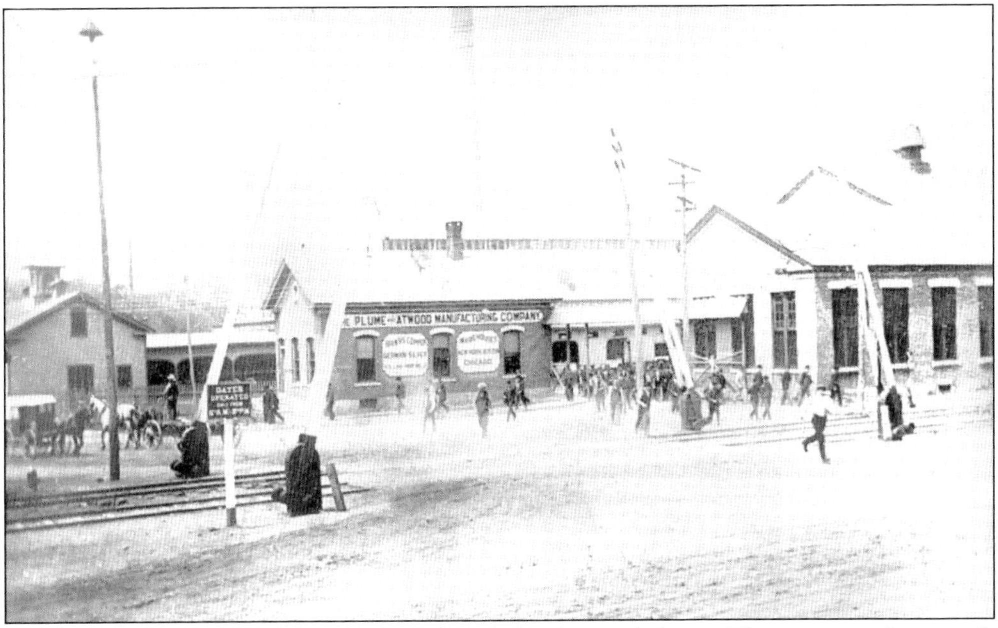

Plume & Atwood workers scurry at the daily dismissal hour. This action photograph demonstrates that traffic c. 1890 was neither as heavy nor as dangerous as today. Crossing East Main Street involved only a leisurely stroll. Note that the railroad track gates operated from 6 a.m. to 8 p.m. The signs illustrate the national nature of Plume & Atwood products, with warehouses in New York, Boston, and Chicago.

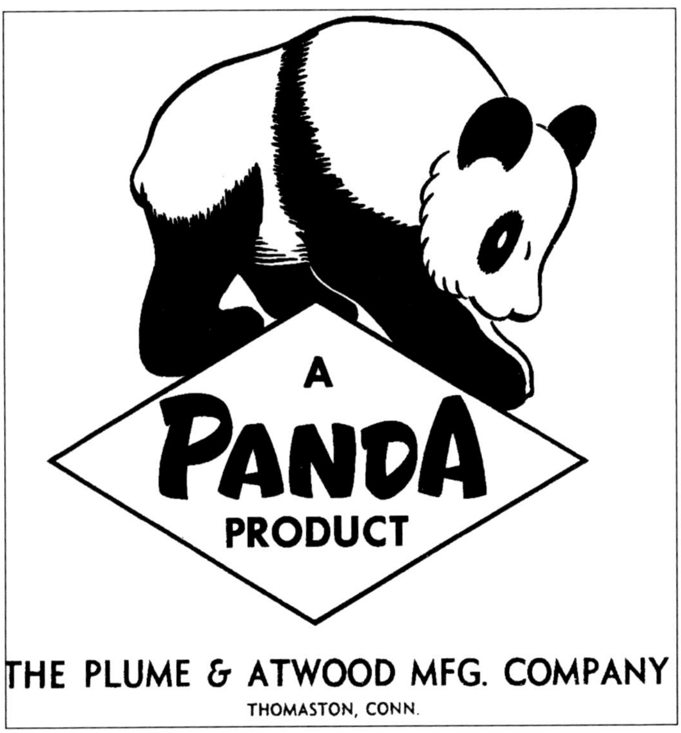

The logo of Plume & Atwood drew upon the first letter in "Plume," the word "and," and the first letter in "Atwood." Its origin is fuzzy, but it became a symbol seen throughout the plant.

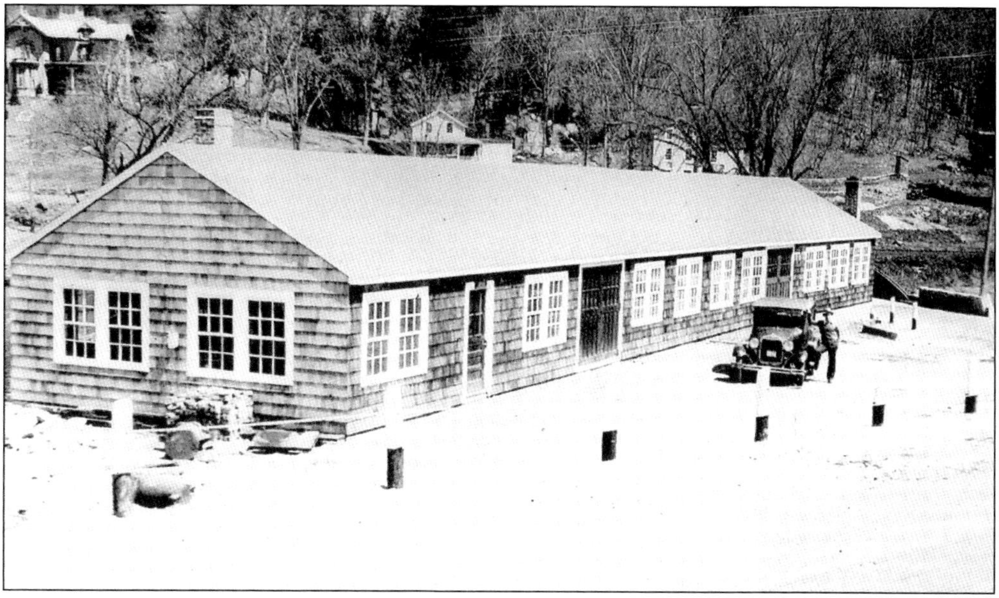

In 1934, the Oris Manufacturing Company made plastic products at the Thomaston Knife Company site. Joseph Oris was the owner. In this photograph, we see a c. 1929 Ford and, beyond the factory, a corner of Terry's Bridge. The Oris family lived in the house on the hill across the river at the left. Sadly, the factory and the bridge were destroyed in the 1955 flood.

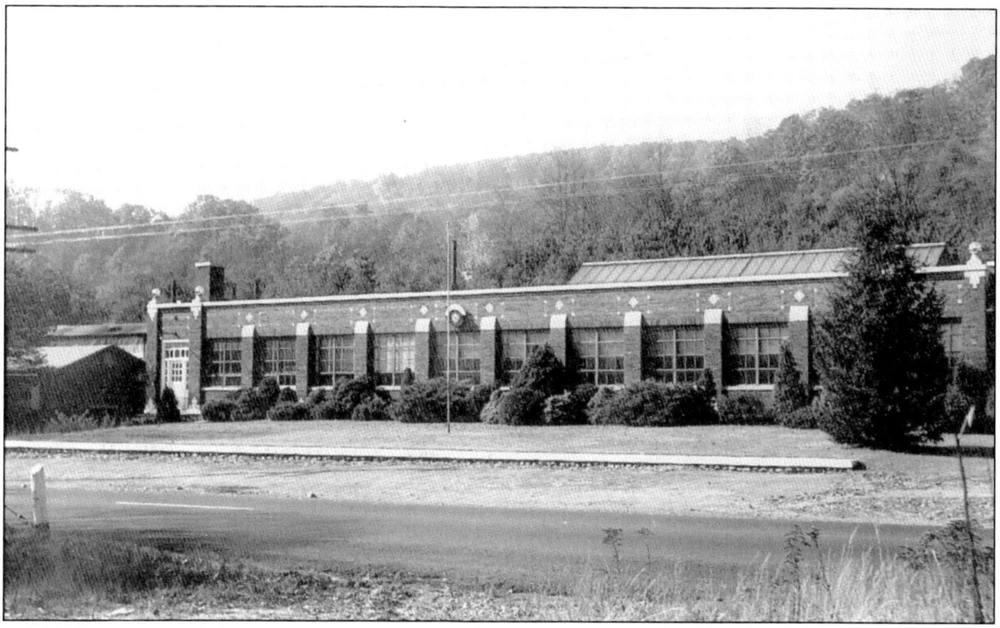

The Eclipse Glass Company was located on the westerly side of North Main Street, at No. 815, immediately south of the Thomaston Dam. It was owned by H. Otto Vogt (1891–1974), originally from Germany, and was a very successful business. Begun in 1927 at Vogt's house (now Black Rock State Park), the company moved to the site of the Oris factory, was burned out, and moved into a new brick building on Torrington Road in 1934. Vogt sold the company in 1966. The building burned in the late 1980s, and the site is now a storage yard for school buses.

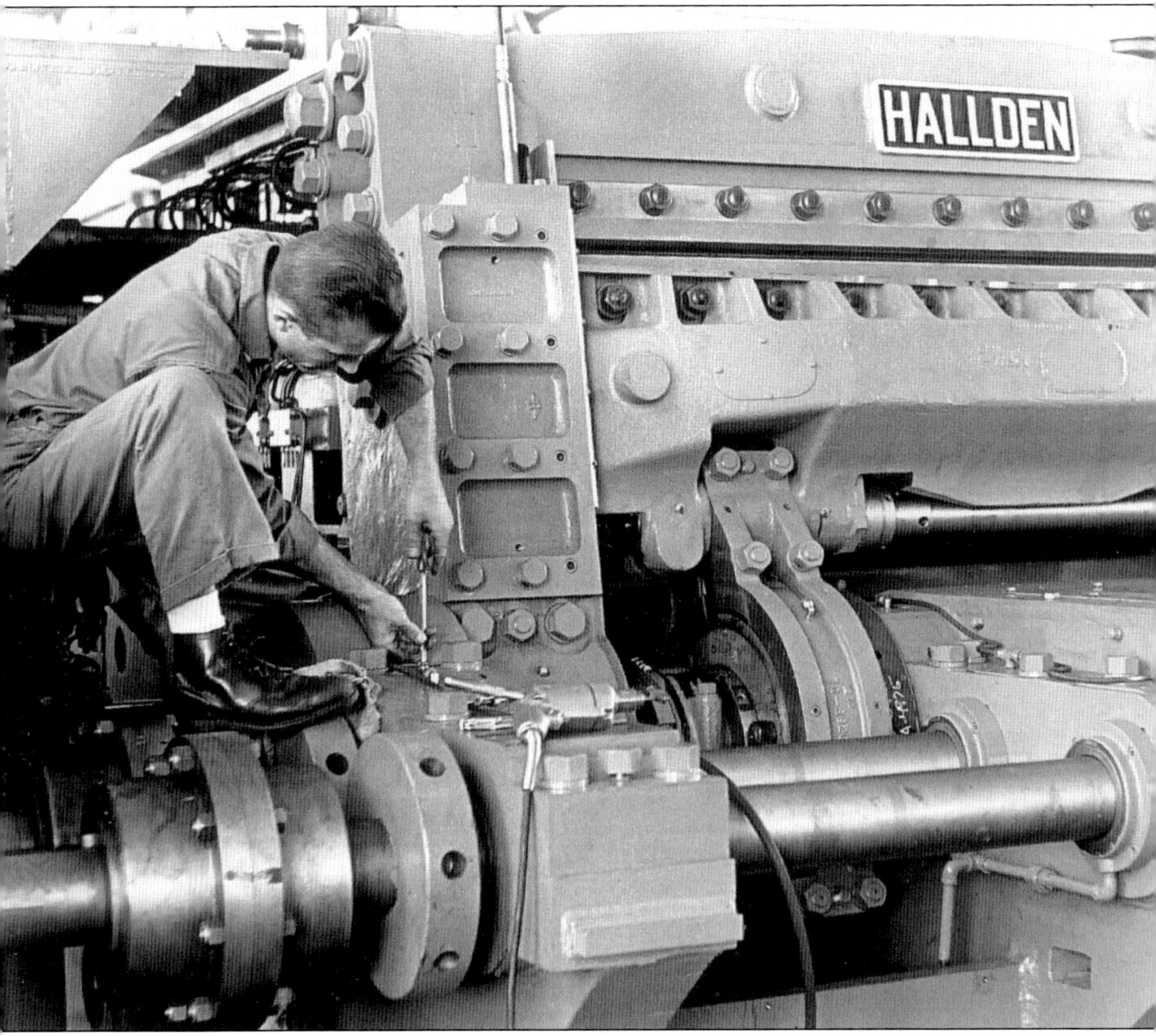

Another major employer in Thomaston was the Hallden Machine Company. Inventor and owner Karl Hallden (1884–1970) was a Swedish immigrant who graduated from Trinity College in Hartford, Connecticut. Roger Gangloff works on the flying shears, the machine prominently displaying the Hallden name, in the early 1960s. The factory was located at the corner of River and Maple Streets in the building that now houses Hayden Industries.

Three

A Cultural View

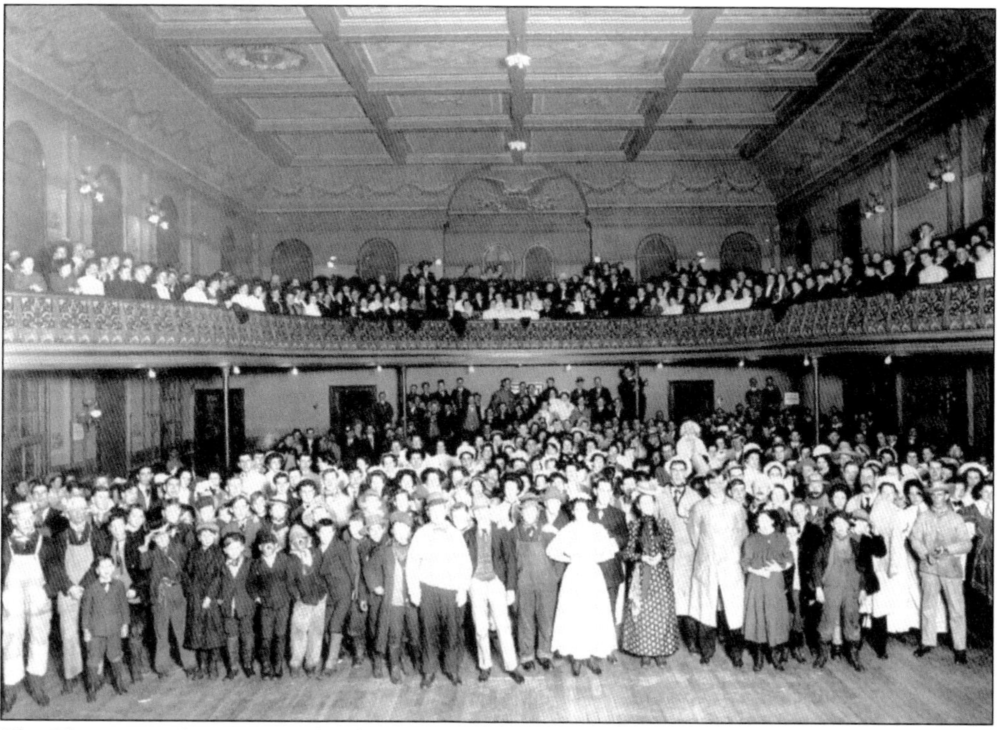

The Thomaston Opera House has been a venue for entertainment, school commencements, and town meetings since its opening in 1884. Sometimes pageants were held involving a large cast, and sometimes the townsfolk gathered at "Hayseed" balls in costume to have fun at Halloween. This panoramic view of the opera house shows the cast of all ages, the well-dressed audience, the lighting fixtures, the American eagle, and the admonition that "spitting is prohibited."

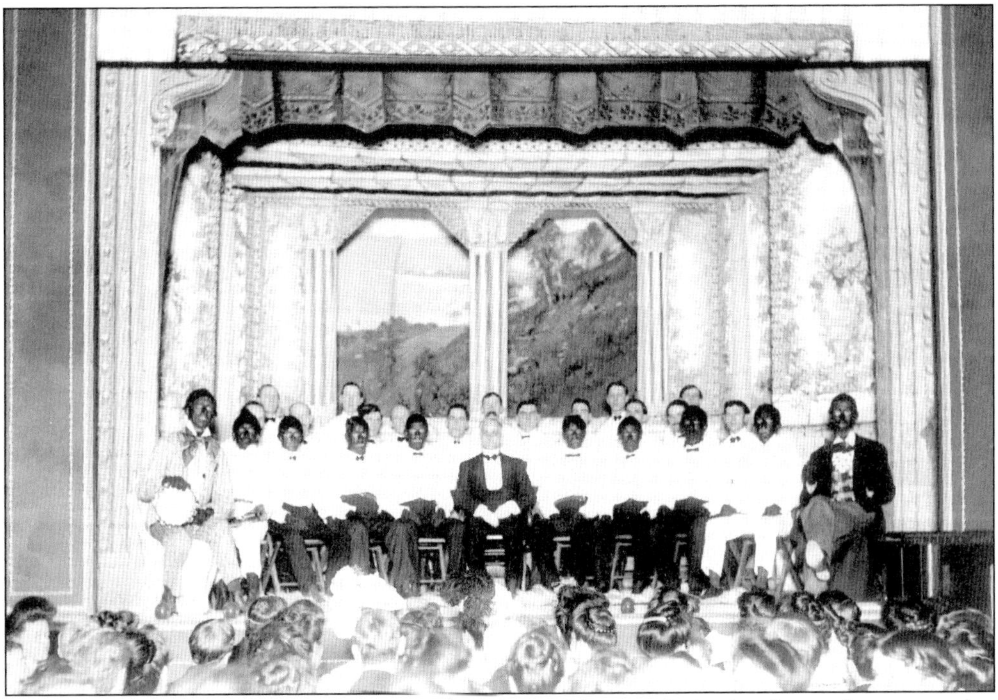

We can date this picture by the women's hairdos and hats and also by the performers in this minstrel show, 10 of whom are in blackface. The year is c. 1900.

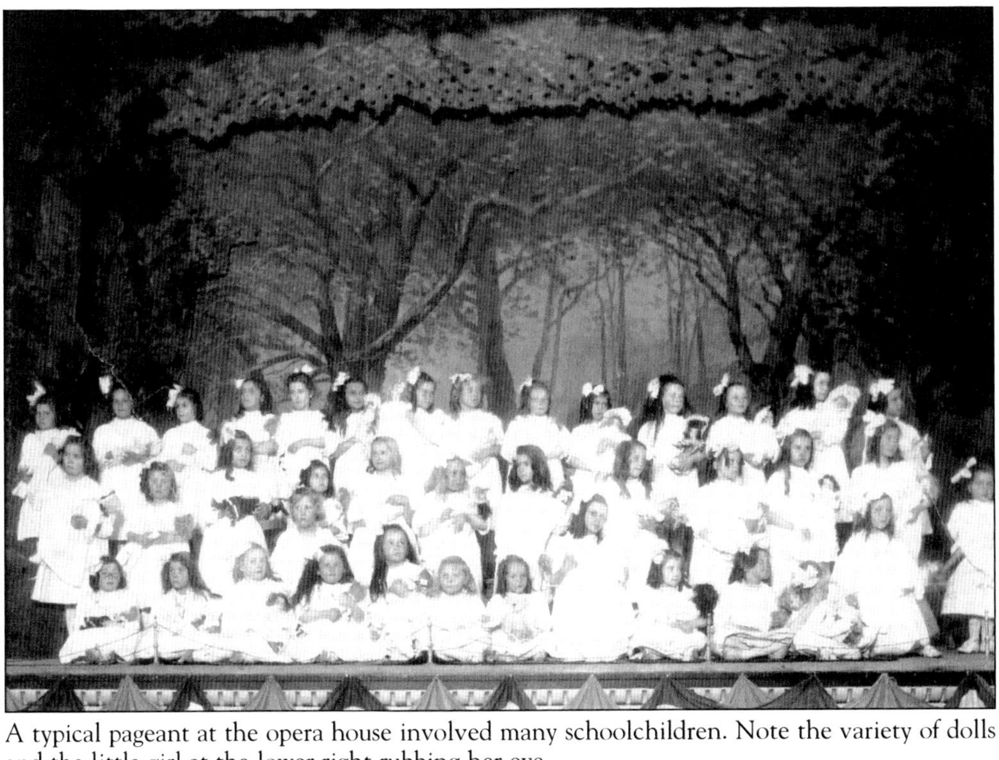

A typical pageant at the opera house involved many schoolchildren. Note the variety of dolls and the little girl at the lower right rubbing her eye.

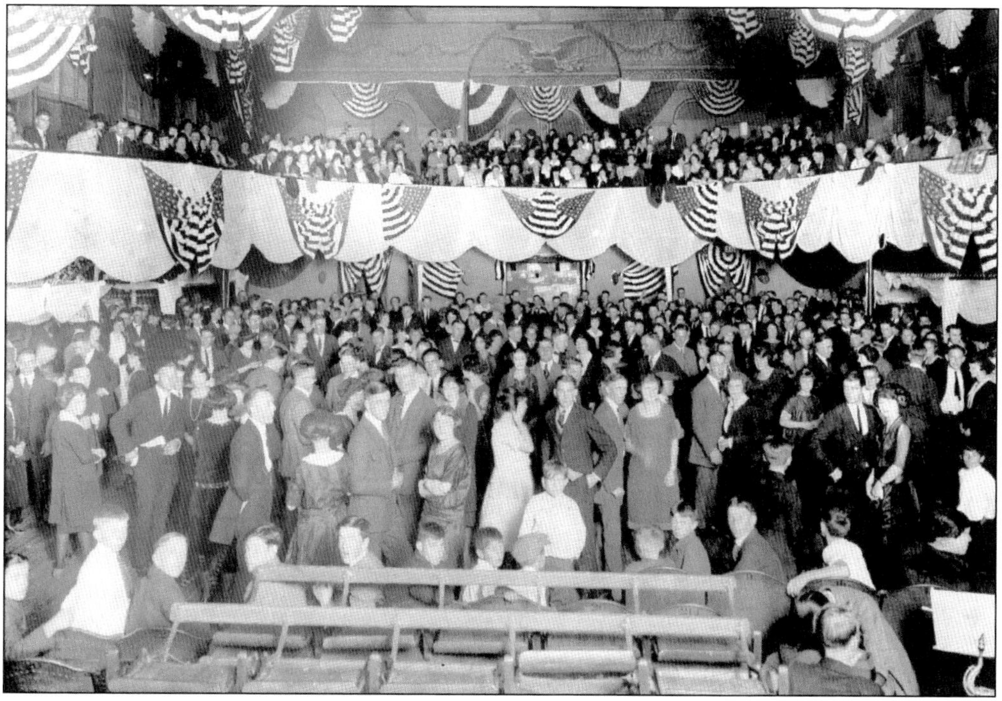

A generation later at the Thomaston Opera House, some enjoy the dance floor while others prefer to watch. Everyone is well dressed. Patriotic bunting is abundant. The eagle is still prominent. Presumably, spitting is still prohibited.

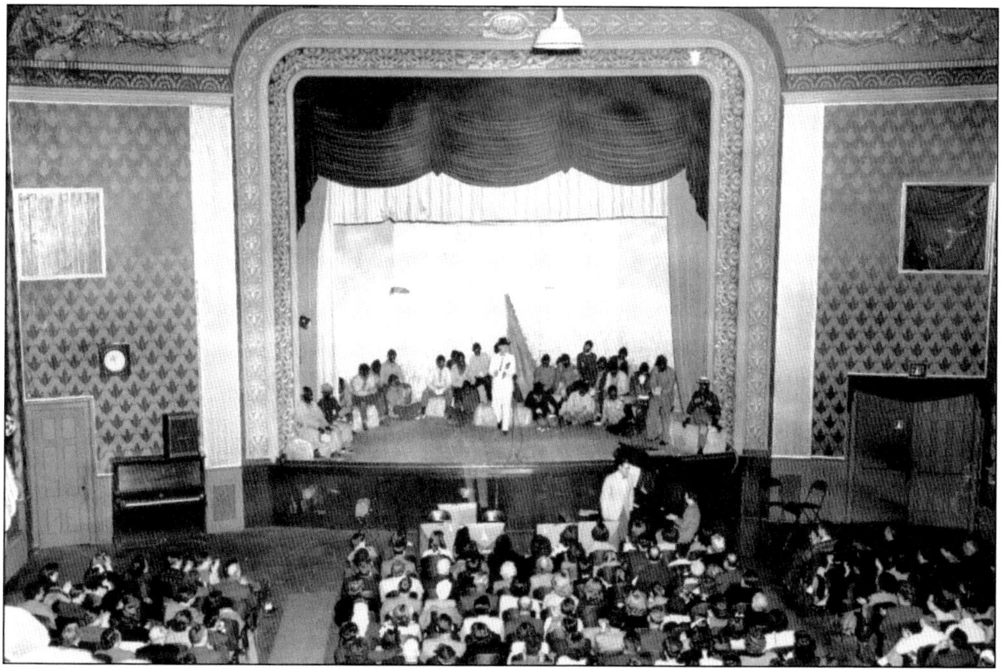

Permanent seating was installed for the Paramount movie theater. The annual Stag Club Minstrel Show, seen here c. 1952, was a popular event in town. Note the difference in hair styles and the performers again in blackface.

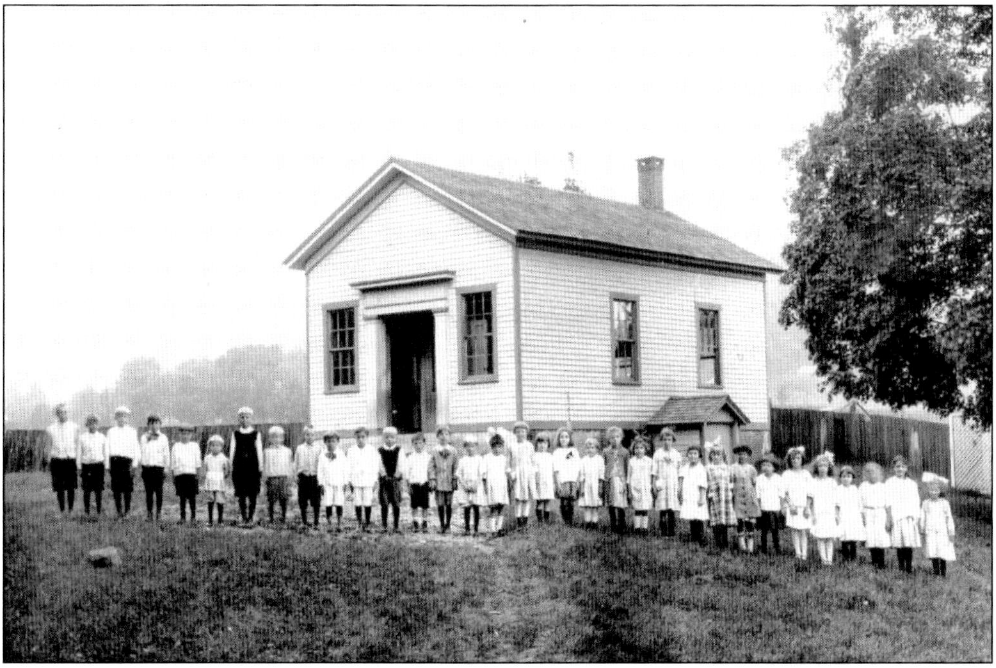

This neighborhood school was the Pine Hill School, located on the north side of Pine Hill Road. These children are lined up in their Sunday best "to have their picture took." The school was closed in 1935. (Courtesy of Robert Magdziarz.)

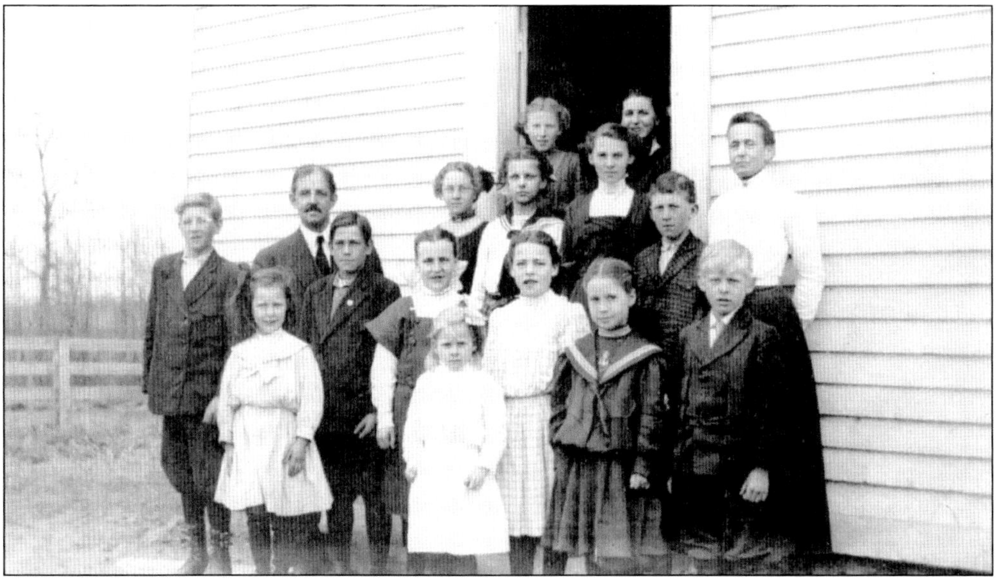

The Walnut Hill School stood near the intersection of Hickory Hill Road, Turner Road, and Babbitt Road. This June 6, 1911, photograph was made into a postcard. The teacher, Bissie Turner, wrote a short letter describing the day's events, now in the collection of the Thomaston Historical Society. Ernest Small was the high school principal and superintendent. In front of Small is Louis Wassong; the second girl to the right of Louis in the light plaid dress is his sister Mary Wassong (Adam).

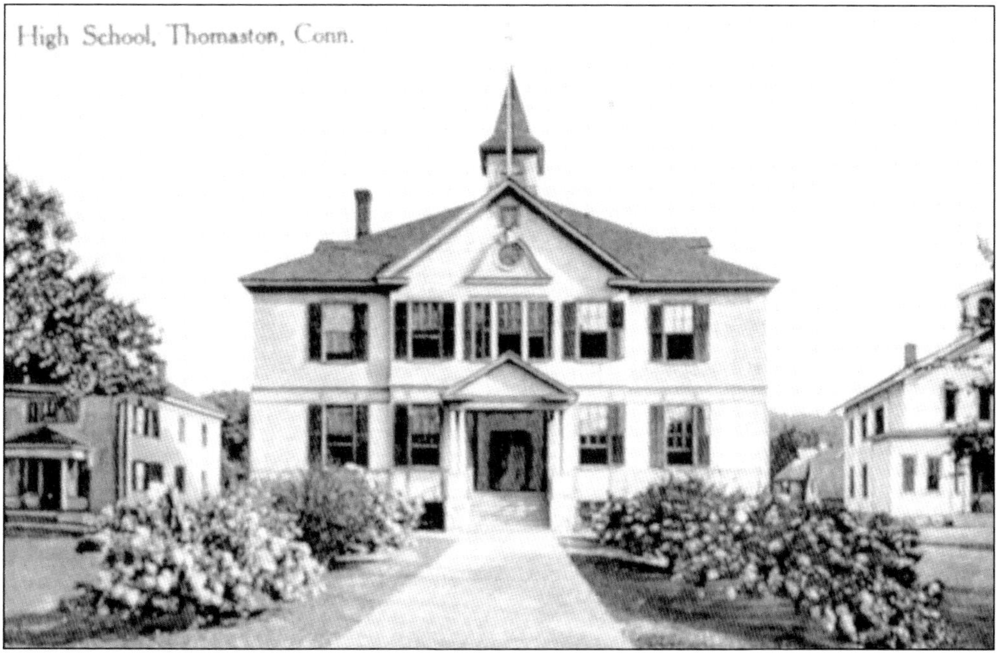

This postcard of Thomaston High shows the relative location of the three schools in the Center School educational complex. It was located just east of the First Congregational Church. The first grammar school, built in 1851, is to the right. The front of the high school was a popular spot for class photographs. The building was demolished for the construction of Green Manor. (Courtesy of Robert Magdziarz.)

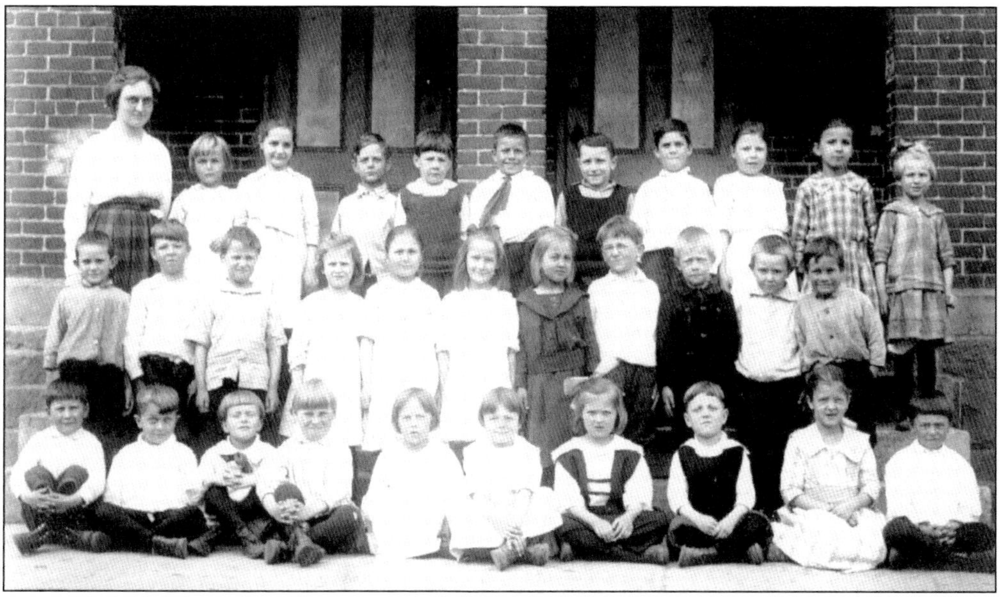

The East Side School was built in 1882 on School Street to serve elementary school children on the east side of town. It was the first school to be built of brick and was popularly known as the Brick School. The school was demolished in 1964 to make room for Route 8. This photograph was taken c. 1925. (Courtesy of Lillian Petke.)

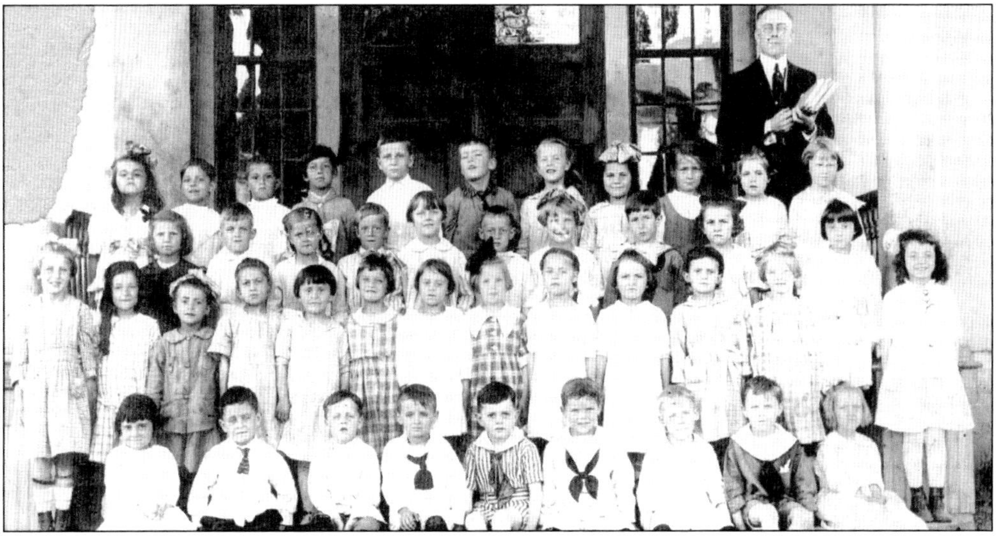

Second-graders at the Old Center School pose in 1918. From left to right are the following: (first row) Jennie Lauretano, George Taylor, James O'Brien, Louis Smith, Fred Flynn, Seth Thomas, Byron Humperville, Francis Czenski, and Grace Anderson; (second row) Margaret Higgins, Madeline Lowther, Esther Lauretano, Mary D'Andrea, Christine McDonald, Grace Pratt, unidentified, Sally Barnum, Loretta Sitkowicz, unidentified, Minnie Byers, Frances Anderson, Gerda Wehrle, and Helen Olcese; (third row) unidentified, Clarence Parson, Stasia Witkowski, Walter Dickinson, Marion Blakeslee, Karl Kiefer, Katharine Woodward, Robert Eckert, and Alice Glennon; (fourth row) unidentified, George Roberts, Robart Yarema, Roy Churchill, Laurence Gilland, Ernest Schinzel, Ruth Benedict, Catharine Danaher, Dorothy Chipman, Amelia Miles, Marion Hellerich, and teacher Leon French, music director. (Courtesy of Gerda Wehrle Grosso.)

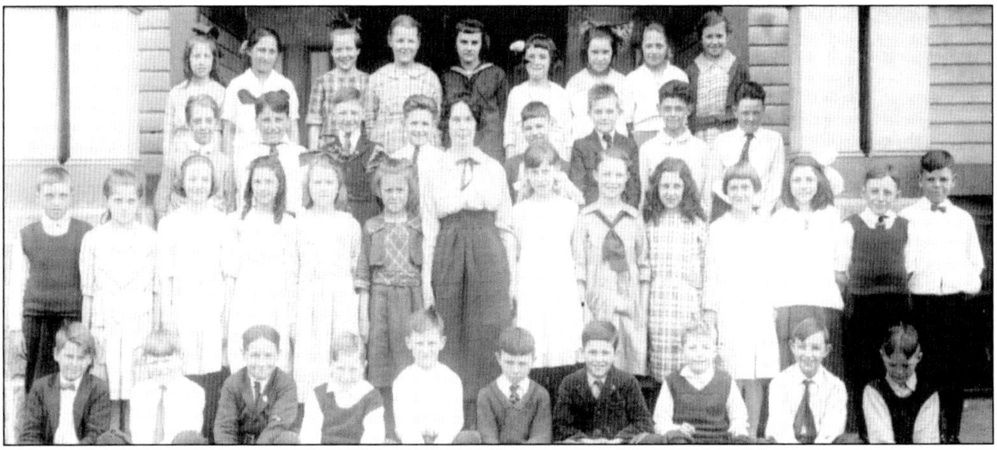

Margaret Hayes's fifth-grade class at the Center School is shown in 1921. From left to right are the following: (first row) unidentified, Levert Tanner, Mike Tripaldi, unidentified, William O'Brien, Robert Goodall, Wesley Rouse, Earl Woods, Raymond Petrke, and unidentified; (second row) unidentified, Ann Grosso, Donna Platt, Erna Wehrle, Ruth Swanson, Ethel Swanson, teacher Margaret Hayes (Wassong), Loretta Warrenburger, Elsie Chipman, Margaret Kaiser, unidentified, Florinda Schiappacasse, unidentified, Gilbert Nase, and unidentified; (third row) Carl Nelson, unidentified, Kenneth Gill, Bill Beardslee, Wesley Anderson, Arthur Parsons, Edward Mattoon, and unidentified; (fourth row) two unidentified children, Florence Thulin, two unidentified children, Mary Hefferman, two unidentified children, and ? Schlauder. (Courtesy of Gerda Wehrle Grosso.)

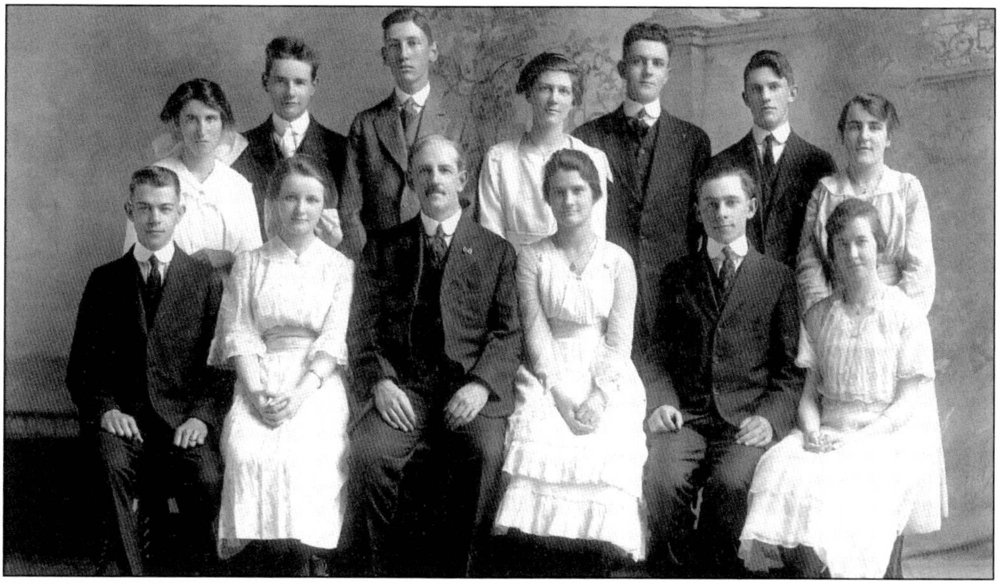

The class of 1917 held its graduation in the opera house two months after the declaration of war on Germany. Graduation speeches by the students included "Americanism," "Lexington," "The American Flag," and "Who Patriots Are." Pictured here are, from left to right, the following: (front row) Raymond Ebner, Olive Barnes, principal Ernest Small, Jennie Byers, Raymond Rafinski, and Maud Bailey; (back row) Doris Parker, Horace Tuttle, Raymond Atwood, Bessie Johnson, Frank Dorner, Wallace Pease, and Hazel Gilbert.

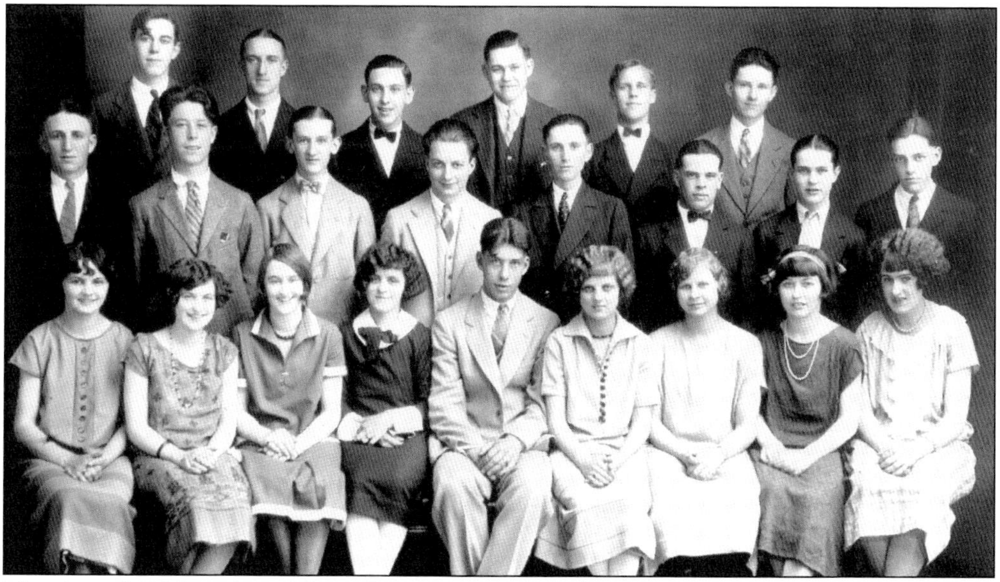

The class of 1925 graduated from the recently built high school on Grove Street in the middle of the Roaring Twenties. From left to right are the following: (front row) Agnes Brellis, Anna Dumont, Lois Biggs, Theresa Schiappacasse, Gardner Hotchkiss, Edith Wood, Elizabeth Holm, Annabelle Madeux, and Loretta Savage; (middle row) Joseph Hefferman, Francis Gilson, Lewis Troland, Herbert Grimshaw, John Luboyeski, Robert Shearer, unidentified, and Paul Gearin; (back row) George Corner, Harold Stuart, unidentified, Frederick Hellerich, Philip Johnston, and Francis Eugene McMahon.

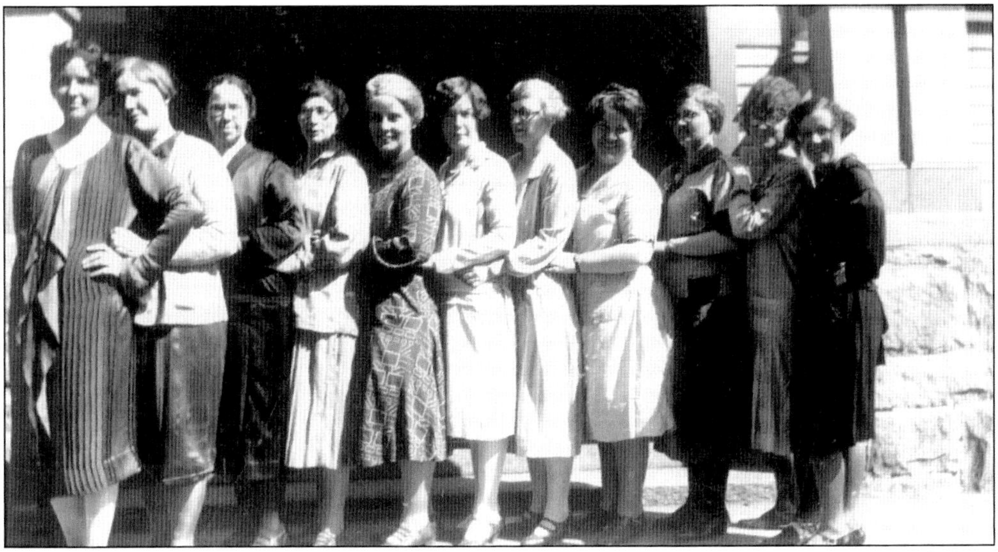

The teachers at the Center School pose for a photograph in the late 1920s. From left to right are Veronica Higgins, Dora Higgins, Nettie Stewart, Lillian Stuart, Edith Miller (Poit), Margaret Hayes (Wassong), Celestine White (Brown), Agnes Sullivan, unidentified, Hazel Ames, and Doris Waters.

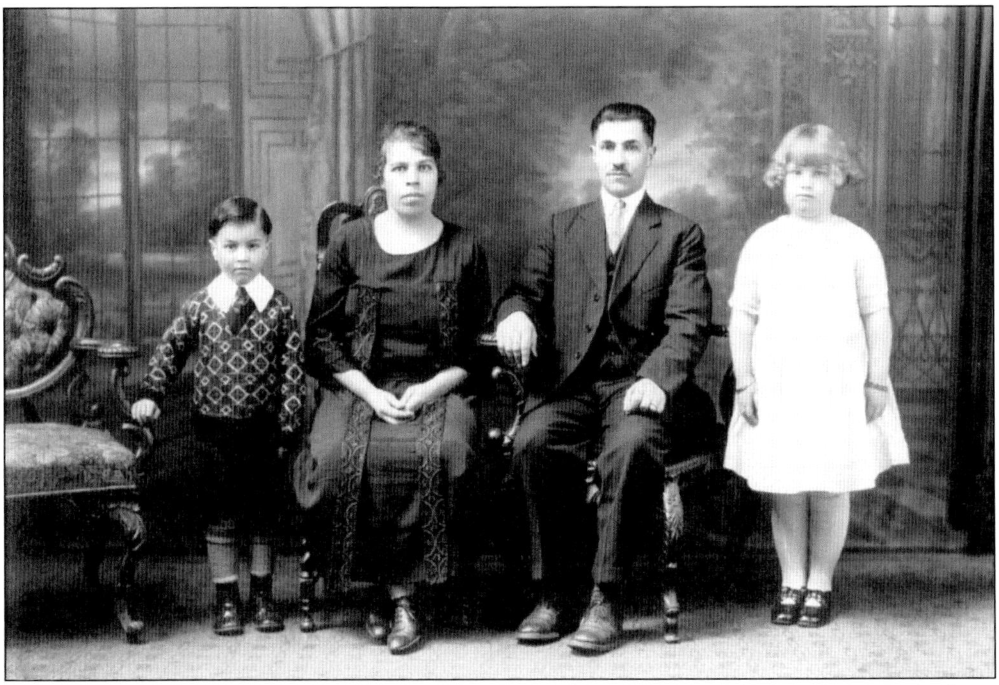

Thomaston has been enriched for at least 125 years by immigrants from a variety of ethnic groups. The family of Stanley Polowy, who emigrated from Ruthenia in the Austro-Hungarian Empire, is portrayed here *c.* 1925. From left to right are Stanley's son John; Stanley's wife, Sophie, who came from a nearby village; and Stanley's daughter Anne (Harris). Sons Lawrence and William were born later. (Courtesy of William Polowy.)

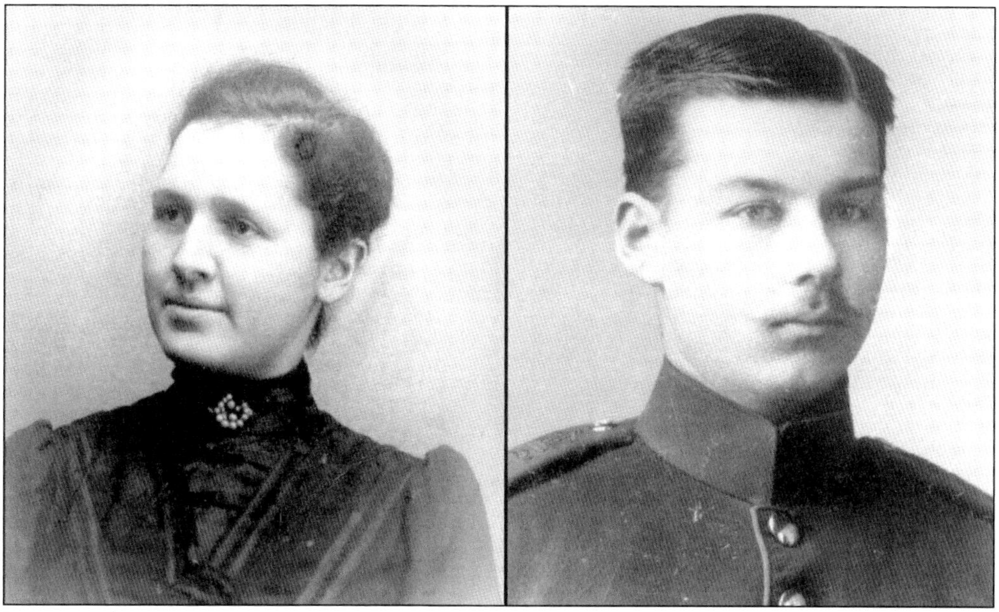

Because Thomaston was a center for clock production, many Germans emigrated to the town. Franz X. Wehrle is pictured here in 1893 at age 23, in the German service. His wife was Agatha Faller, who was 25 at the time of this photograph. Wehrle came to America in 1902 and invited Faller soon after to join him. They were married in Waterbury that same year and established their home at 268 Litchfield Street. They had four children: Frank, Erna (Lilliefelt), Gerda (Grosso), and Armin. (Courtesy of Gerda Wehrle Grosso.)

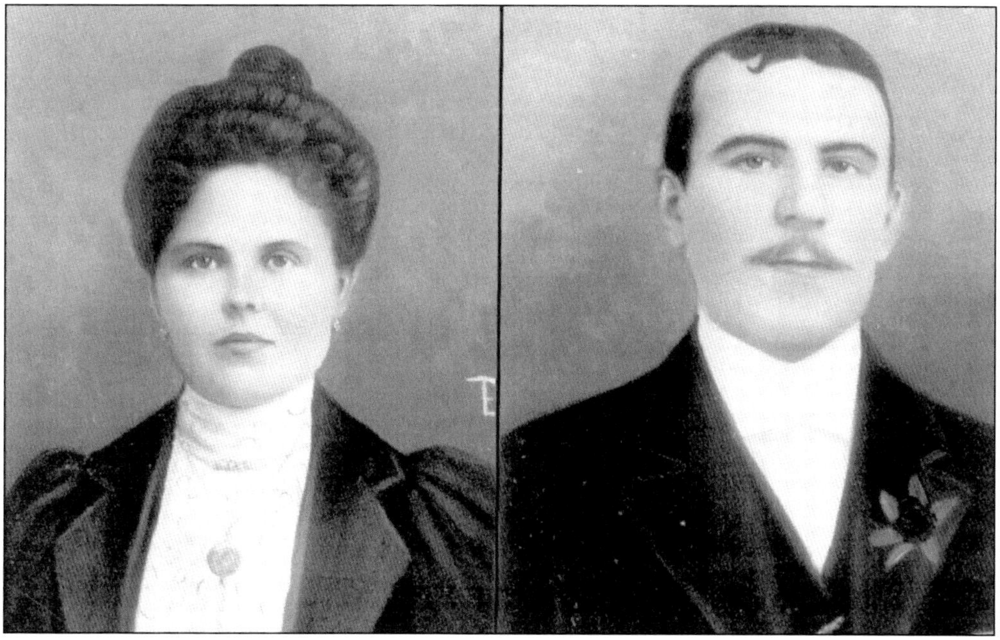

The section of town east of the river was home to many Polish immigrants. Among them were the Krayeskis, pictured here. Anthony (1878–1964) and Julia (Waskowski) (1878–1955) were born in Warsaw, at the time part of Russia. Their daughter Helen married Enos Ptachcinski, who owned a market on Railroad Street. (Courtesy of Dorothy P. Vigeant.)

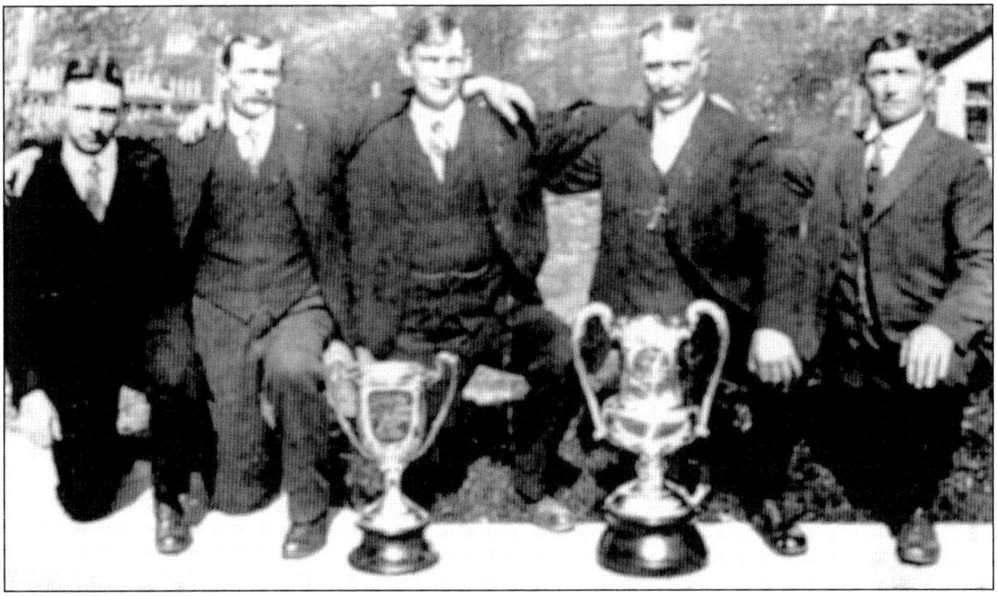

Charles J. Johnson took the initiative in 1904 to organize a fraternal lodge of the Vasa Order. It was organized by 28 Swedish men. The Oscar II Lodge No. 69 Order of Vasa was the result. On the annual Vasa Day, they participated in a tug of war in competition with other lodges. Winning the contest six times in seven years, they retired the trophy at the right in 1917, which is now part of the collection of the Thomaston Historical Society. Pictured, from left to right, are Alfred Johnson, Theodore Nelson, Hilding Hackenson, John Thulin, and Charles J. Johnson. Charles J. Johnson was the father of Philip and Kenneth Johnson.

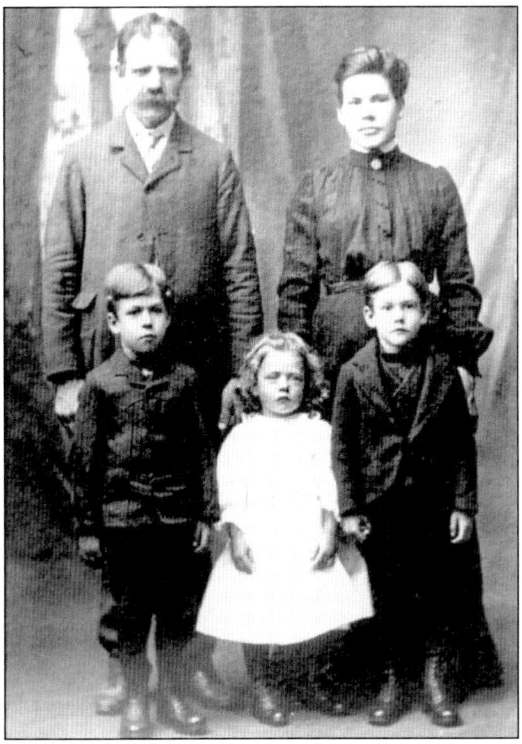

This studio photograph portrays the Joseph Wassong family *c.* 1903. Joseph was born in the French village of Uberach in 1866. His wife, Mary (Gangloff), was born in the same village eight years later, although it had become German. When Joseph brought his family to Thomaston, he could not have expected that he would be the first of four Joseph Wassongs to live here. The three children are, from left to right, Joseph Jr., Mary (Adam), and Louis.

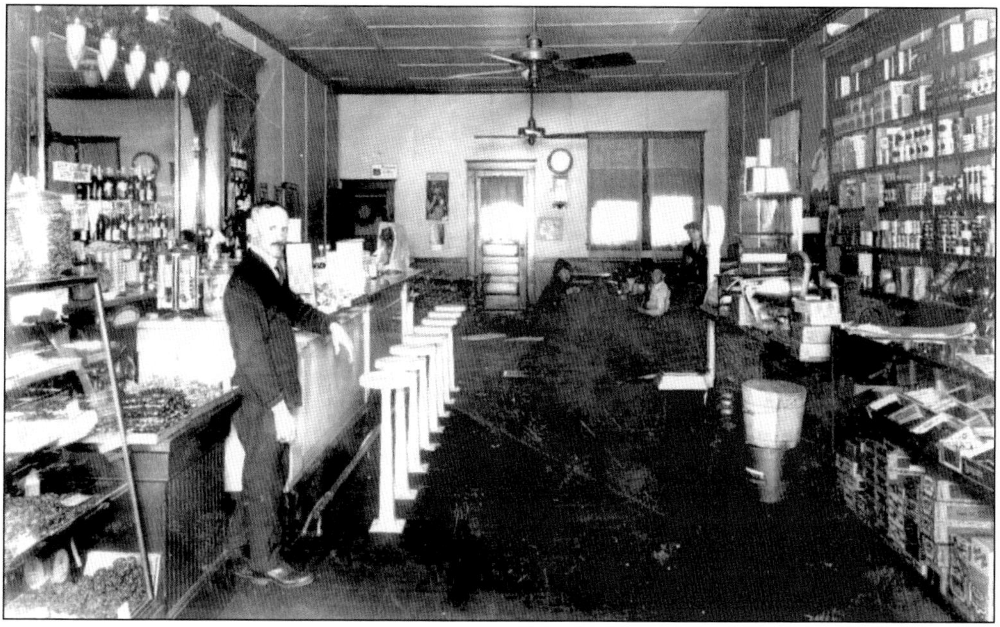

Louis Gardella is pictured in his store at 89 Main Street *c.* 1925. He had been in partnership with Louis Schiappacassee for 15 years at Candyland. Dissolving the partnership in 1923, Gardella became the sole owner. Selling a variety of products and produce, from cigars to soda, are first- or second-generation Italian-Americans Daniel Ciafardone, Patsy DiMaria, and Michael Tripaldi.

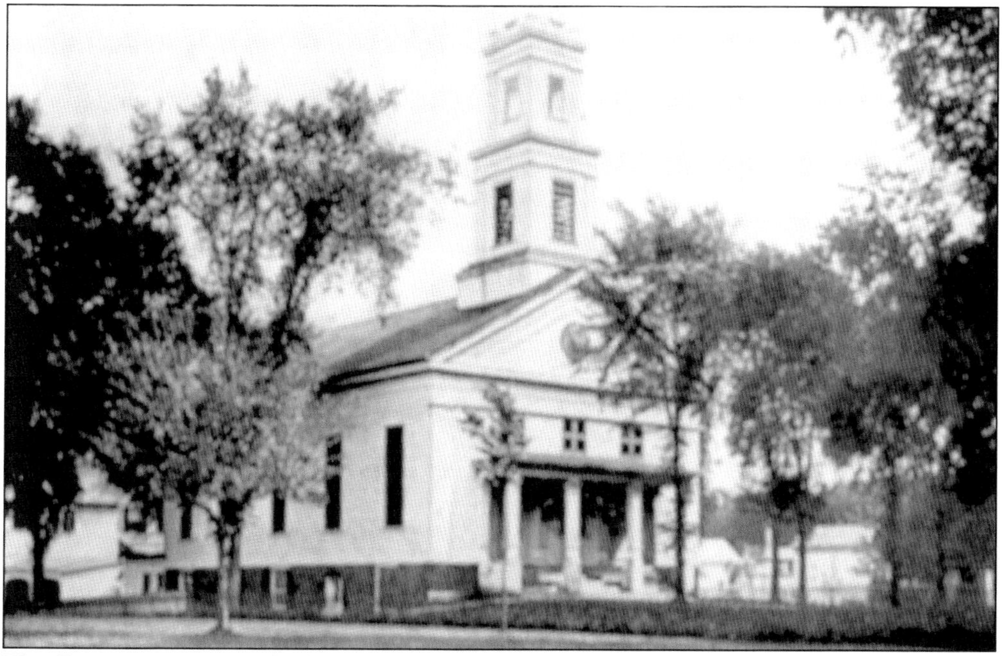

The First Congregational Church was organized in 1837, long before Thomaston separated from Plymouth. Greek Revival in design, it is one of the downtown's showpieces. Its Seth Thomas tower clock is one of only three remaining in town. The others are atop the town hall and the Seth Thomas factory building. (Courtesy of Robert Magdziarz.)

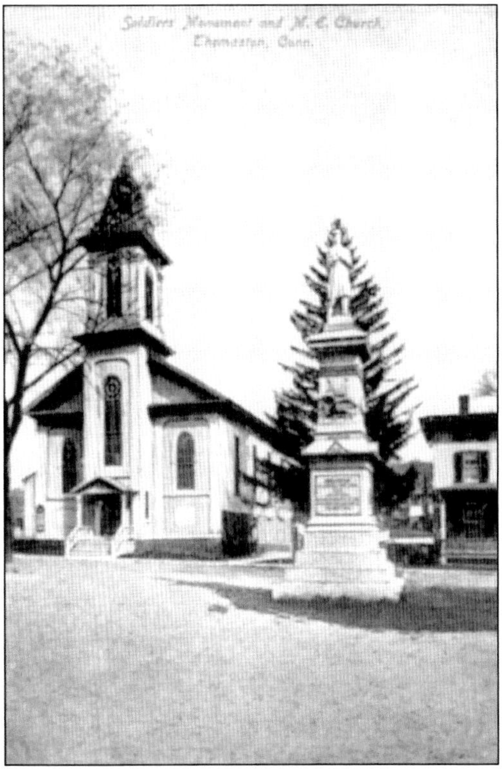

Churches have often been the subjects of postcards. The Methodist Episcopal church overlooks Veterans' Park. Built in 1866, it is the second-oldest church in Thomaston. (Courtesy of Robert Magdziarz.)

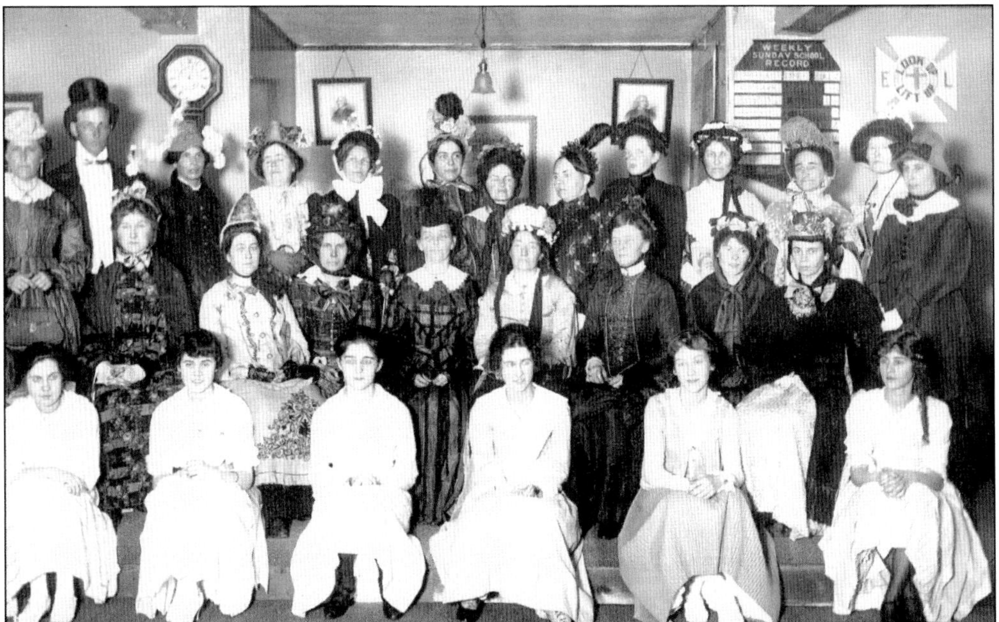

This church play was performed by members of the Methodist Episcopal church *c.* 1920. The various facial expressions suggest that this was a talented cast, although the lone male performer looks a little downcast. We see a Seth Thomas regulator on the wall, pictures of the Wesleys, and the "Weekly Sunday School Record."

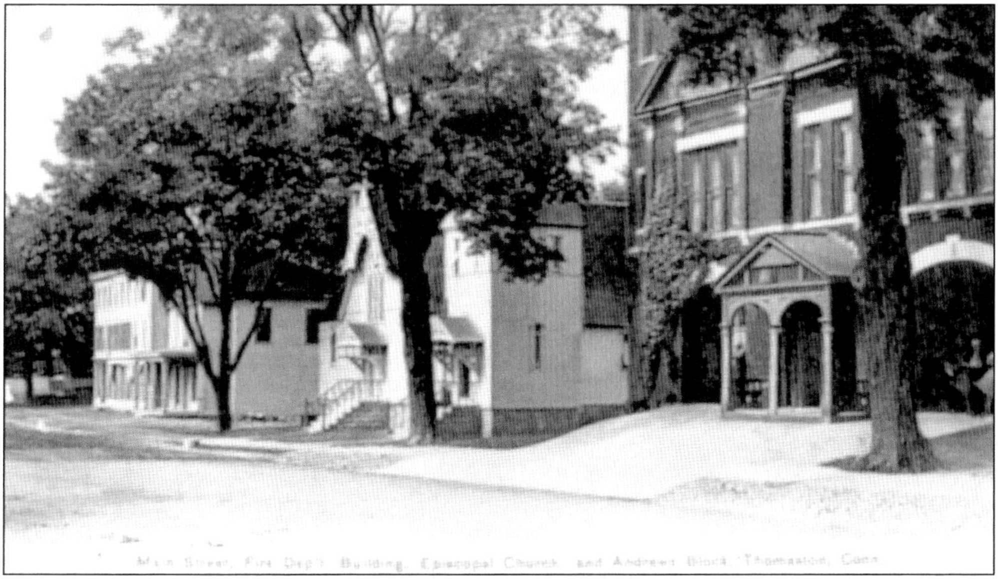

This postcard was mailed in 1907 to Collinsville. The Trinity Episcopal Church is in the center, and the former chapel is in its new location. The stepping stone in front of the church assisted parishioners as they alighted from their carriages. (Courtesy of Robert Magdziarz.)

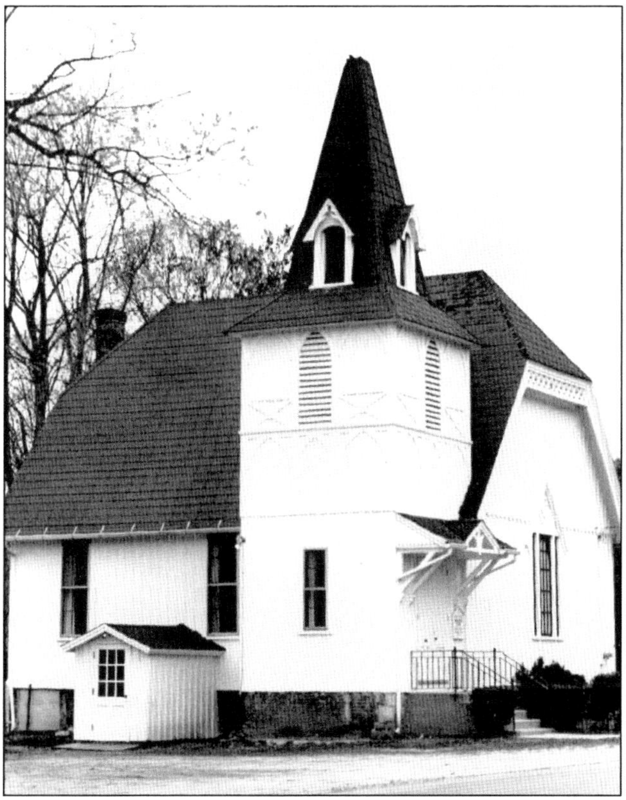

The Eagle Rock Congregational Church was established in 1878, mainly serving the Reynolds Bridge neighborhood.

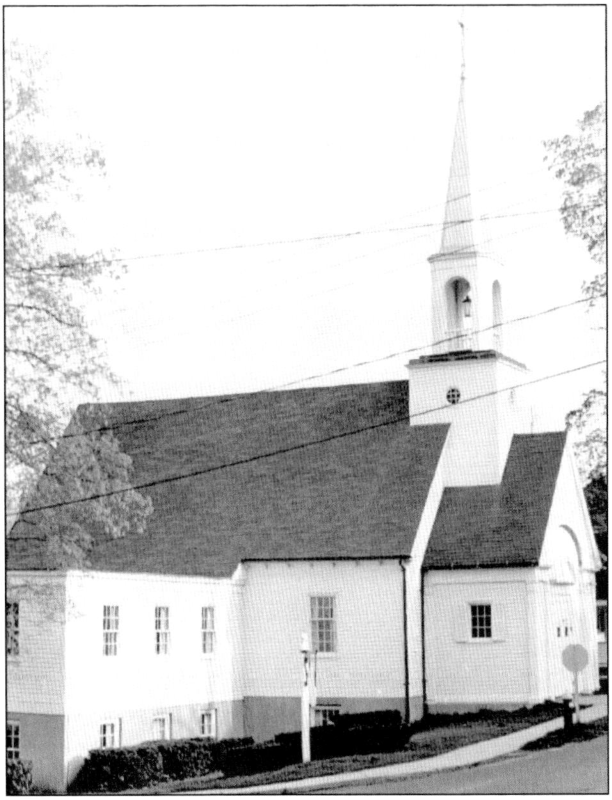

The Covenant Church, on Grove Street, was built in 1892. Another of the downtown area churches, it is pictured here with its addition, which was constructed in 1962.

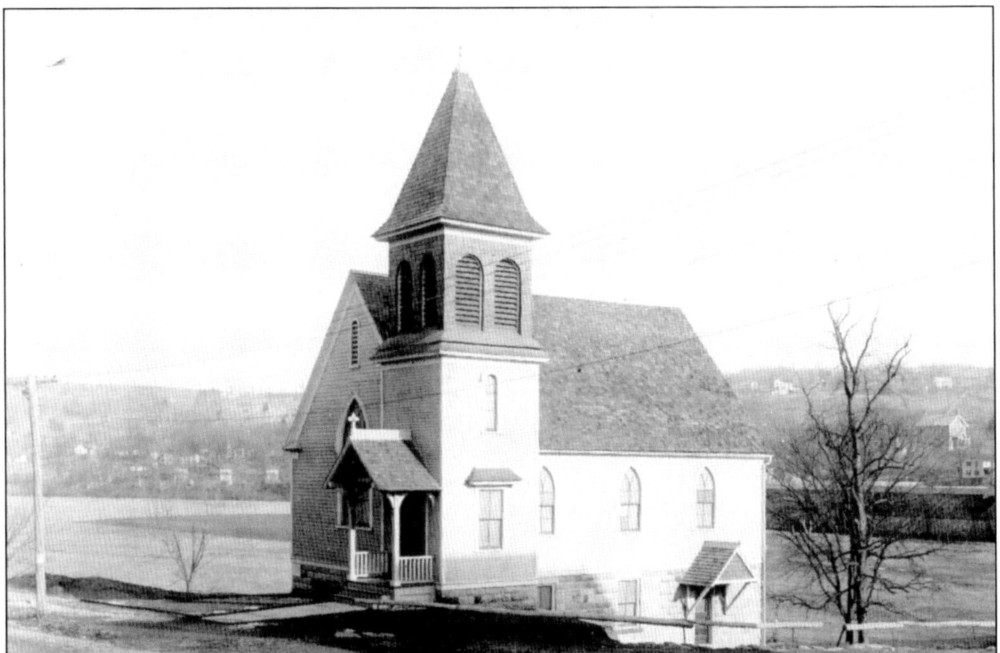

The newly constructed Bethlehem Lutheran Church, seen here in 1909, was situated at the northern corner of Electric Avenue and North Main Street.

Fr. Michael McGivney (1852–1890) is a candidate for sainthood in the Roman Catholic Church. He is best known as the founder of the Knights of Columbus in 1882. Appointed as pastor of St. Thomas Church in November 1884, he served until his death from a respiratory illness on August 14, 1890, two days after his 38th birthday. St. Thomas was the only pastorate served by the young priest.

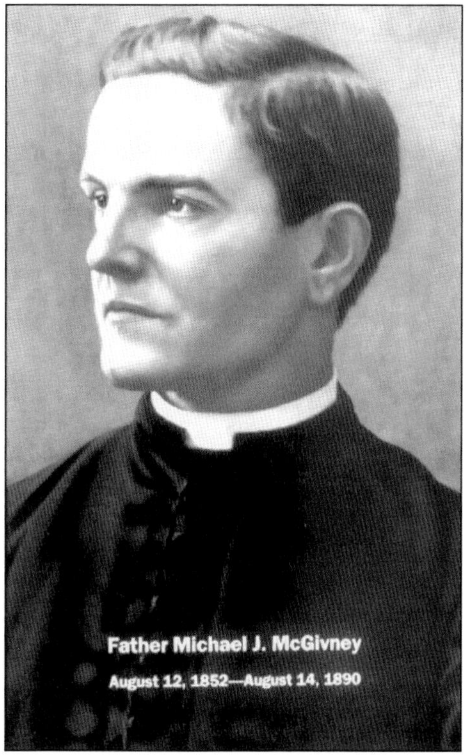

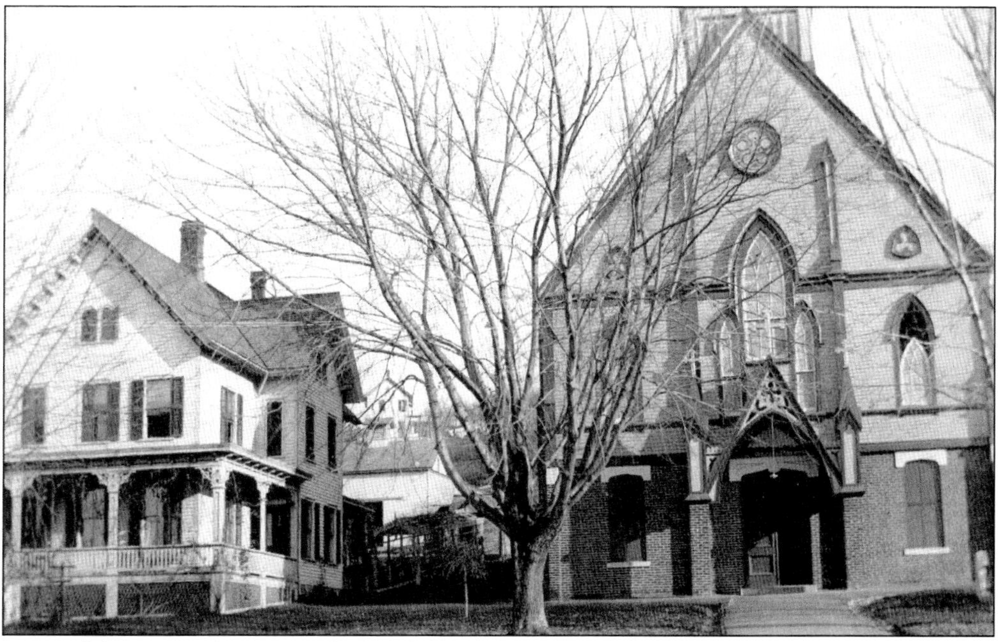

Pictured here are the original church and rectory of St. Thomas, served by Fr. Michael McGivney. Built in 1876, the church was located on the east side of Chapel Street, close to the homes of its Irish and Polish parishioners. The present St. Thomas was built in 1906. These buildings and most of the residences on Chapel Street were demolished in the 1960s during the construction of Route 8.

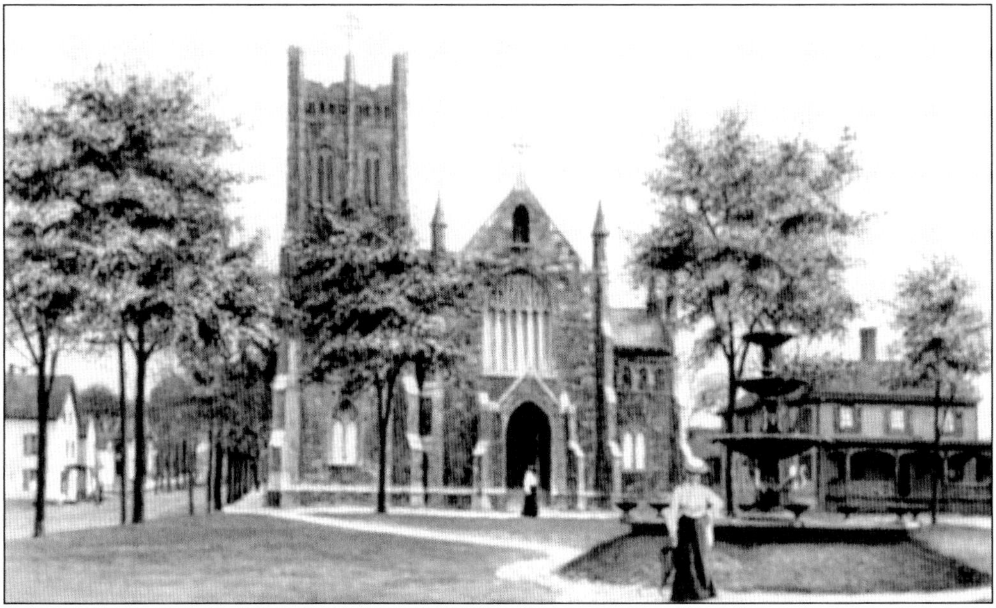

A pleasant place to promenade was in the park in front of the new St. Thomas Church. Built in 1906, it is the largest of Thomaston's churches. A magnificent neo-Gothic structure, it suffered significant damage when the gold cross on the tower was struck by lightning. Without a tower for many years, it was restored during the pastorate of Fr. John J. McGrath in 1940. (Courtesy of Robert Magdziarz.)

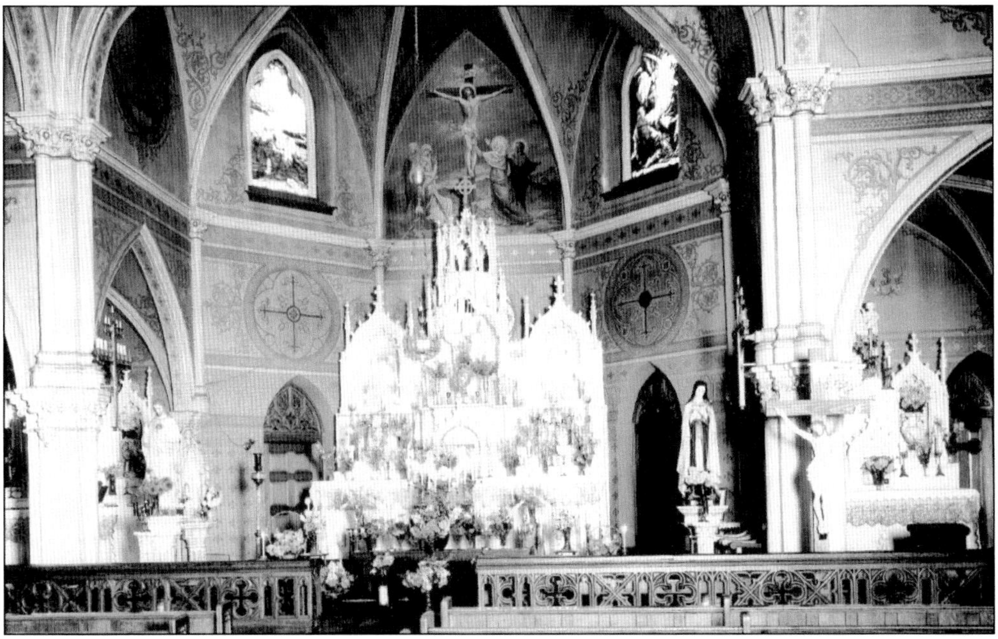

This study of the interior of St. Thomas shows the rich decor and elaborate design of the main altar and surroundings. The statuary and the flowers add to the setting, and the arches, columns, and decorative panels are appealing. This is a historic picture, since the interior underwent significant alteration in the early 1970s at the direction of Archbishop John Whealon.

Four

SPORTS AND SERVICE

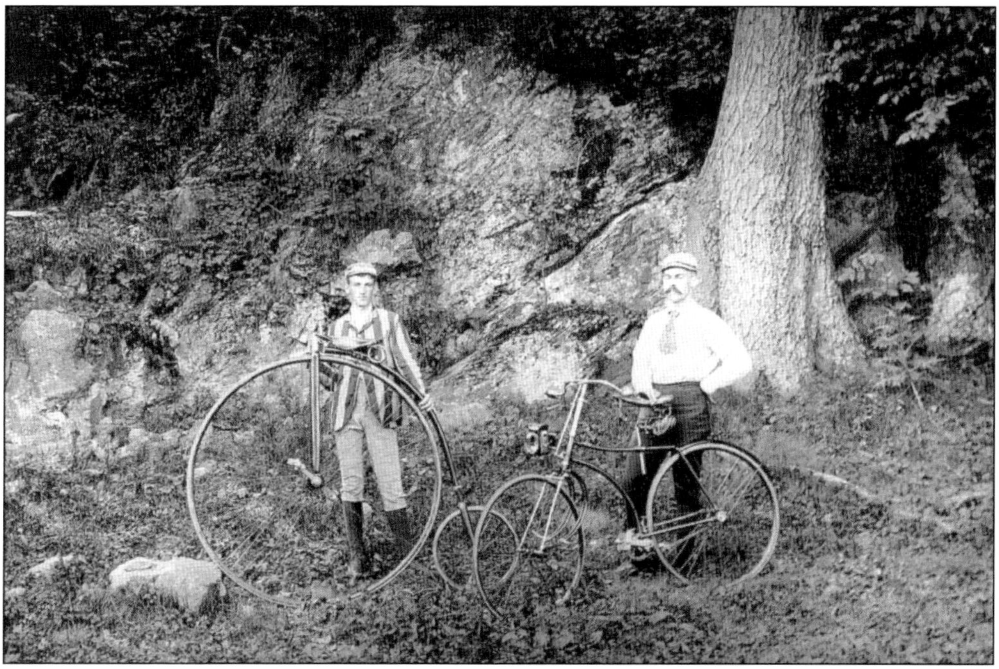

Sports activities have always been a part of the Thomaston scene. These two dandies are all set for a Sunday bicycle ride. Called an "ordinary," the bicycle at the left was designed in 1870 and remained in production until c. 1890. The dapper young gentleman with the necktie is the picture of confidence. The other, with a flamboyant jacket, looks a bit more apprehensive.

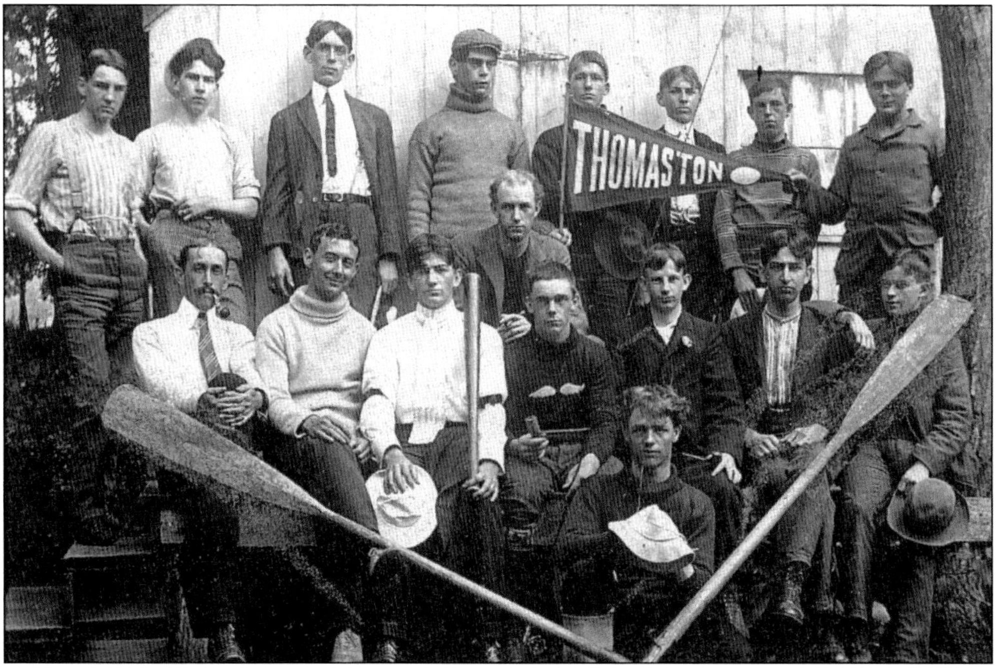

A group of men has gathered for an afternoon of sport—rowing and baseball. Note the variety of dress, from their high-laced shoes to their hats. Harold DeWolfe Hotchkiss, president of the Thomaston High School class of 1906, was the owner of the photograph. The only ones we can identify are Robert Welton, holding the bat, and Arthur Bold, wearing the cap in the center of the back row.

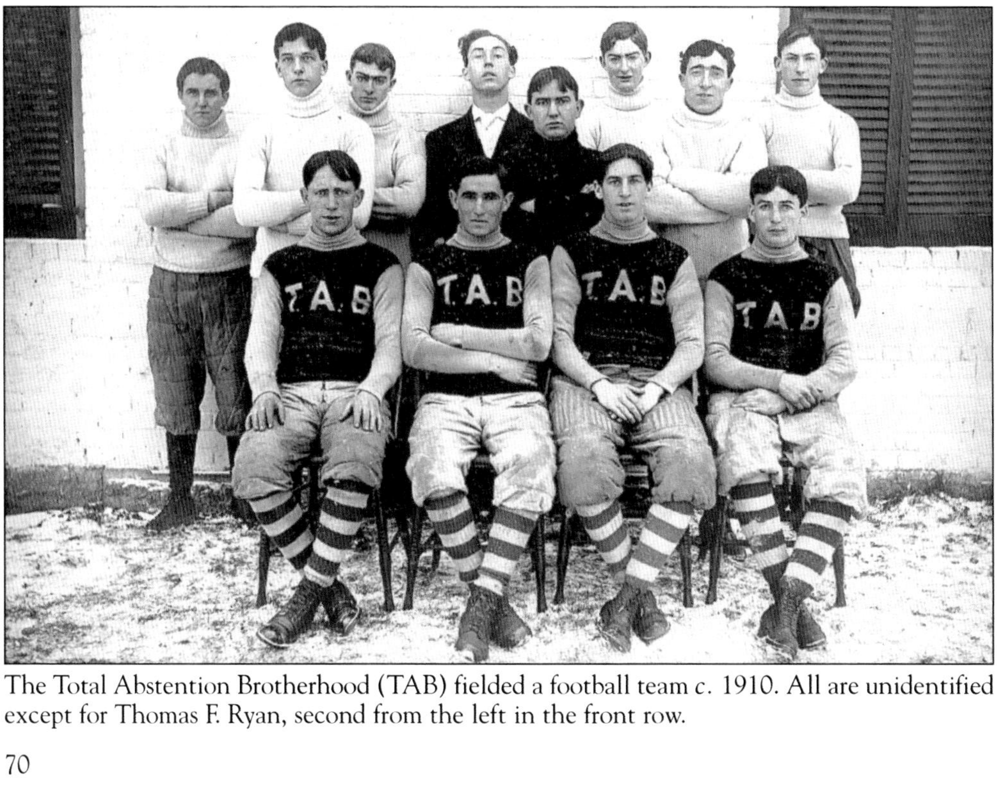

The Total Abstention Brotherhood (TAB) fielded a football team *c.* 1910. All are unidentified except for Thomas F. Ryan, second from the left in the front row.

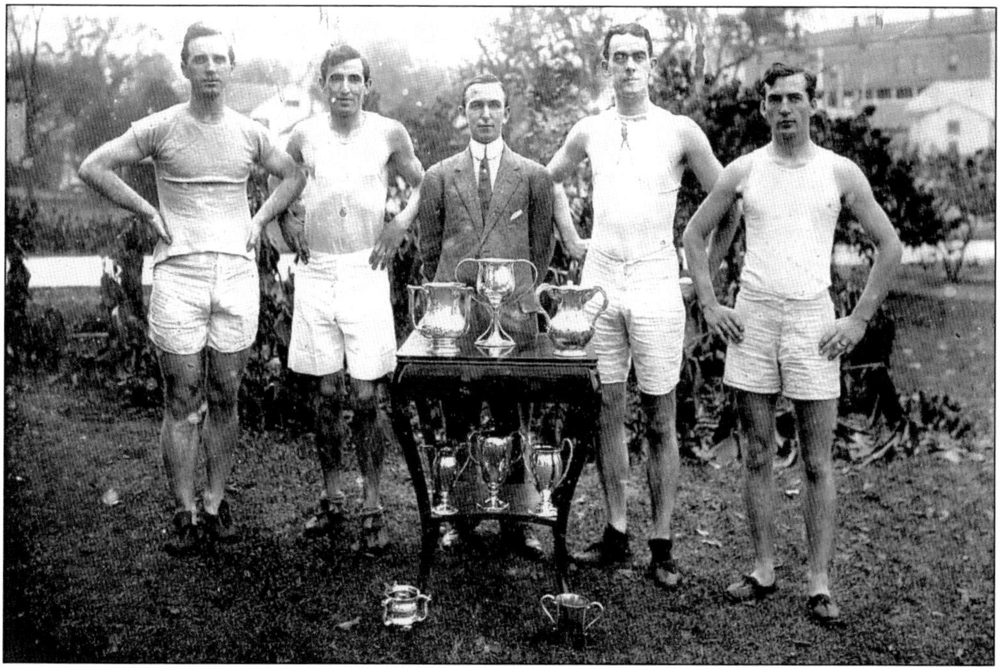

In 1911, the Total Abstention Brotherhood's relay team was very successful, as evidenced by the number of trophies in the photograph. A major victory was the defeat of the New York Athletic Club at Groton Point. Pictured here are, from left to right, B.A. McDonald, Thomas F. Ryan, manager John Waters, James J. Carr, and J. Monahan.

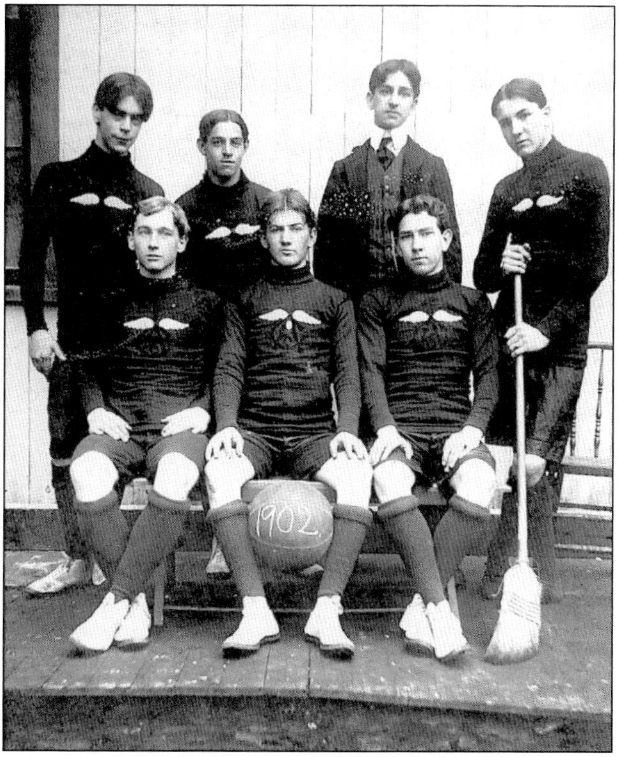

Organized team sports became more common in the early 20th century. This vintage basketball team has warm stockings, long shorts, and stylish hairdos. The manager looks somewhat disconsolate, but at least he did not have to sweep the floor. That was evidently the job for the sixth man. Robert Welton holds the ball, while Arthur Bold strikes a pose at the left in the back row.

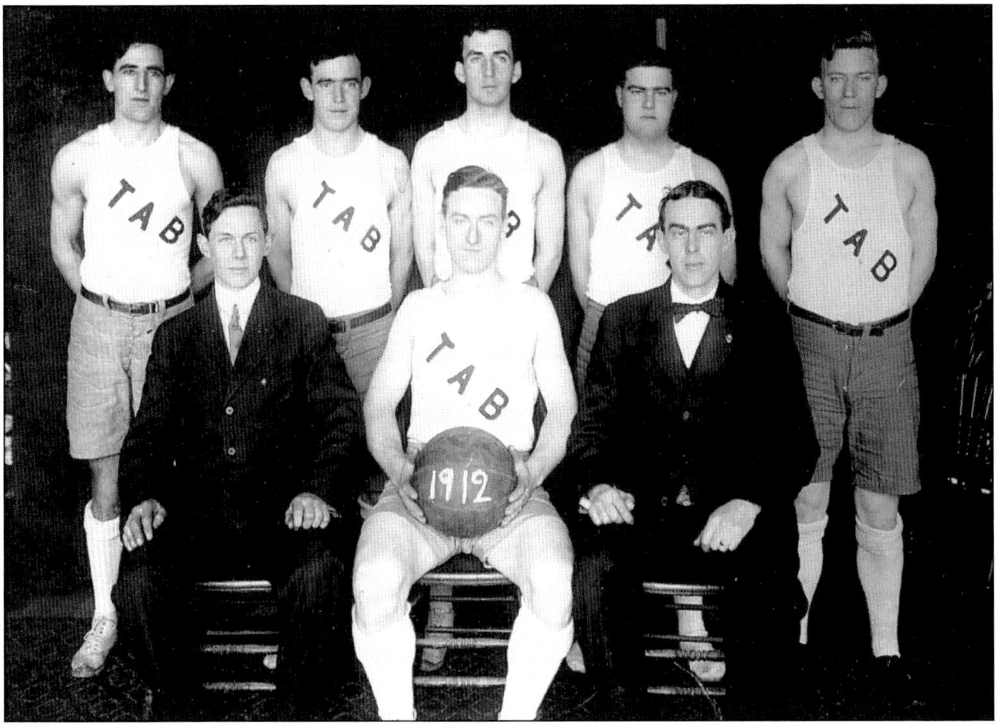

Basketball has always been popular in Thomaston. Apparently, at least two teams existed in 1912. The Total Abstention Brotherhood's players are, from left to right, as follows: (front row) Jerry Reardon, Ed Glennon, and James J. Carr; (back row) Thomas F. Ryan, Mike Flemming, Jim Monahan, Henry Langford, and Tom Fruin.

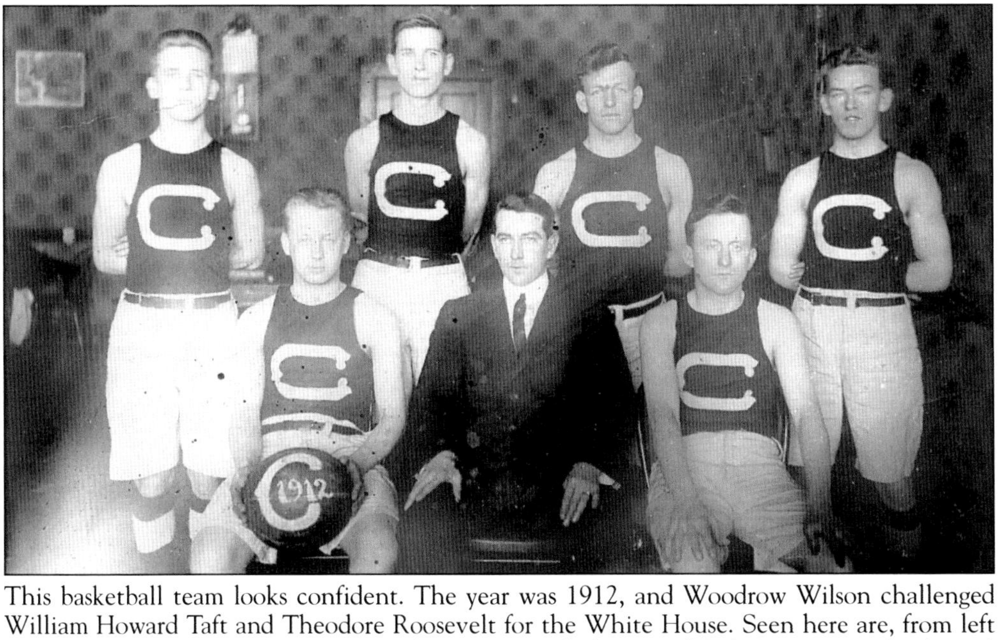

This basketball team looks confident. The year was 1912, and Woodrow Wilson challenged William Howard Taft and Theodore Roosevelt for the White House. Seen here are, from left to right, the following: (front row) Fred Latimer, Fred Flynn, and Bob Cummings; (back row) Pete Martin, Chuck Albecker, John Lynch, and Joe Glennon.

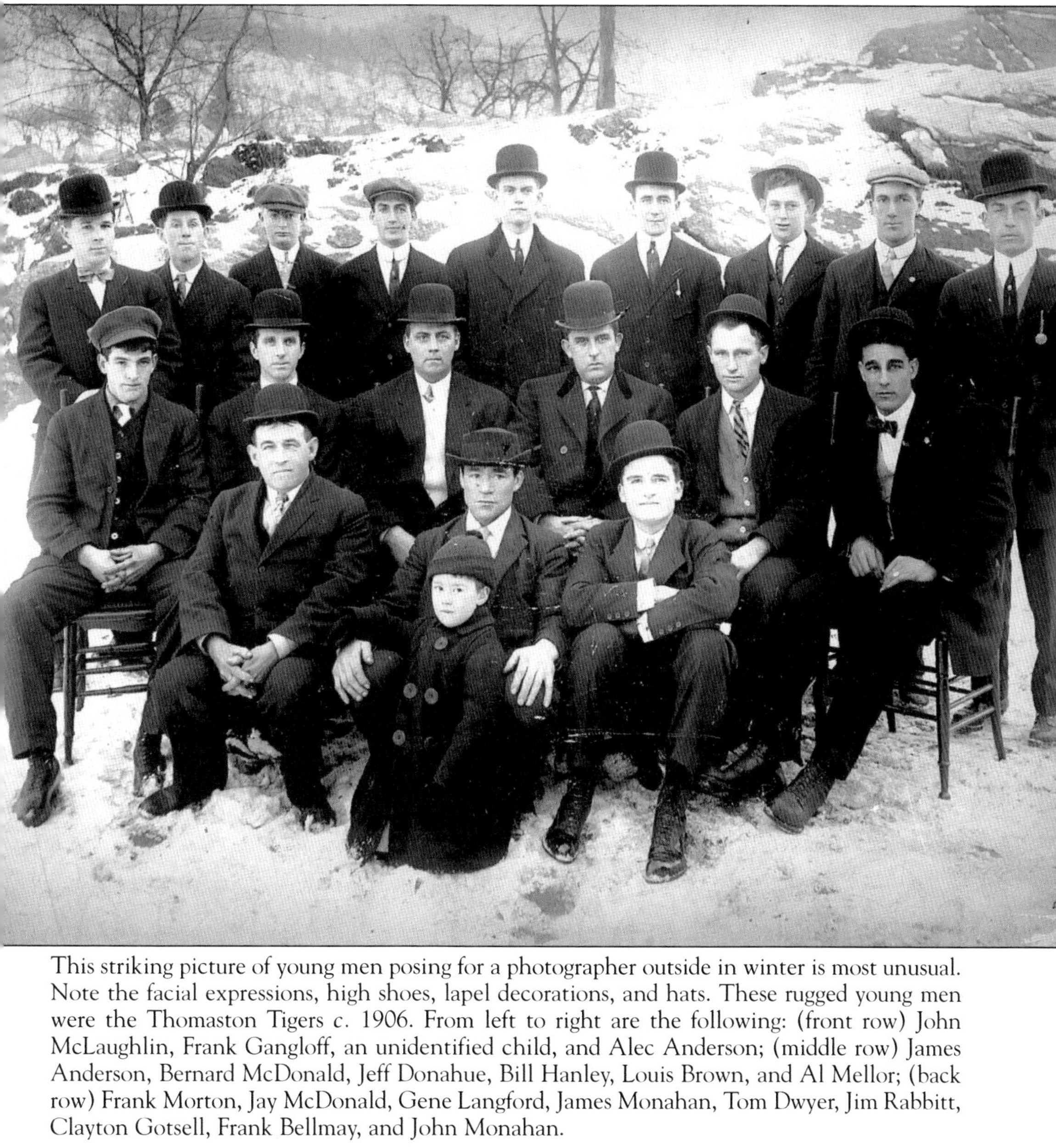

This striking picture of young men posing for a photographer outside in winter is most unusual. Note the facial expressions, high shoes, lapel decorations, and hats. These rugged young men were the Thomaston Tigers *c*. 1906. From left to right are the following: (front row) John McLaughlin, Frank Gangloff, an unidentified child, and Alec Anderson; (middle row) James Anderson, Bernard McDonald, Jeff Donahue, Bill Hanley, Louis Brown, and Al Mellor; (back row) Frank Morton, Jay McDonald, Gene Langford, James Monahan, Tom Dwyer, Jim Rabbitt, Clayton Gotsell, Frank Bellmay, and John Monahan.

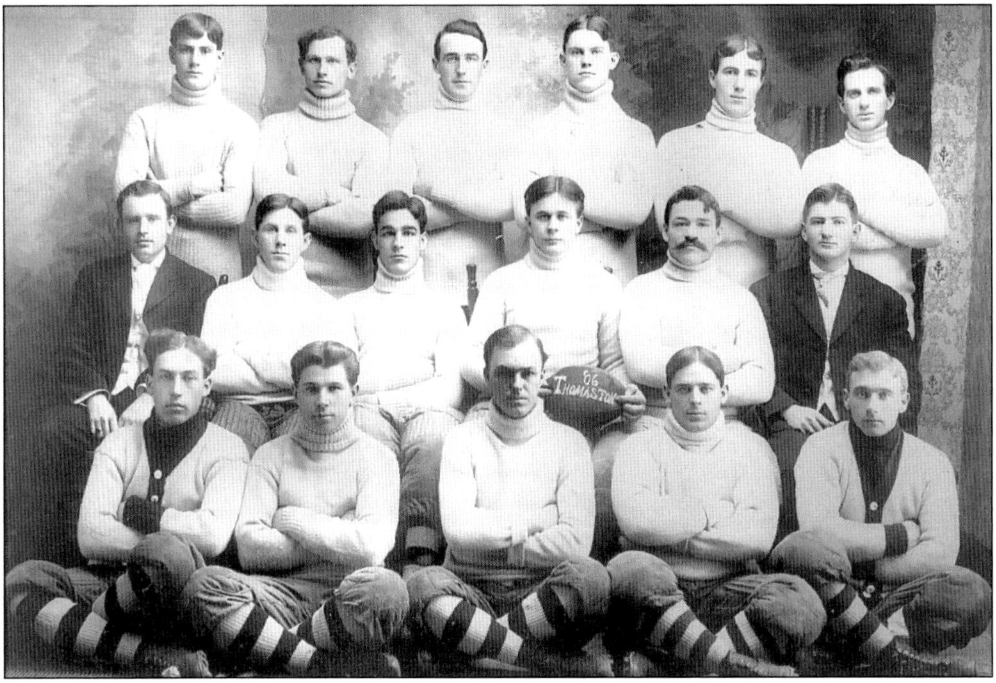

The Thomaston Tigers led the way for the Ponies of the 1920s. The 1906 team includes, from left to right, the following: (front row) John Monahan, Frank Morton, Bill Parke, Ralph Remson, and Harry Stubs; (middle row) Eugene Purdy, Jay McDonald, Al Mellor, Frank Platt, Frank Gangloff, and Robert Welton; (back row) Ed "Duke" Klocker, Louis Brown, Jim Rabbitt, Tom Dwyer, Frank Bellmay, and Bernard McDonald. (Courtesy of Mario DePecol.)

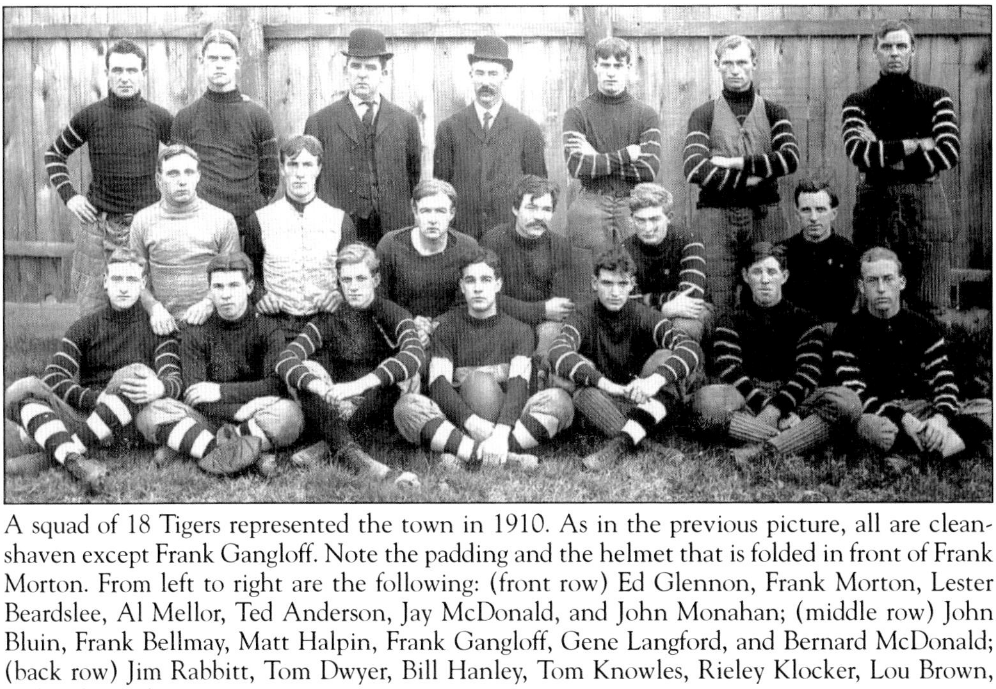

A squad of 18 Tigers represented the town in 1910. As in the previous picture, all are clean-shaven except Frank Gangloff. Note the padding and the helmet that is folded in front of Frank Morton. From left to right are the following: (front row) Ed Glennon, Frank Morton, Lester Beardslee, Al Mellor, Ted Anderson, Jay McDonald, and John Monahan; (middle row) John Bluin, Frank Bellmay, Matt Halpin, Frank Gangloff, Gene Langford, and Bernard McDonald; (back row) Jim Rabbitt, Tom Dwyer, Bill Hanley, Tom Knowles, Rieley Klocker, Lou Brown, and Jeff Donahue.

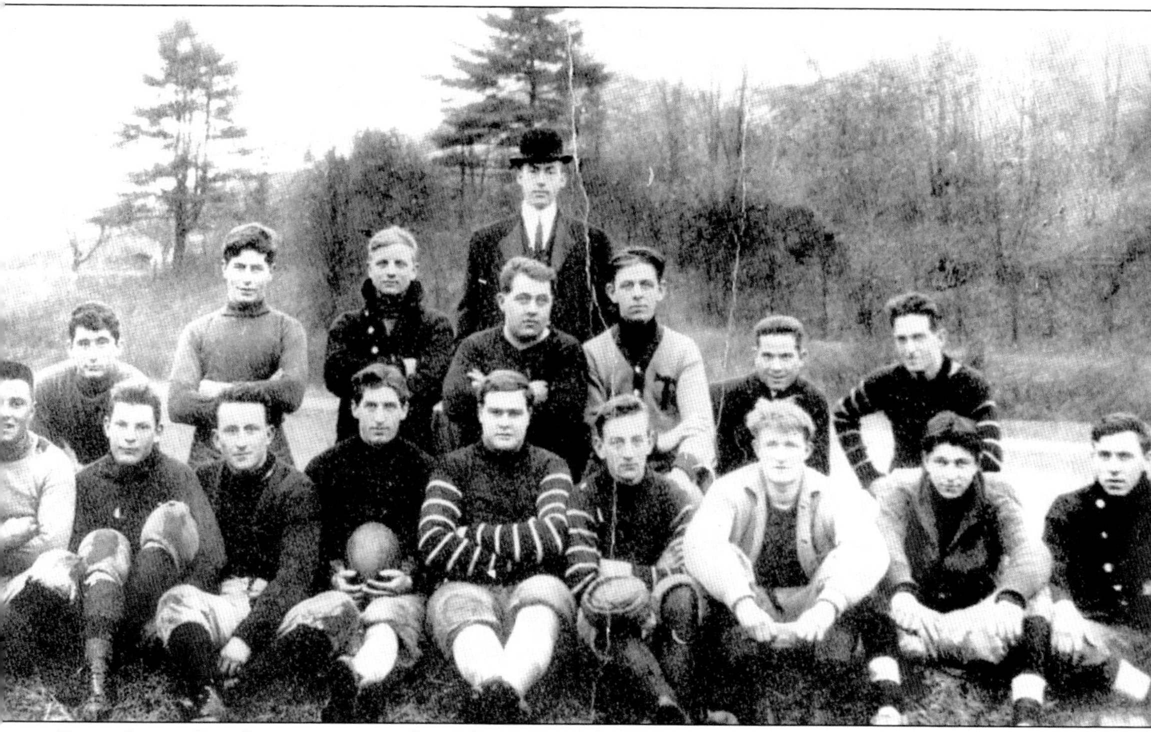

Sports have played a prominent role in the town's life for decades. The 1911 and 1912 Tigers set a high standard as Naugatuck Valley champions with an undefeated record. Pictured in the front row are, from left to right, James P. "Taft" Ryan, Wesley Billings, Bob Cummings, unidentified, Henry Langford, three unidentified players, and John J. Callahan. The men in the back row are unidentified. The manager was John Waters. (Courtesy of Joan Eileen Flynn Raccio.)

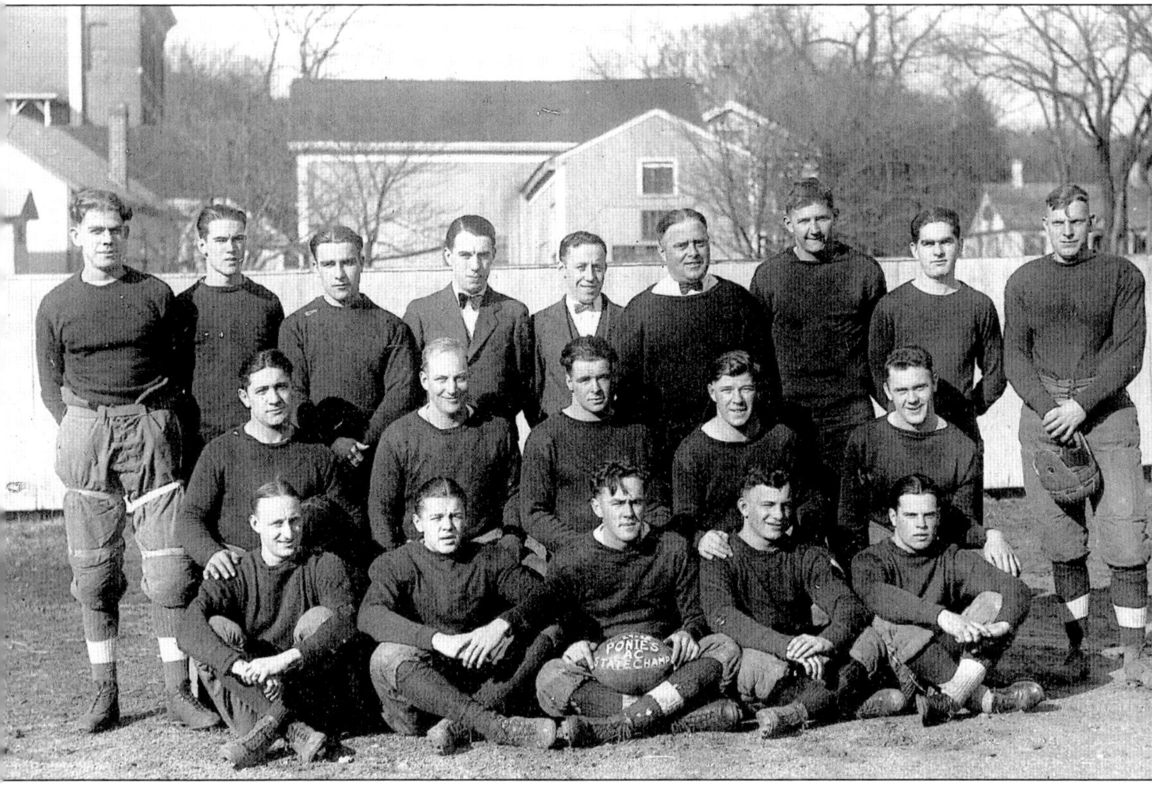

The tradition of championship football was upheld by the Thomaston Ponies, coached by James "Taft" Ryan, who served later as the town's police chief. The 1924–1925 team includes, from left to right, the following: (front row) Arthur Dodge, Rudy Novakowski, Harry Hearn, Myron Klaneski, and Robert Shearer; (middle row) Bill Richie, Herbert Thulin, William Shearer, Otto Harbert, and Louis Mozonski; (back row) William Rupenski, George Callahan, Ben Gilland, Edward Coates, Peter Rein, coach Ryan, Harold "Percy" Atwood, Thomas Lyons, and Wesley Billings.

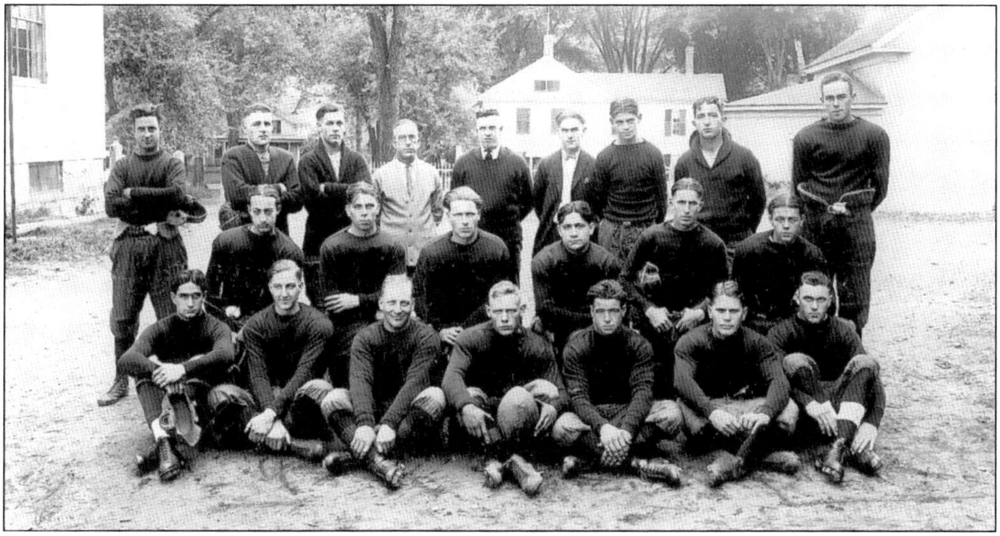

Harry Lynch succeeded Taft Ryan as coach of the Ponies. The team is pictured here in the Old Center School yard. Elm Street appears in the background. Note the helmets and pads. From left to right are the following: (front row) unidentified, Edward Johnson, Herbert Thulin, ? Boniveer, William Shearer, unidentified, and Louis Bristol; (middle row) Bub Koegel, Josh Innocent, three unidentified players, and Rudy Novakowski; (back row) Shoot Simpson, unidentified, Leese Perbeck, George Dewell, Harry Lynch, Tom Lyons, two unidentified players, and Labart Hearn.

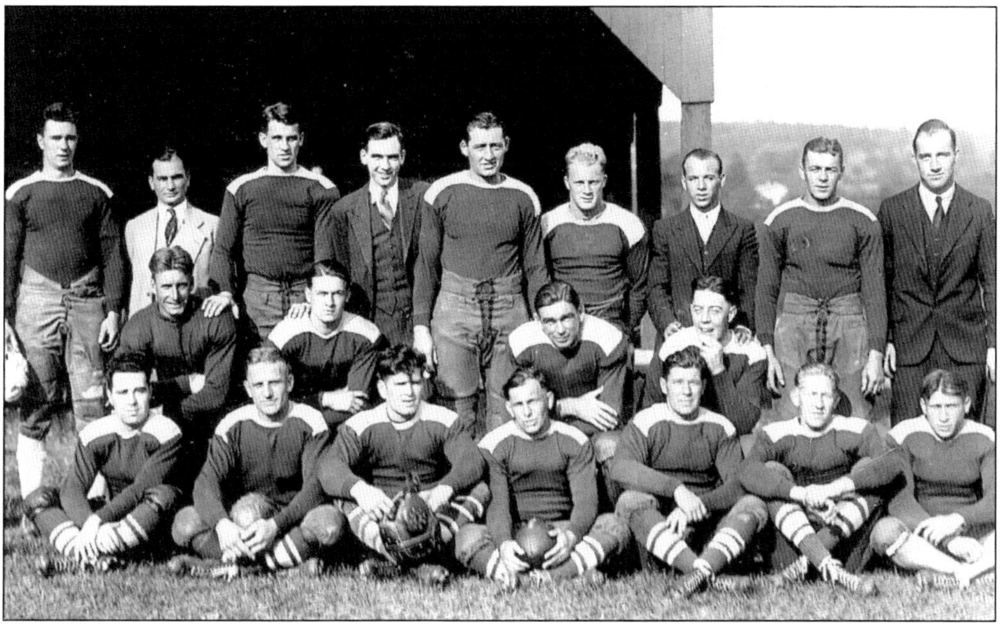

In 1930, the Ponies were coached by the Yale great Fay Vincent. They played their games at Risdon Field. Pictured here are, from left to right, the following: (front row) Joe Concannon, Bill Welnitz, Jake Hamel, Myron Klaneski, Otto Harbert, Bill Bertnagel, and Milo Morton; (middle row) George Klug, Mickey Fill, Leo Smith, and Dave Kane; (back row) George Smith, Ernest Ruggie, Art Rode, Henry Brophy, Beans Leary, Cliff Gleason, Joe Boguslawski, Rudy Novakowski, and coach Vincent.

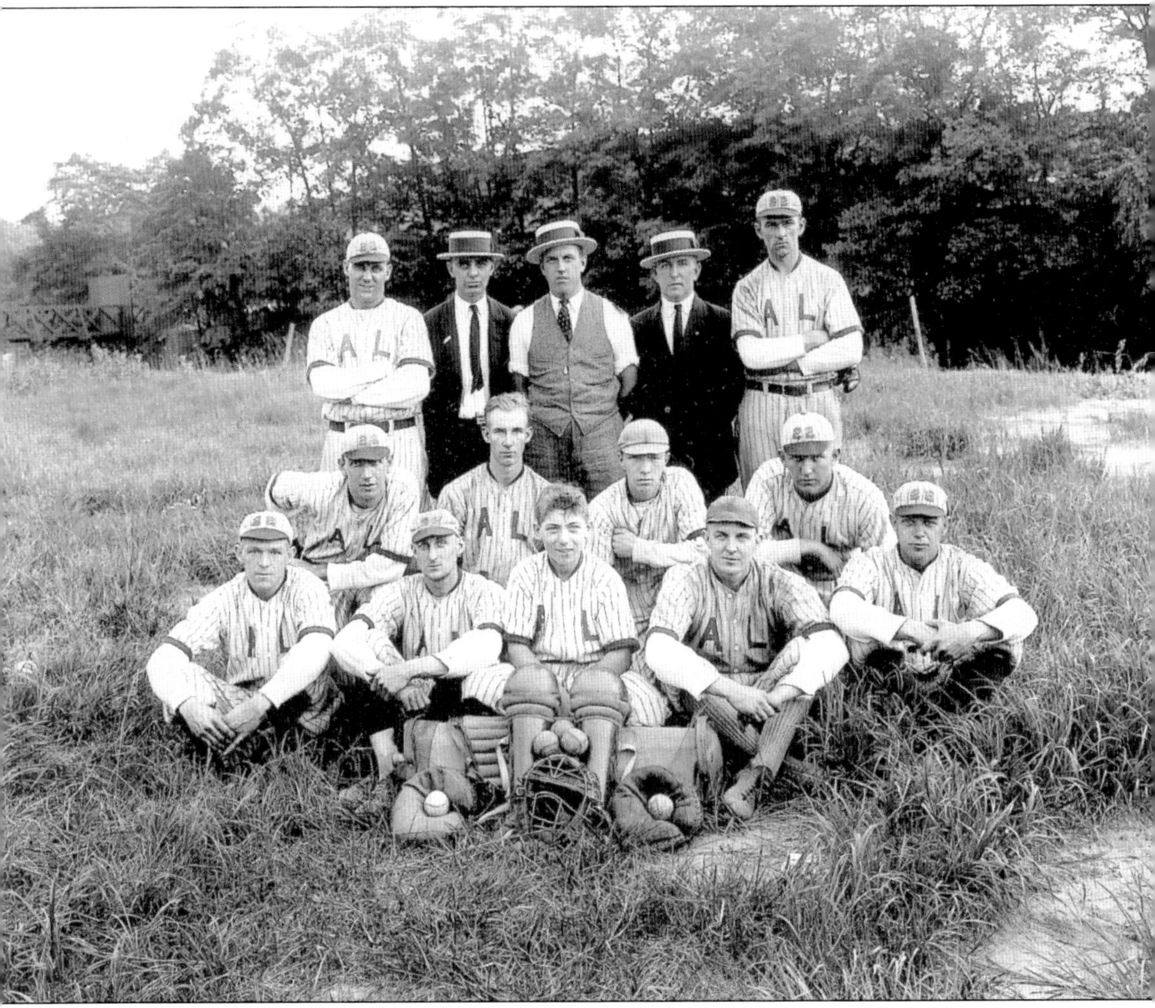

Thomaston played baseball for 30 years in competition with other towns. Harry Lynch was the longtime manager. His American Legion team c. 1925 consisted of the players shown here. From left to right are the following: (front row) Harold Dayton, Art Dodge, ? Ostroski, ? McLeary, and Ray Ebner; (middle row) "Hung" Waters, "Lefty" Beach, "Beck" Robinson, and Harold "Percy" Atwood; (back row) Andrew O'Neill, George "Tip" Bernatchez, Harry Lynch, John Waters, and Steve Handlowich.

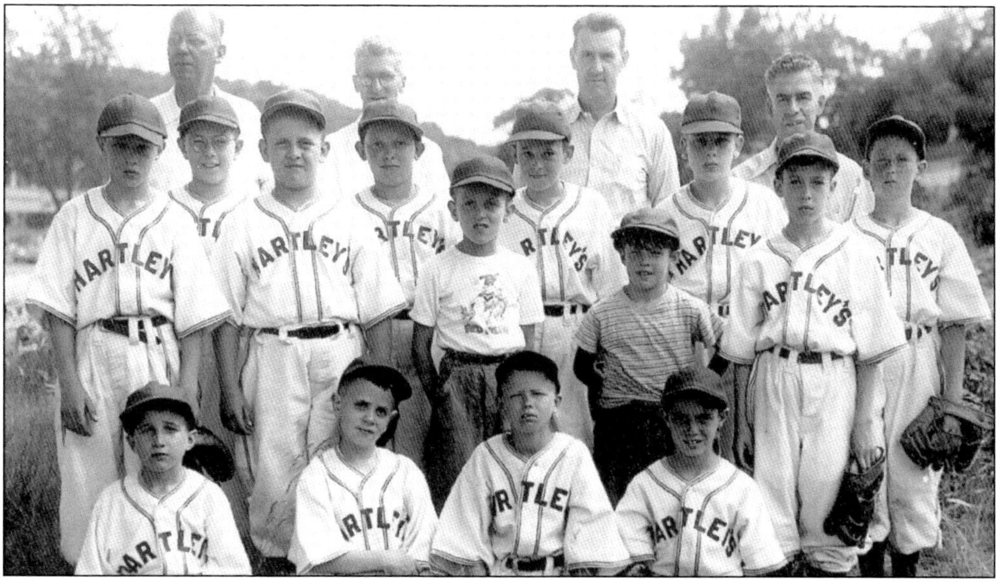

In 1949, Thomaston joined the nationwide Little League. The league had four teams that first year, sponsored by Hallden's, Hartley's, Innes Brothers, and the Knights of Columbus. Games were played on what is now Risdon Field. Pictured here are, from left to right, the following: (first row) Anthony Damiano, Michael Conway, Ronald Rogozinski, and Ronald Reed; (second row) Robert Brink, Edward Adam, William O'Connor, Edward Knox, and Joseph Wassong Jr.; (third row) John Oris, Richard Beruk, Francis Savage, Scott Clemens, and William Sofield; (fourth row) coaches Andrew O'Neill, Patrick Ryan, Francis Conway, and Joseph Wassong Sr.

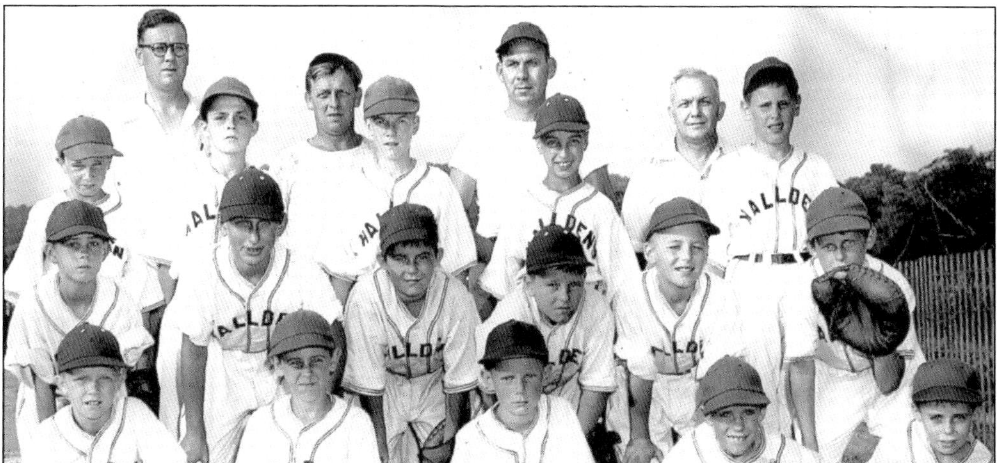

During the first year, the outfield fence was a makeshift snow fence of vertical slats. For the second year, a real stadium fence was built, with space for advertising. Sadly, the field was ruined during the 1955 flood. Shown here are, from left to right, the following: (first row) James Mathews, Clifford Kean, Robert Fox, Peter Farrell, and Julian "Bucky" Vidou; (second row) Donald Sholtis, John Vita, George Dennison, William Foley, Richard Acker, and Eugene Finkle; (third row) Bruce Brink, William Gangloff, Raymond Smith, William Polowy, and Robert Monroe; (fourth row) Herbert Koenigsbauer, George Knox, John Boguslawski, and Henry Fox.

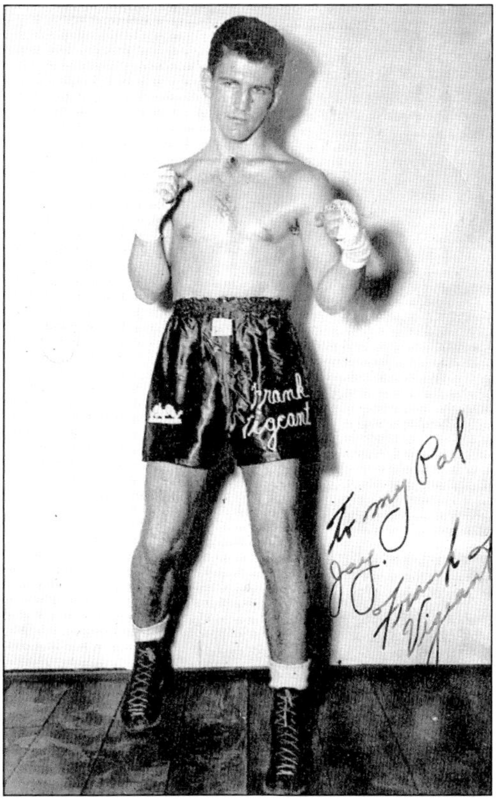

Boxing was a major sport in Connecticut in the 1940s, and featherweight champion Willie Pep of Hartford was a national celebrity. Thomaston had its own "Thomaston Express"—Frank Vigeant, who fought in the welterweight class. After a three-and-a-half-year tour in the U.S. Navy, Vigeant turned professional, winning 26 of 41 bouts, with 4 draws. Certainly the high point in his career was his reign as state welterweight champion from 1947 to 1949. (Courtesy of Frank Vigeant.)

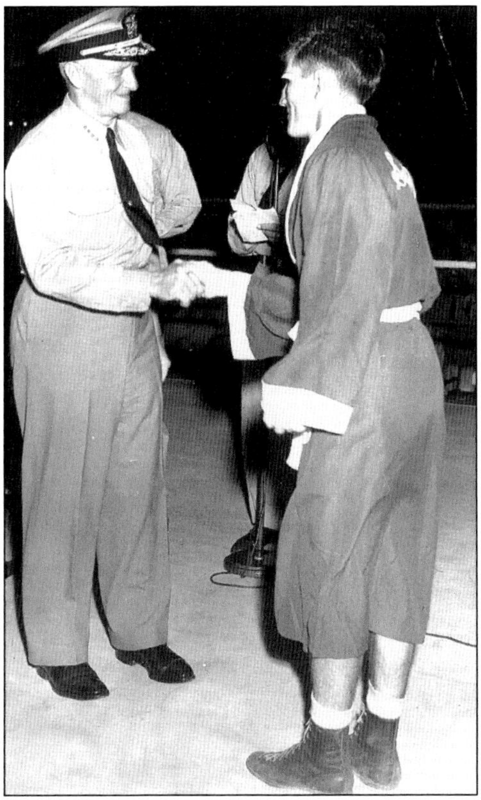

Frank Vigeant served in the South Pacific during World War II. Here, he is congratulated by Adm. Chester Nimitz, commander in chief, Pacific Theater, in 1943 for winning a bout while representing the U.S. Navy. (Courtesy of Frank Vigeant.)

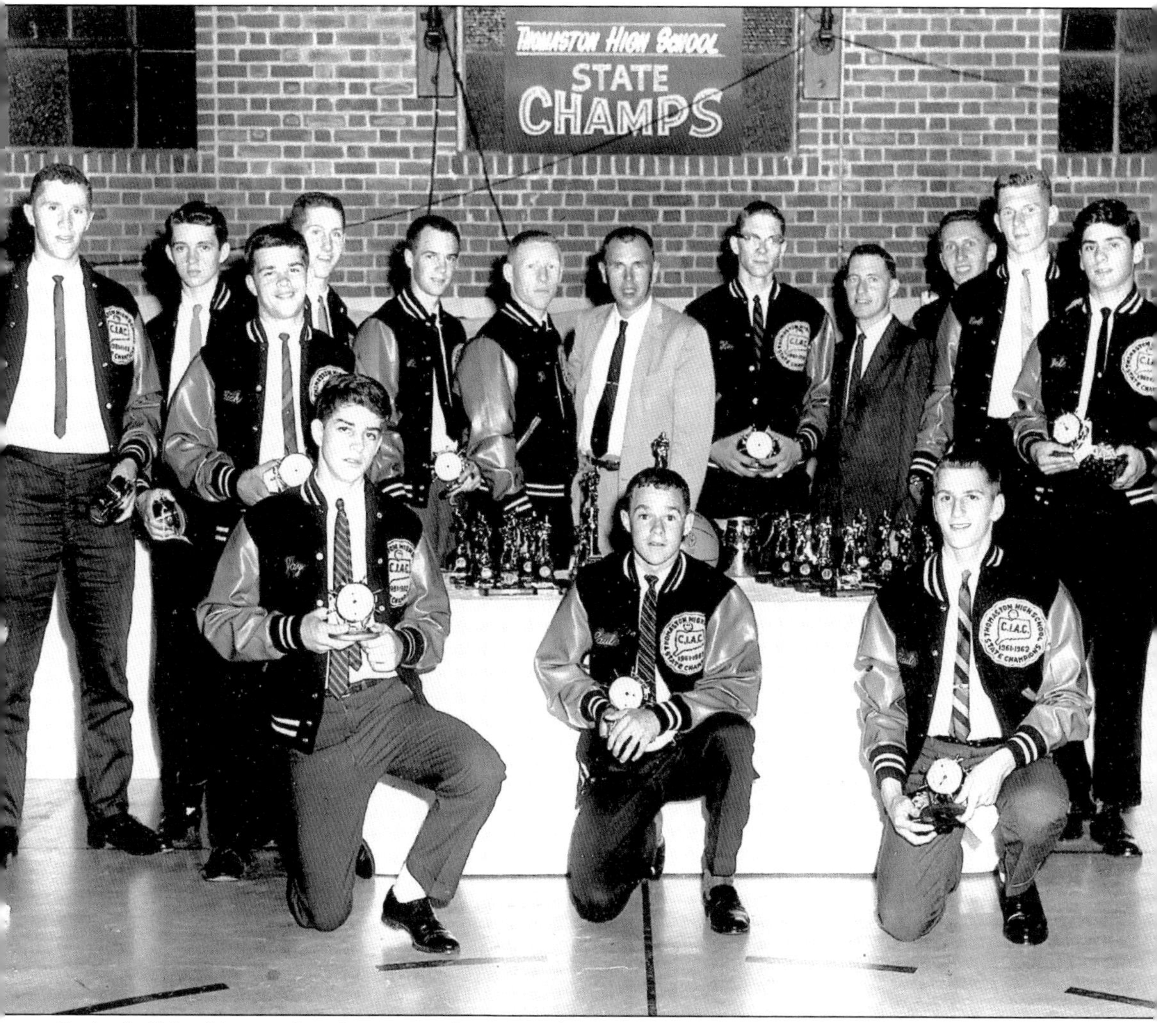

Basketball had been played in town for more than 60 years until the 1962 Thomaston High School Bears hit the heights with a state championship. They have new jackets, clocks, and memories. Seen here are, from left to right, the following: (front row) Jay Lyons, Paul Raider, and Paul Luboyeski; (back row) Ray Watrous, Jim Hannon, Rick O'Connell, John Benedict, Pete Raider, "Red" Root, coach John Kennedy, Ken Linsley, assistant coach Ray Ryan, Ray Cwick, Bob Wotysiak, and Cesare DelVaglio. (Courtesy of Richard O'Connell.)

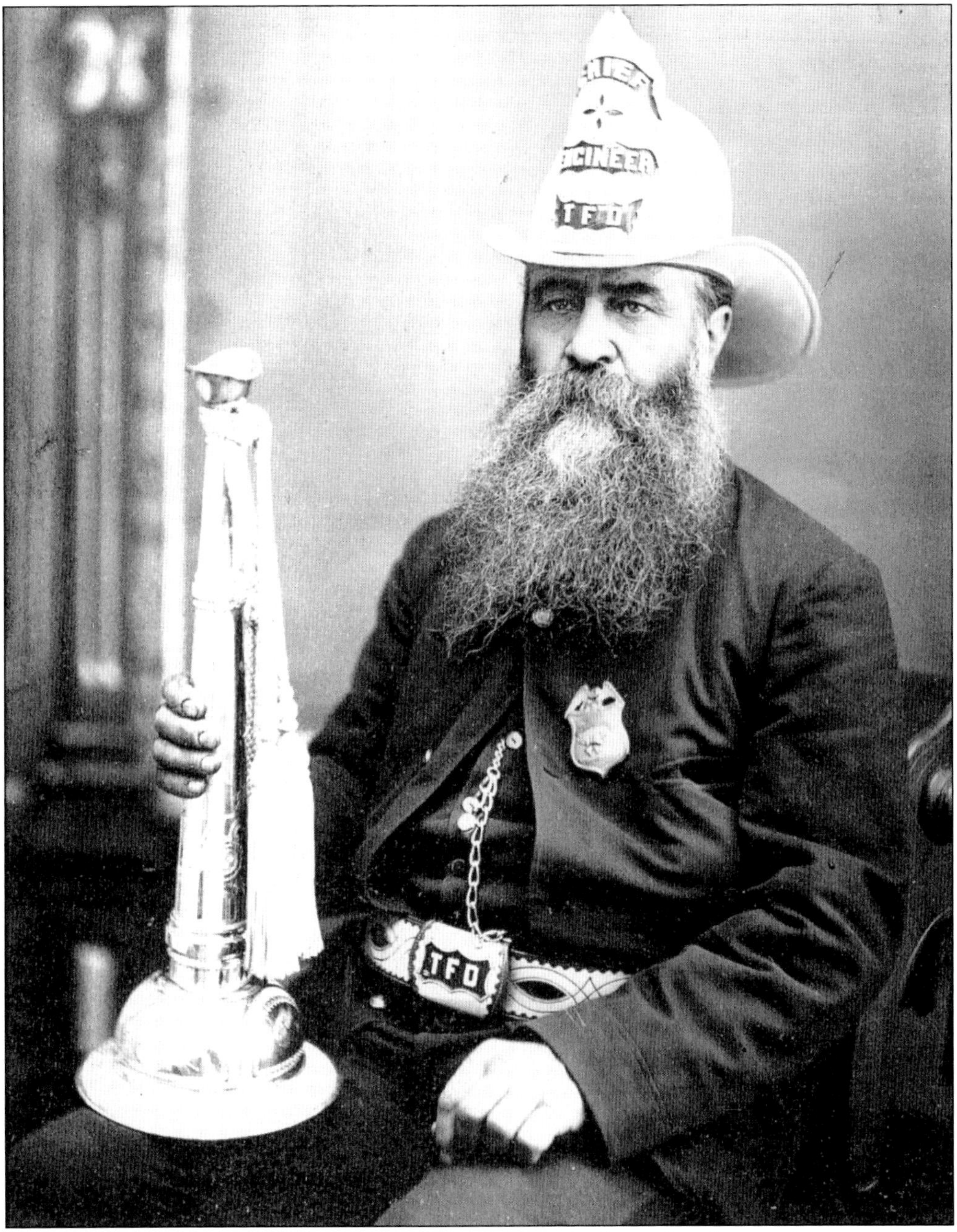

The Thomaston Fire Department has a proud tradition. Not long after the town's incorporation, the firemen elected their first chief in 1882. In this formal portrait, John R. Hoyt wears the badge and helmet of office.

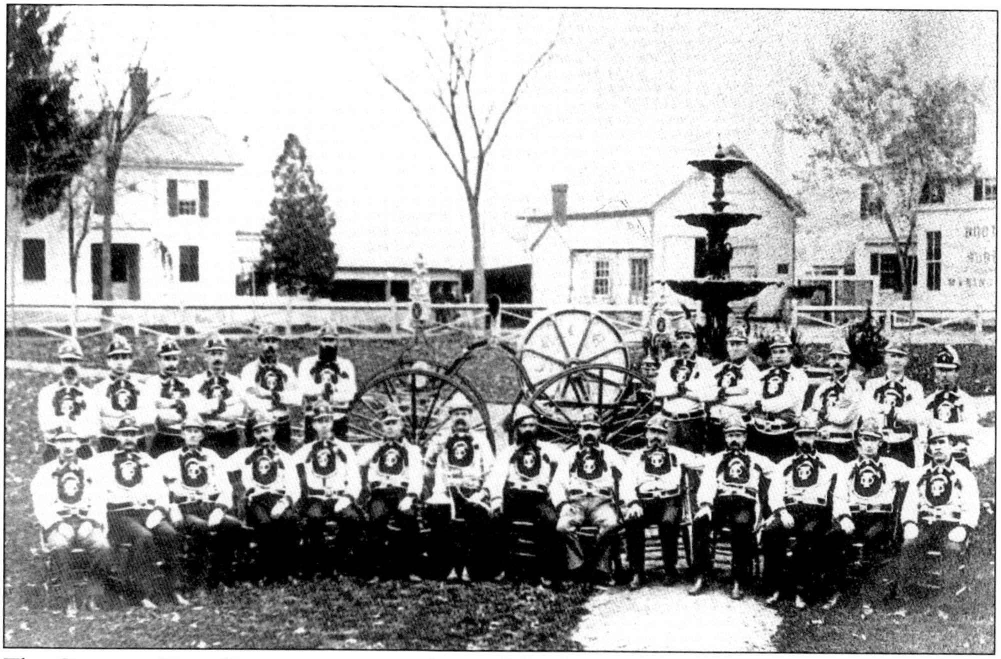

The Crescent Hose Company poses in front of the fountain on the green *c.* the 1890s. This view, looking north, predates the naming of the park after Edith Kenea, in recognition of her contributions to the town's beautification.

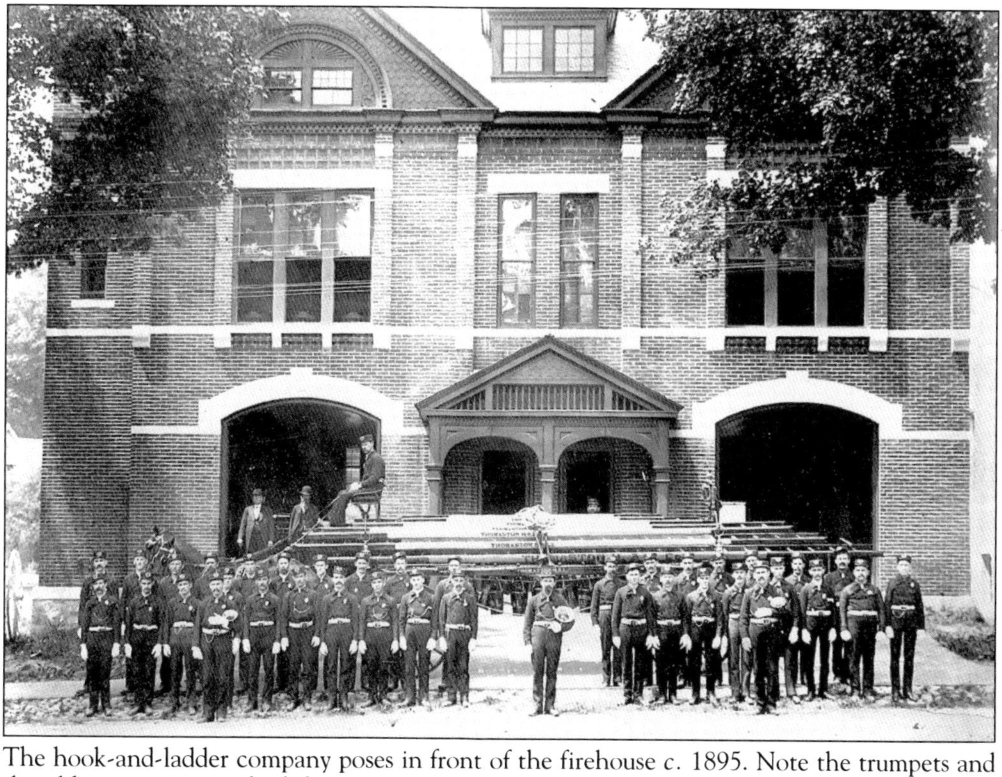

The hook-and-ladder company poses in front of the firehouse *c.* 1895. Note the trumpets and the older apparatus at the left rear.

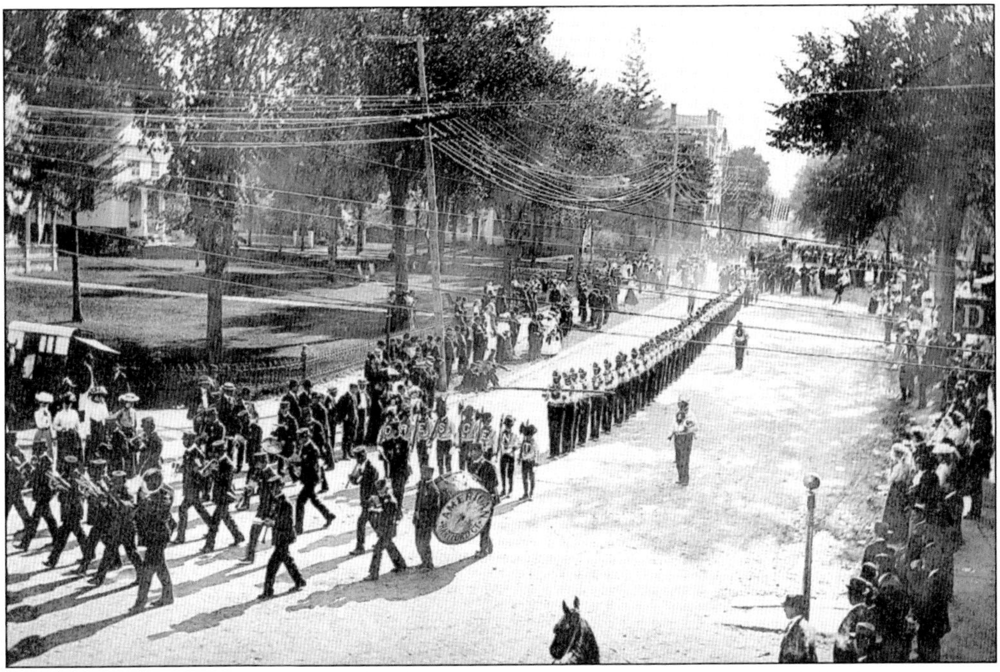

The Crescent Hose Company of the fire department stands at attention while the American Band from Hartford marches along Main Street. Women in long dresses and colorful hats and even one curious horse focused on the parade as the marchers passed in front of the First Congregational Church and the Etheridge house, prior to turning into East Main Street. The occasion was the Firemen's State Convention parade, held on September 11, 1902. One hundred years later, the State Convention returned to Thomaston.

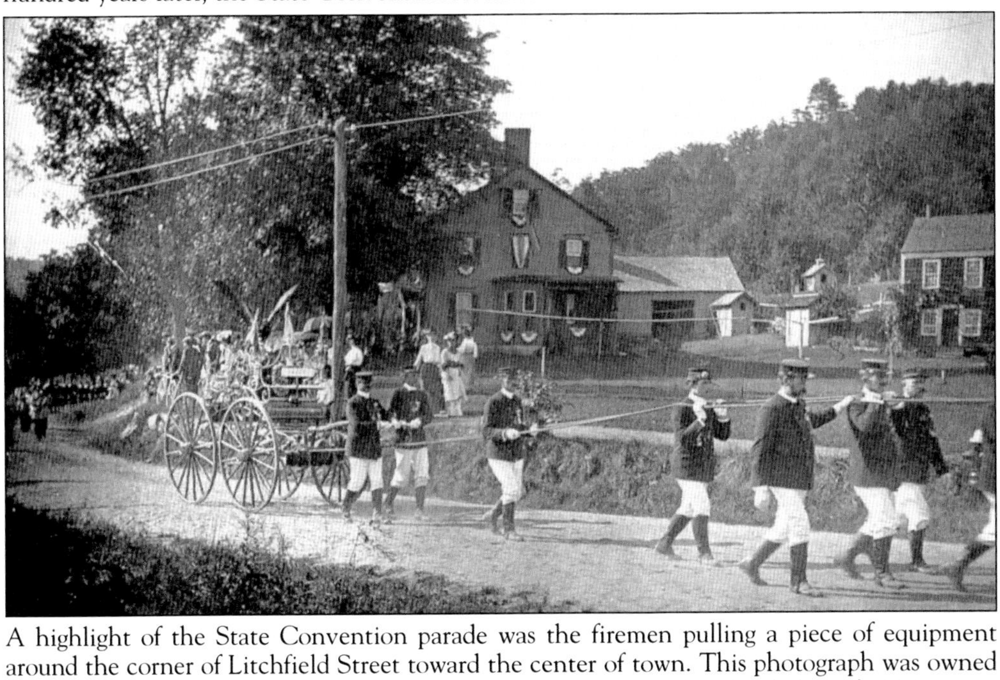

A highlight of the State Convention parade was the firemen pulling a piece of equipment around the corner of Litchfield Street toward the center of town. This photograph was owned by Harold DeWolfe Hotchkiss, a member of the Thomaston High School class of 1906.

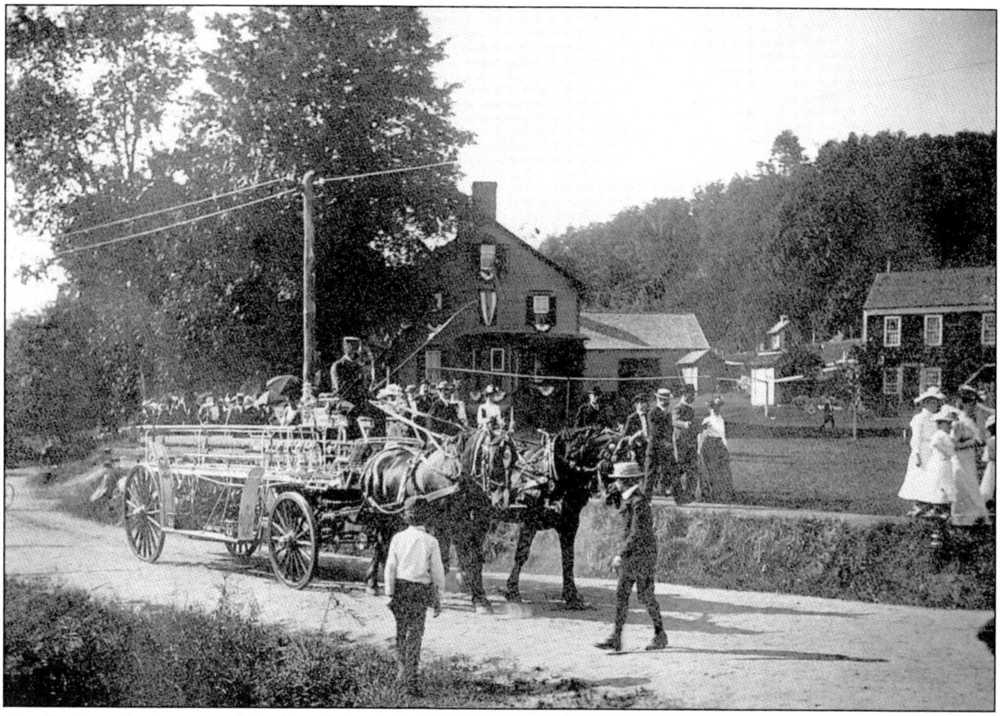

As the last fire wagon filled with hoses turns the corner, the crowd begins to disperse. Note how well dressed everyone is, even the boys in the foreground. A parasol in the background shields a woman from the sun, which casts long shadows late in the afternoon.

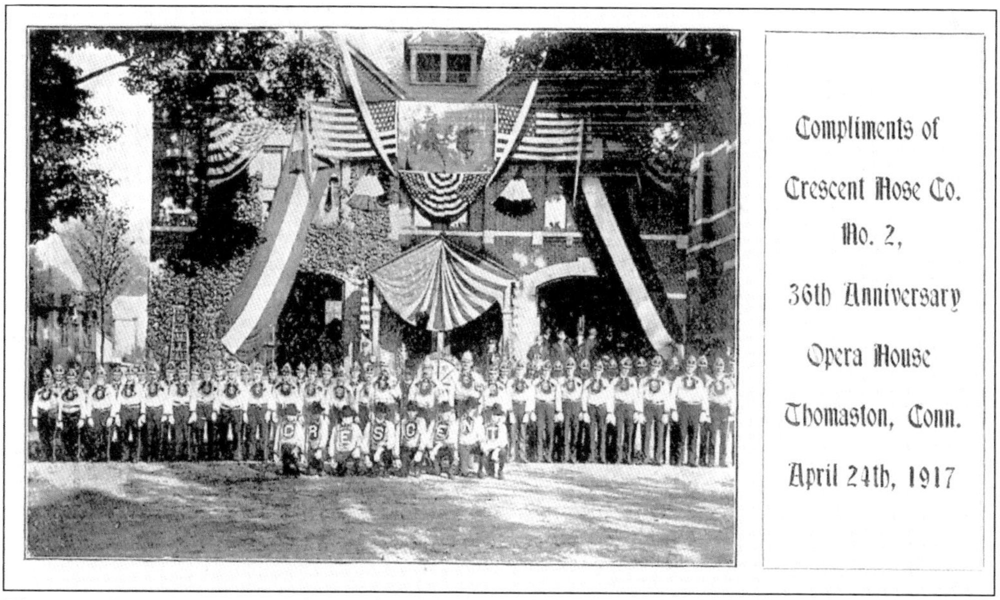

The complimentary postcard-size photograph of the Crescent Hose Company's celebration of its 36th anniversary coincided with the nation's declaration of war upon Germany a few days before. A special patriotic program, detailed on the back of this card, was held in the opera house on April 24, 1917.

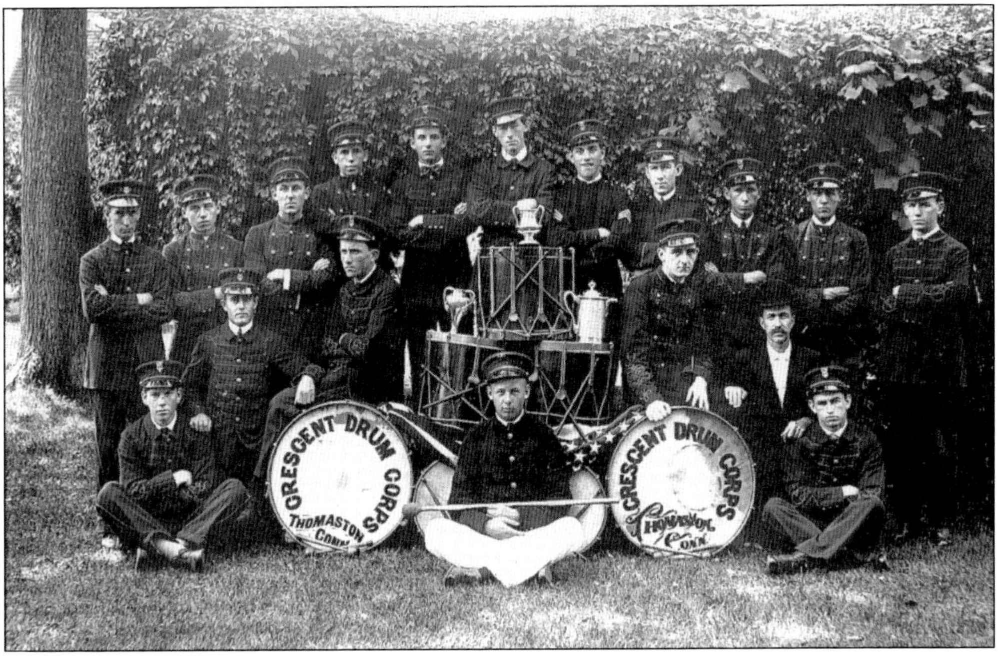

The Crescent Drum Corps was an award-winning band, judging from its trophies. The corps consisted of 17 members, including a sergeant and a drum major.

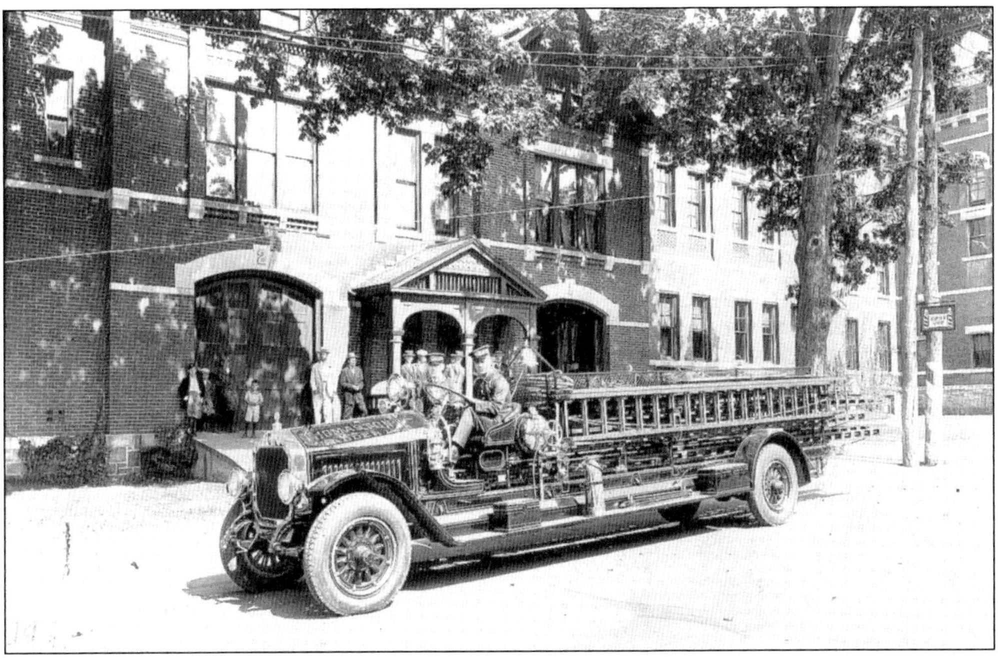

In 1926, the first motorized ladder truck was purchased. The driver is Andrew O'Neill, and the assistant driver is Lawrence Barrett. Andy O'Neill was pictured earlier as a Little League coach. This Goodwin Court resident worked for Connecticut Light and Power but still donated his time to the town like so many others who make Thomaston special. Note the barber shop sign on the pole at the right.

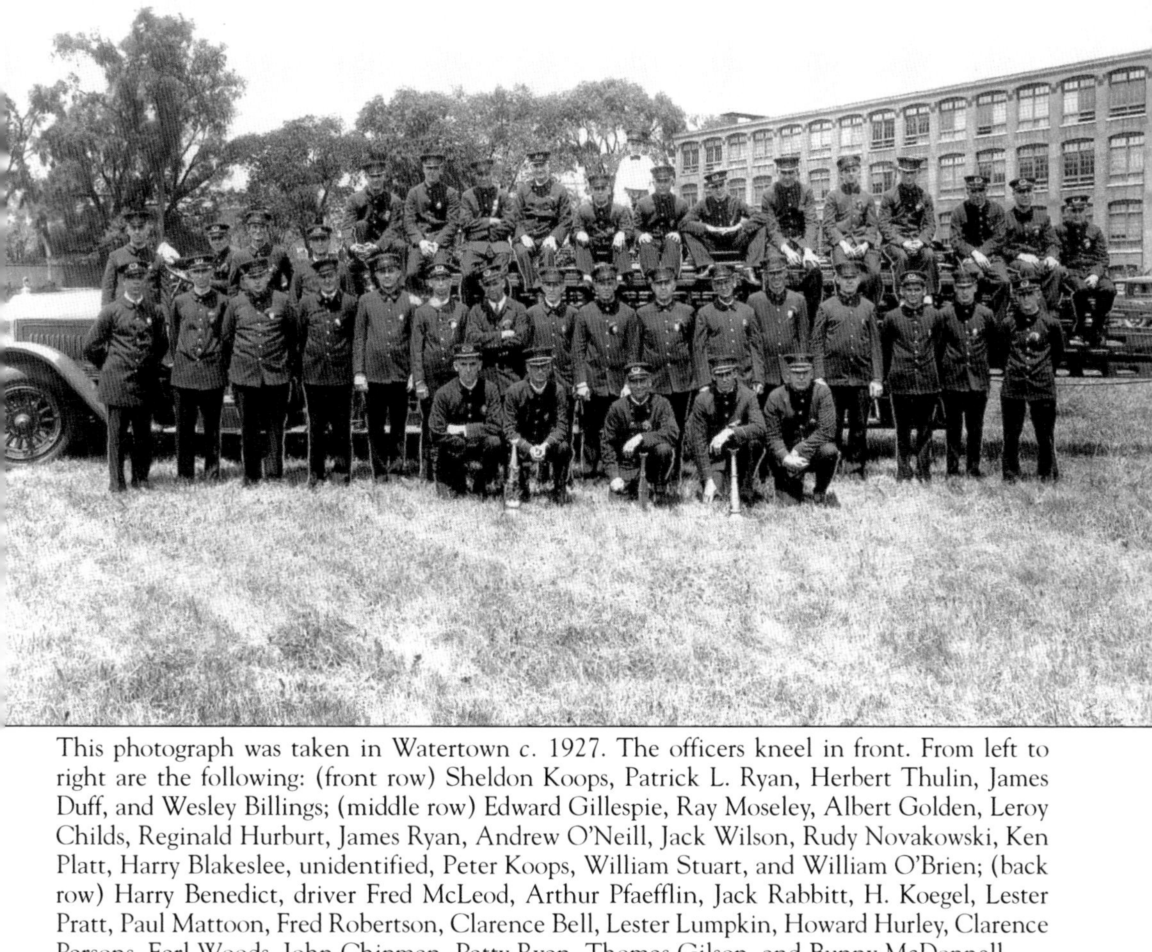

This photograph was taken in Watertown *c.* 1927. The officers kneel in front. From left to right are the following: (front row) Sheldon Koops, Patrick L. Ryan, Herbert Thulin, James Duff, and Wesley Billings; (middle row) Edward Gillespie, Ray Moseley, Albert Golden, Leroy Childs, Reginald Hurburt, James Ryan, Andrew O'Neill, Jack Wilson, Rudy Novakowski, Ken Platt, Harry Blakeslee, unidentified, Peter Koops, William Stuart, and William O'Brien; (back row) Harry Benedict, driver Fred McLeod, Arthur Pfaefflin, Jack Rabbitt, H. Koegel, Lester Pratt, Paul Mattoon, Fred Robertson, Clarence Bell, Lester Lumpkin, Howard Hurley, Clarence Parsons, Earl Woods, John Chipman, Patty Ryan, Thomas Gilson, and Bunny McDonnell.

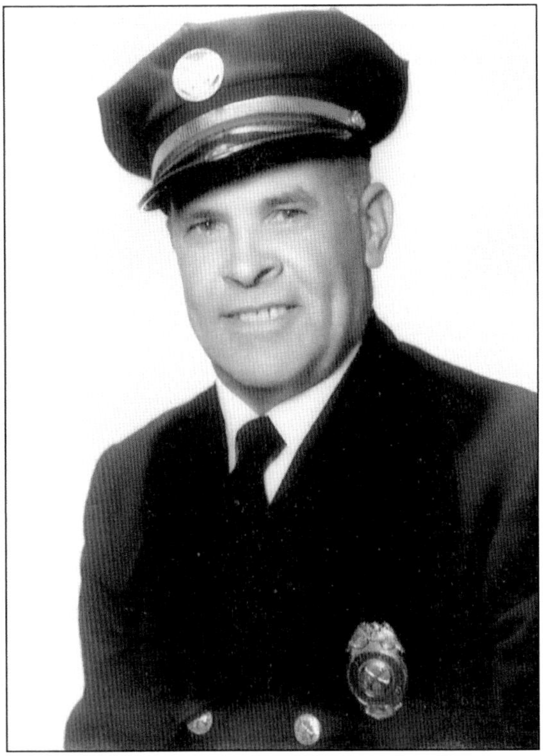

Bob Shearer was a captain and assistant chief with the Crescent Hose Company. We have seen him earlier with the class of 1925 and with the Thomaston Ponies. In the State Convention held in Thomaston in 2002, the 95-year-old was the parade's grand marshal. (Courtesy of Christine S. St. Denis.)

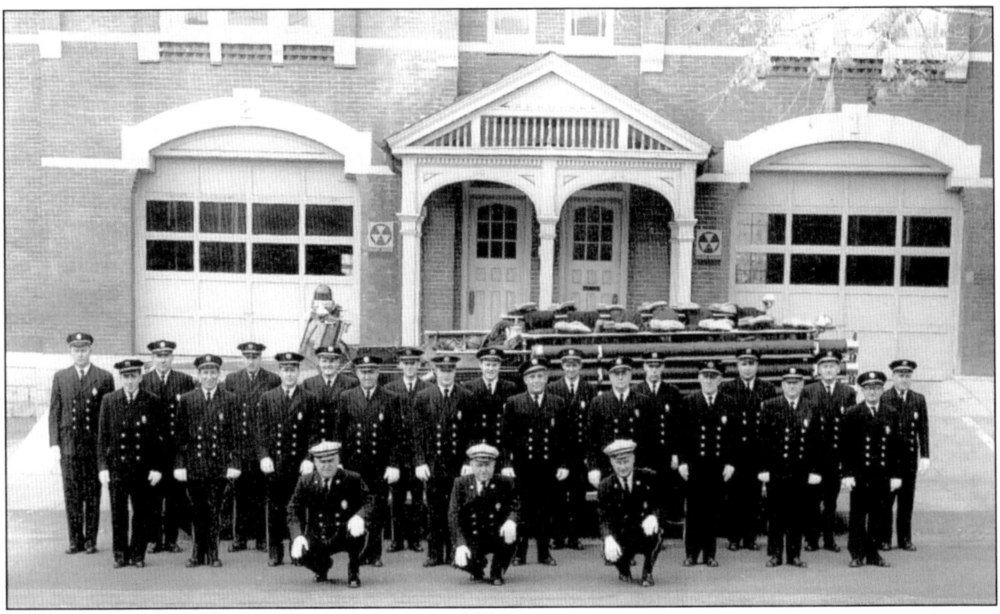

The Crescent Hose Company poses in front of the hose truck in 1966. From left to right are the following: (front row) 2nd Lt. D. Barnett, Capt. James Wilson, and 1st Lt. Robert Brown; (middle row) E. LeClair, Peter Rayder Jr., James DeBisschop, Eugene Torrence, Robert Brink, John Mendicino, William Shearer, J. Wilson, Robert Ray, and A. Cook; (back row) George Skerstonas, Robert Golden, Robert White, Donald Cables, William O'Connor, B. Berling, D. Cables, C. Williams, Donald Norton, John Wilson, and Albert Wilson.

Five

WARS AND PEACE

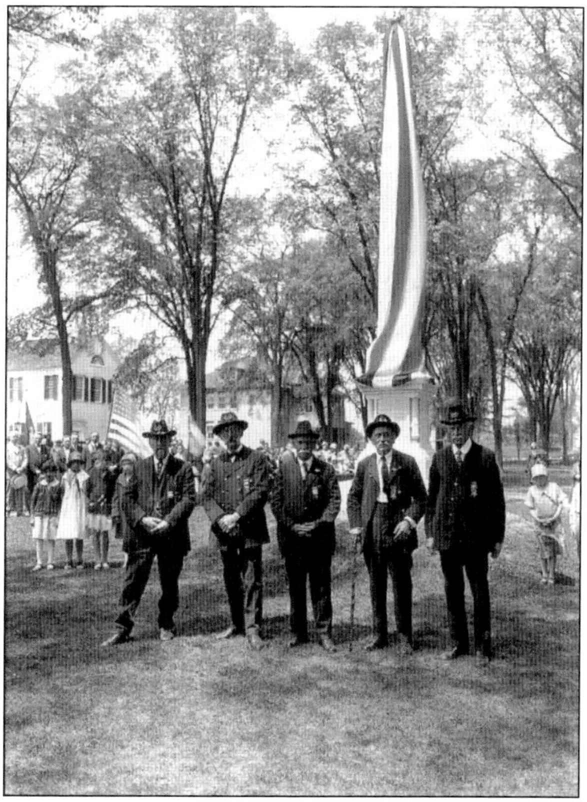

Thomaston has always done its part in serving our country. The Civil War began even before the town was incorporated, two years after the death of Seth Thomas. The men portrayed here *c.* 1925 were the last survivors of the scores that served. Posing on the Plymouth Green are, from left to right, Charles B. Harrison, W.F. Bellmay, Charles Morse, Joseph Simpson, and George Washington Purdy. Morse was the last survivor, dying on September 15, 1935, at age 89.

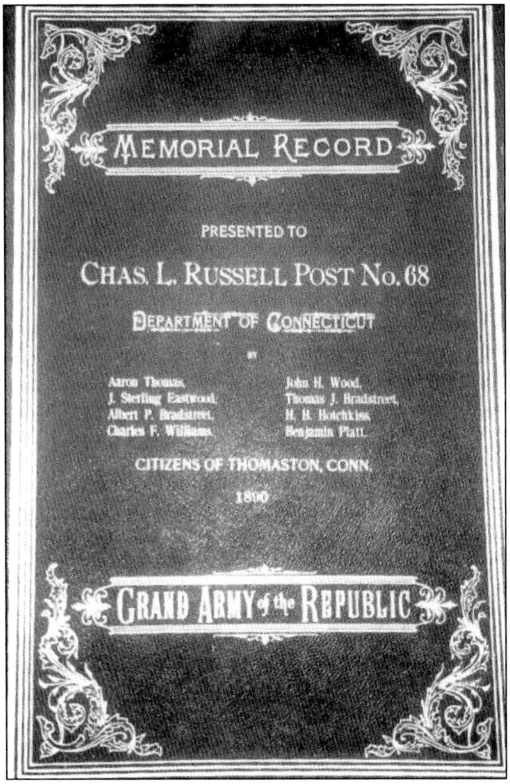

The Grand Army of the Republic Memorial Record was presented to Charles L. Russell Post No. 68 by Aaron Thomas, J. Sterling Eastwood, Albert P. Bradstreet, Charles F. Williams, John H. Wood, Thomas Jefferson Bradstreet, H.H. Hotchkiss, and Benjamin Platt in 1890.

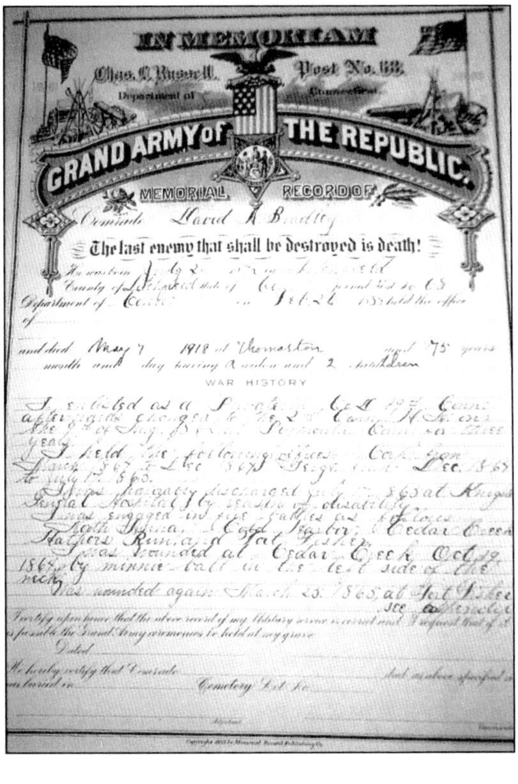

This is the entry of David Bradley, who was born in 1842 in Litchfield. He was wounded by a "minnie" ball in the neck at Cedar Creek, Virginia. Thomaston men fought at Cedar Creek, Cold Harbor, Gettysburg, and were present at Appomattox Courthouse at the end of the war. Bradley died in Thomaston on May 7, 1918, when the nation was once again engaged in conflict.

The nation entered World War I in April 1917. Thomaston supplied more than 220 soldiers, sailors, and nurses, all listed on the monument in Veterans' Park. Born in Sheffield, England, Herbert Truelove (1896–1972) enlisted in the army at 21. When he was honorably discharged, he was a sergeant in the Chemical Warfare Service. His daughters, Claire Lyon and Carol Smith, gave his foot locker and uniform, including his gas mask, to the Thomaston Historical Society.

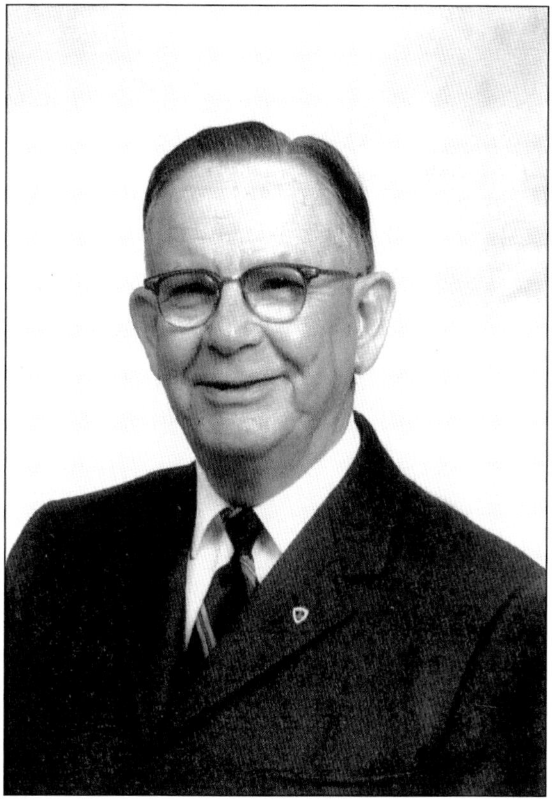

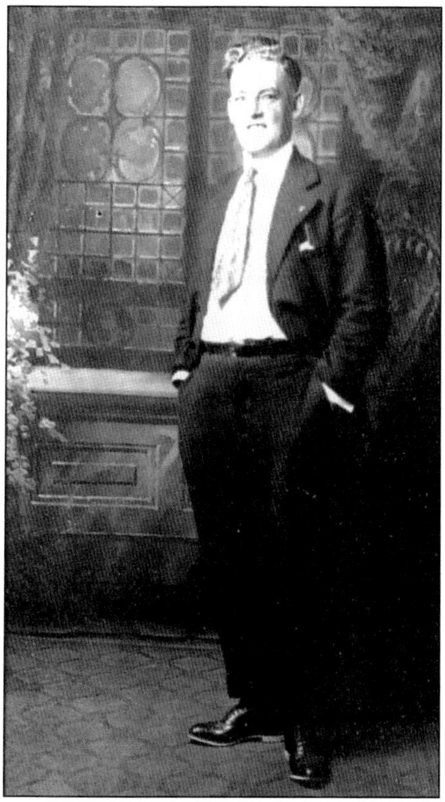

Pvt. Joseph M. Glennon (1891–1998) was wounded in France and was given the Purple Heart. He wore the patch and received the medal of the Second Division, which lists the battles in which he fought. The State of Connecticut medal was awarded to its servicemen, and the World War I Campaign Medal lists campaigns and allies of the United States. All of these are in the Thomaston Historical Society's collection.

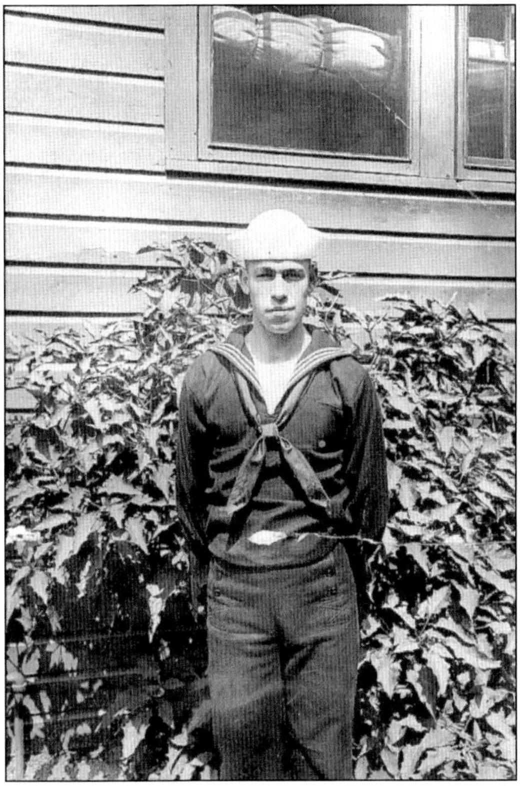

Joseph F. Wassong (1896–1973) was born in Warren, Connecticut, the second of four to bear that name and live in Thomaston. An enlistee in the Connecticut Home Guard from April 1917 until June 1918, when he joined the Naval Coast Defense Reserve, Wassong was called to active service in September 1918. A navy seaman second class, he served at the naval station in Pelham Bay, New York. After his honorable discharge from the reserves in 1921, he worked for M.J. Daly and for Seth Thomas Clocks as a steamfitter.

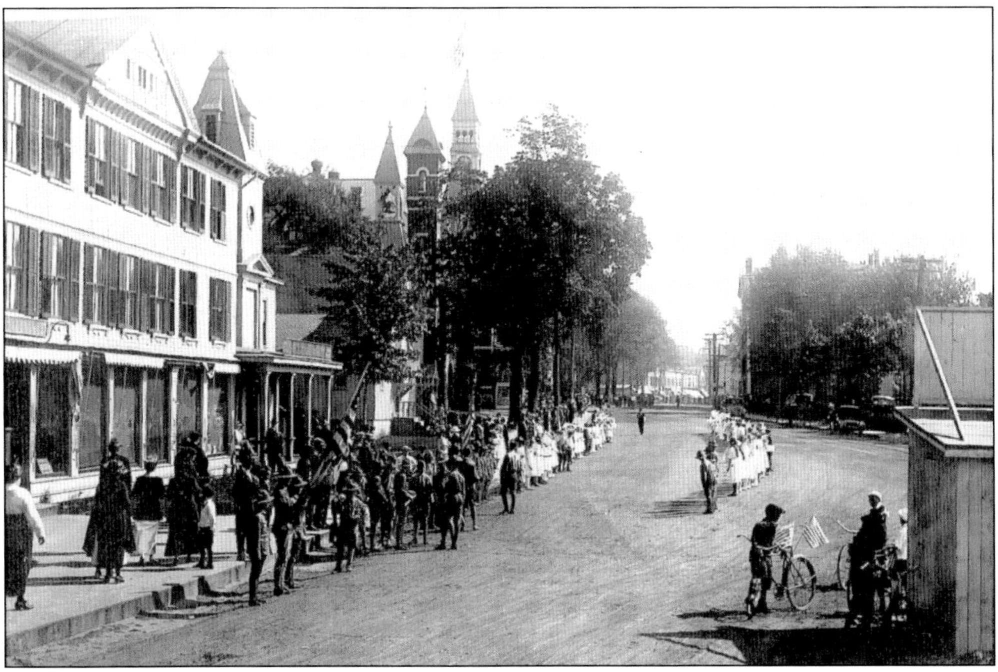

A morning parade heads toward Hillside Cemetery, probably on Memorial Day in 1919. On the left is the Andrews Block. In the center are soldiers. On the right, girls in white dresses and boys with bikes hold flags in anticipation of the marchers.

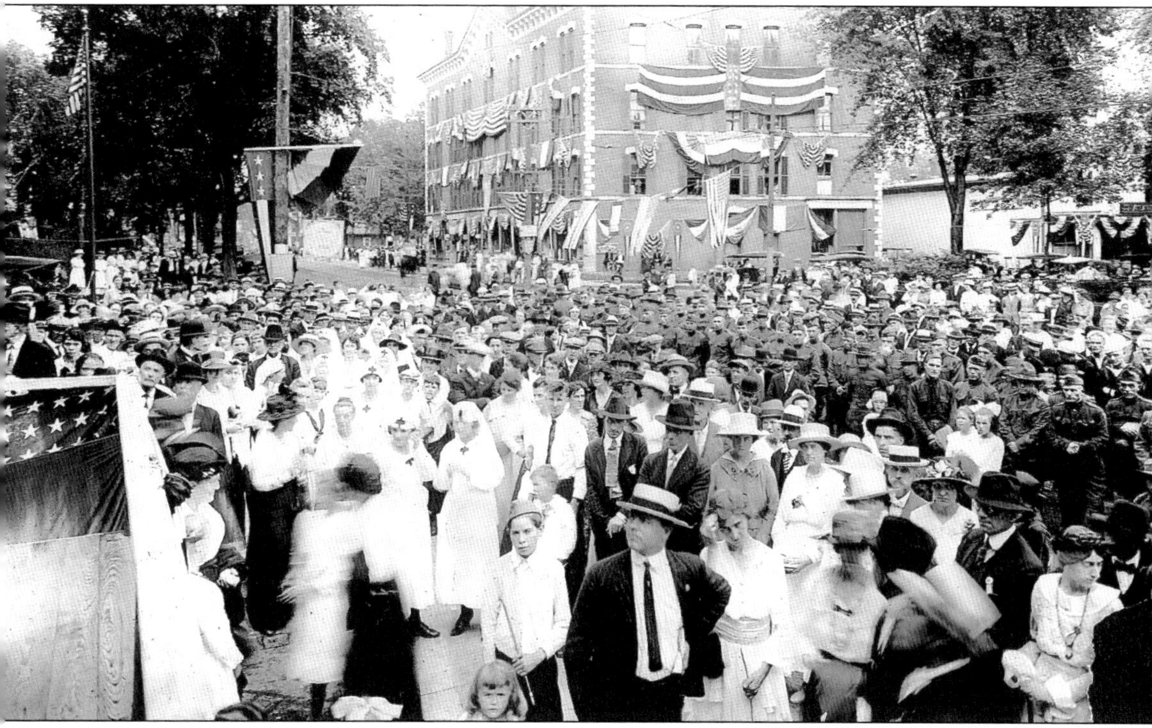

On July 19, 1919, a beautiful Saturday, Thomaston held its welcome home ceremony for its soldiers, sailors, and nurses. This photograph shows the gathering in front of the reviewing stand. Many of the honorees are visible, while two veterans of the Grand Army of the Republic can be seen at the left, one peering around the corner of the reviewing stand and the other standing in full profile facing the town hall. In the background are the Bradstreet Block and the A & P.

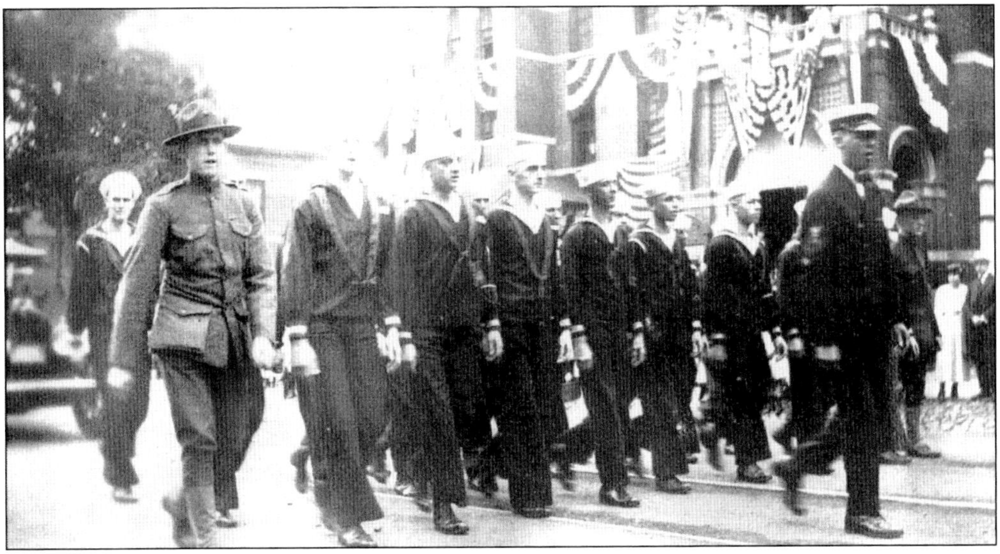

Here we see the sailors on parade in a photograph taken from an Innes family album. The view points west toward the decorated town hall. The first sailor on the right, below the bunting, is Joseph Wassong. (Courtesy of Marion Innes DePecol.)

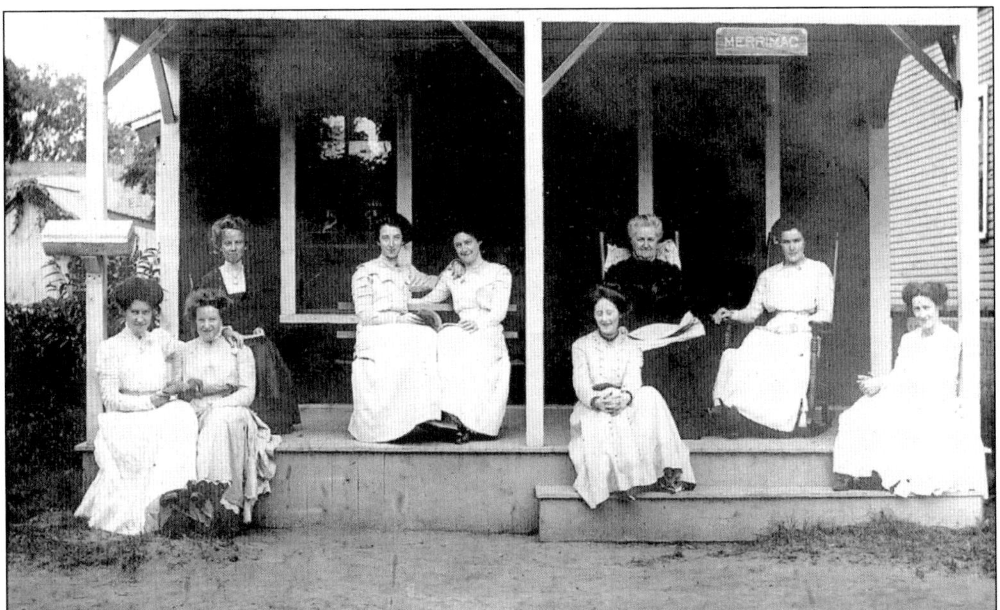

With the war over, people pursued their normal peacetime activities. These young women from Thomaston enjoyed a vacation at the beach. The site is unknown, but the photograph was printed in a postcard format. Pictured on the porch of the Merrimac are, from left to right, two unidentified women, Ruth Sandel (Rabbitt), Mary Doyle, unidentified, Agnes Ryan (Hennessey), unidentified, Dora Higgins, and unidentified. Dora Higgins was a second-grade teacher, and Mary Doyle, also a teacher, was later postmistress.

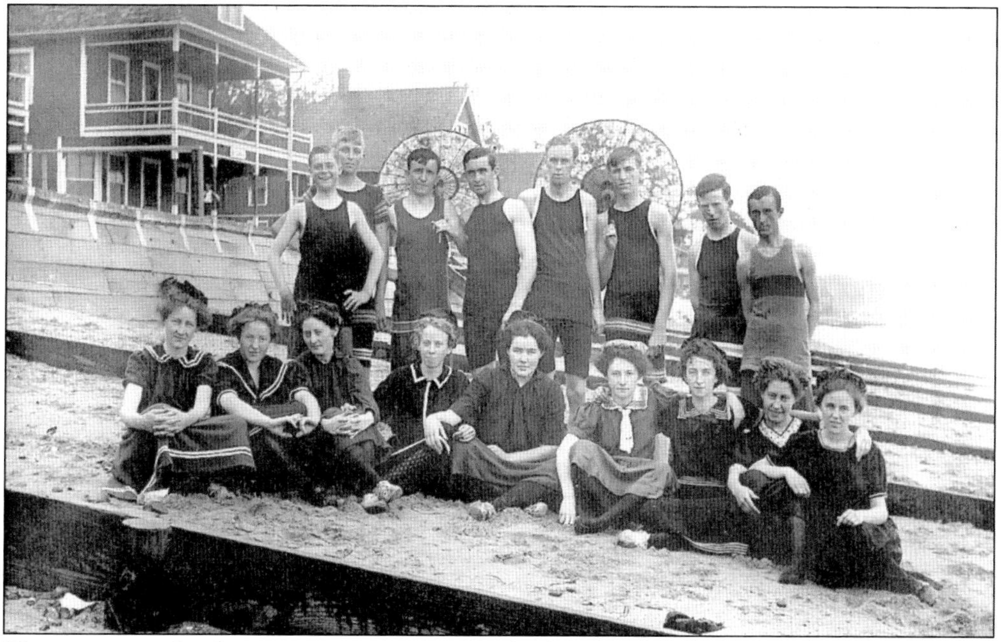

The women evidently met some young men at the beach for a group photograph—eight men, two with Chinese parasols, and nine women. Where is the ninth man? We assume he was the one taking the picture. In the front row are, from left to right, two unidentified women, Agnes Ryan (Hennessey), Ruth Sandel (Rabbitt), Dora Higgins, an unidentified woman, Mary Doyle, and two unidentified women.

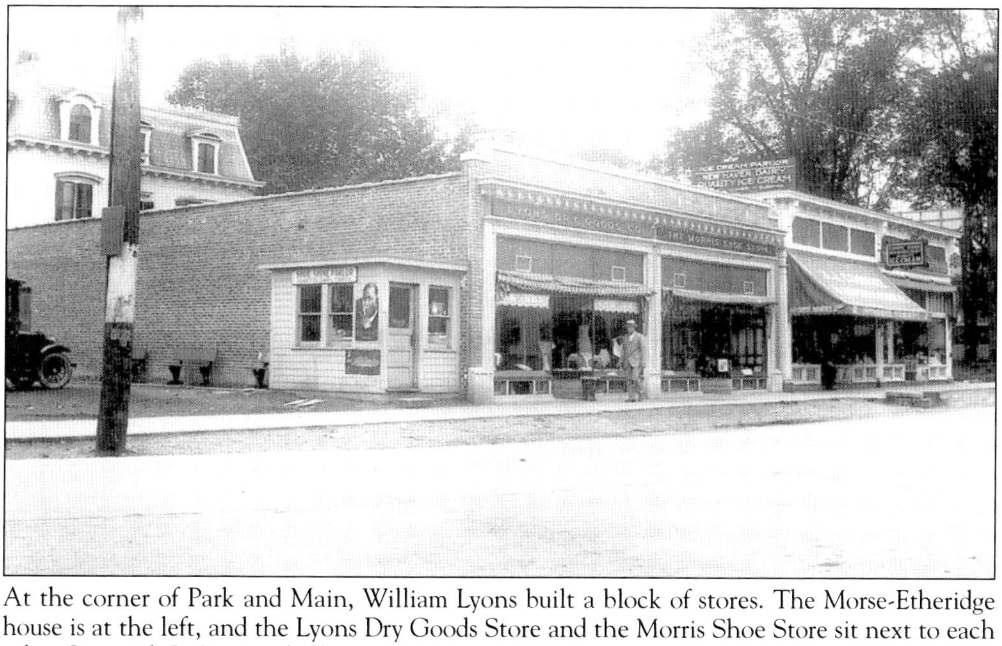

At the corner of Park and Main, William Lyons built a block of stores. The Morse-Etheridge house is at the left, and the Lyons Dry Goods Store and the Morris Shoe Store sit next to each other. Jeremiah J. Conway had a men's store next. He was custodian of the Grand Army of the Republic Memorial Record, given to the Thomaston Historical Society by his daughter Eleanor Conway. The last store on the right is Candyland, owned by Louis Gardella.

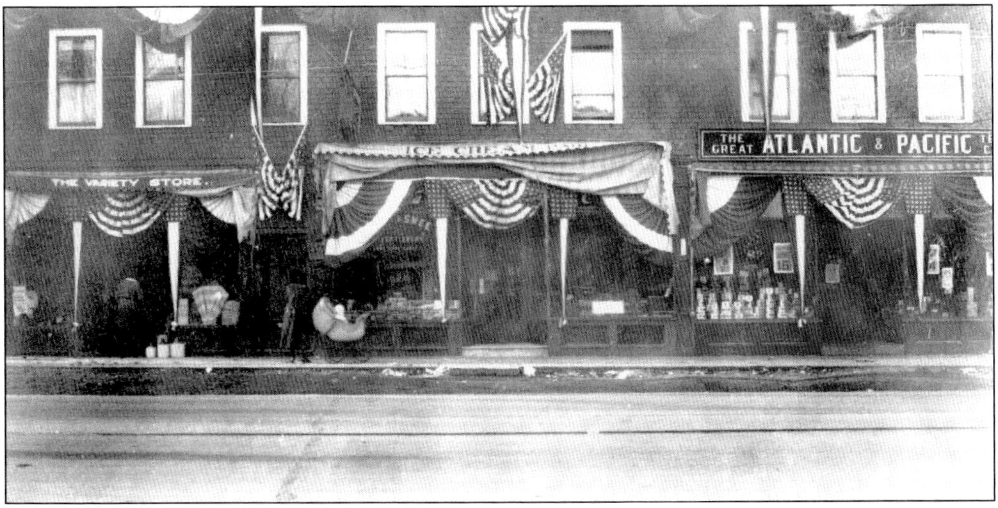

The Lipman building was located across Main Street from the Lyons Block. It housed a variety store, an ice-cream parlor, and the A & P. The A & P had moved from its Union Street location, and its manager was William Noack. (Courtesy of Frank Noack.)

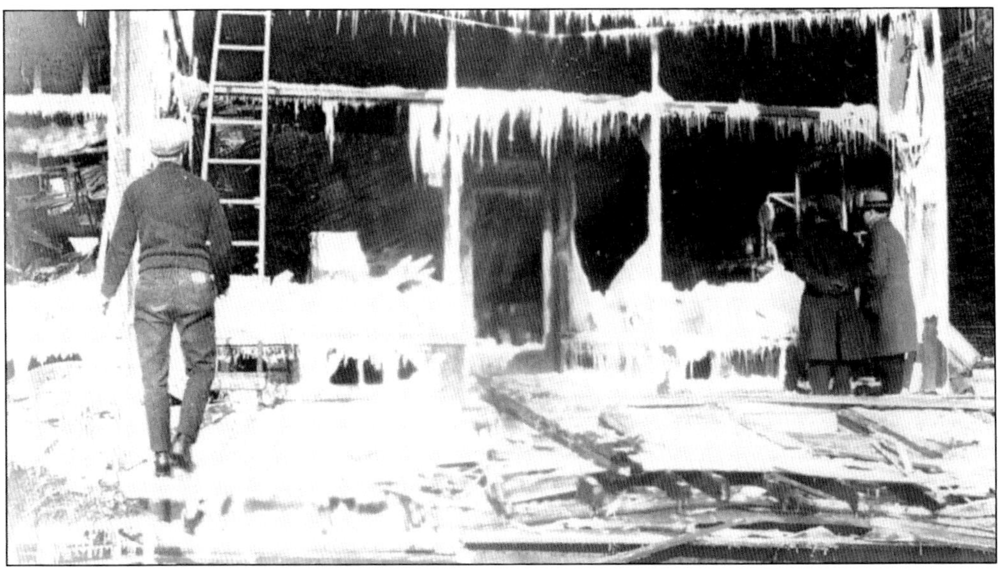

William Noack was the manager of the A & P from 1914 to 1940. In the winter of 1924, a devastating fire destroyed the Lipman building. (Courtesy of Frank Noack.)

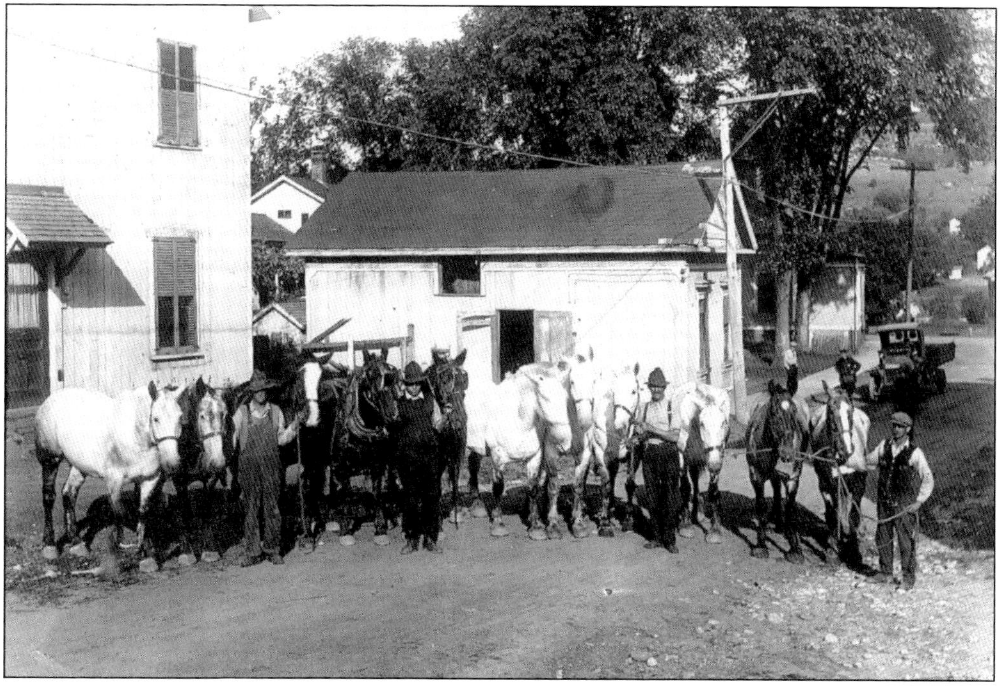

This view of Park Street, looking toward Elm, was taken *c.* 1925. The men pictured are, from left to right, Gus Matz, unidentified, Robert Woods, and Wilbur Graham. The 11 horses and the truck belong to Peter Conaghan.

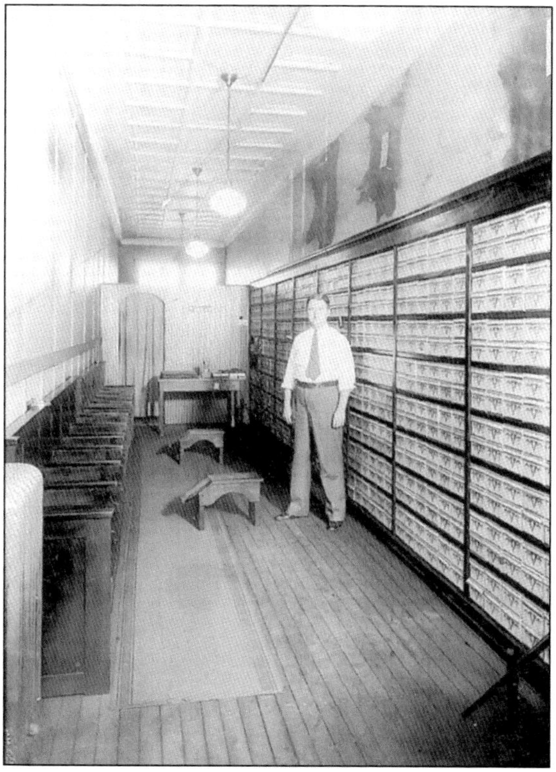

When the Lipman building was rebuilt, one tenant was Flynn's Shoe Store. The new ceiling was made of tin. The stool near the owner's foot is in the collection of the Thomaston Historical Society. Enlarged somewhat, in 1934 Flynn's became Stanley's Shoe Store, owned by Stanley Kaniewski. Today it is the Stanley Room of Vi-Arms Restaurant.

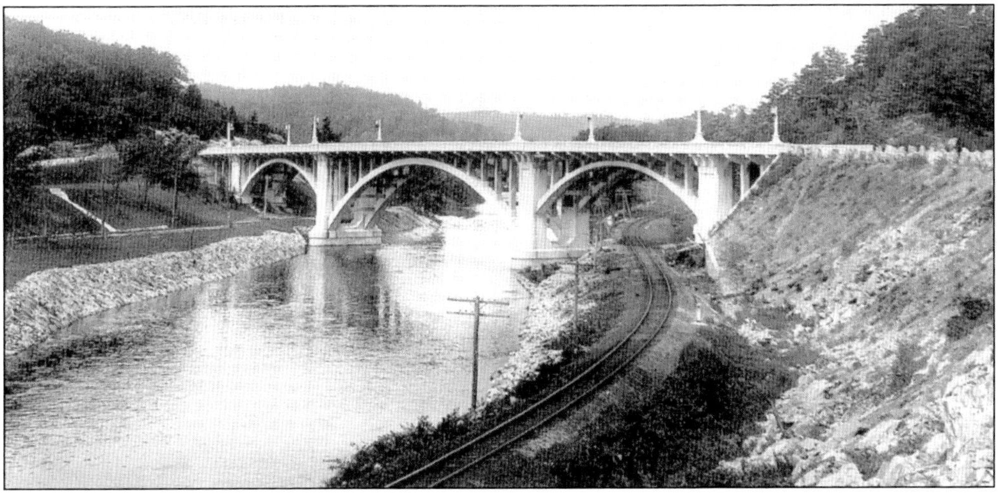

When completed in May 1928, Reynolds Bridge was reportedly the second-longest concrete span in the country. Nearly 500 feet long, the bridge was surpassed in length only by one in Minneapolis. This view is looking north.

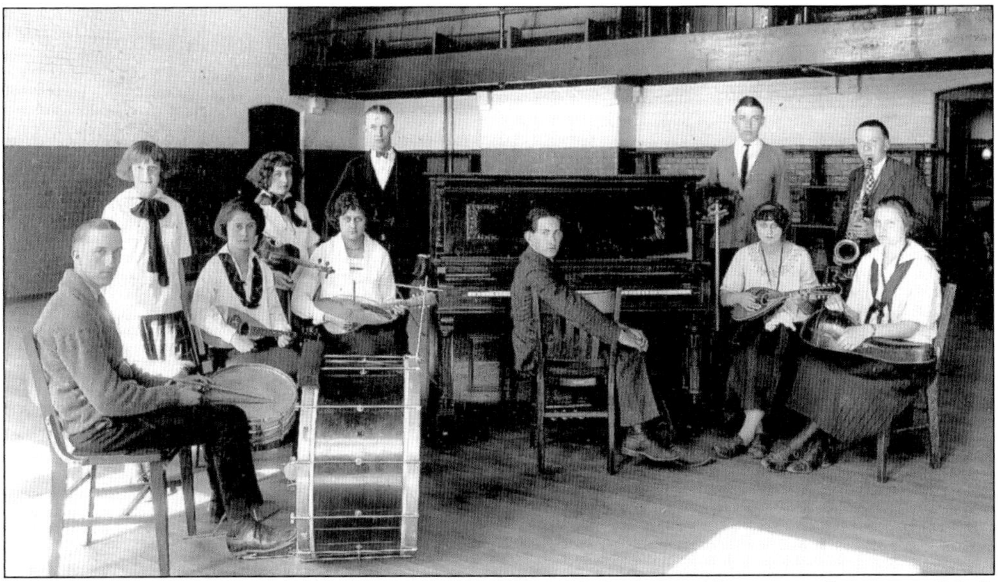

Student musicians pose *c.* 1925. The drummer at the left is Harold Stuart, Thomaston High School class of 1925. The practice session was held in the gymnasium of the Grove Street School, then the high school. Note the variety of musical instruments.

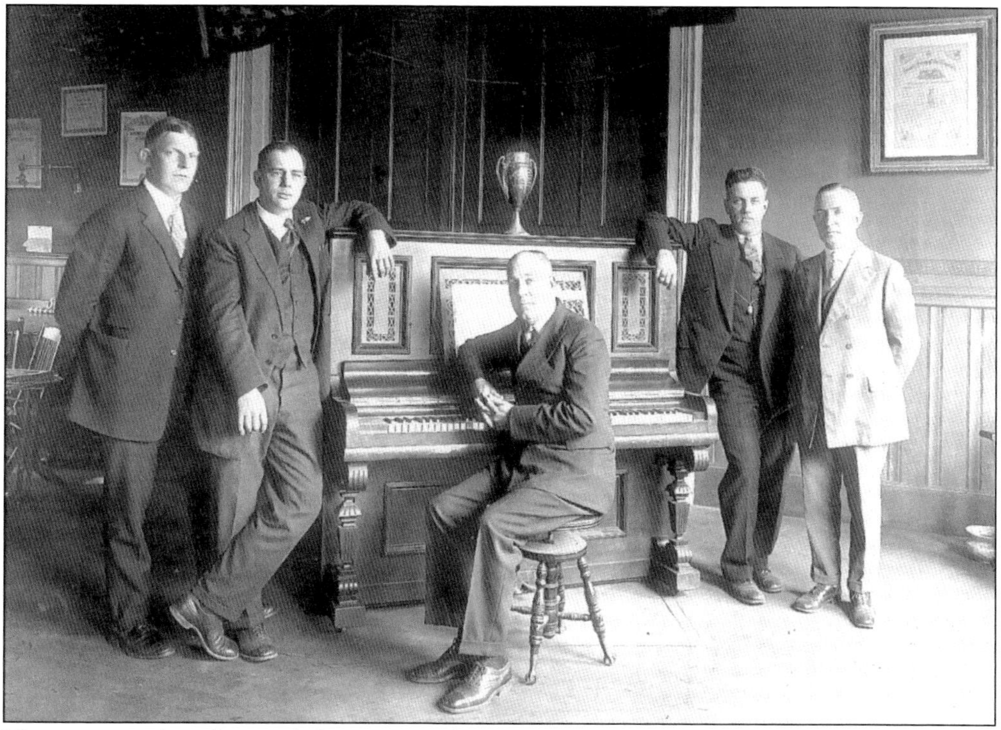

These men gathered around the piano and struck a pose. The photographer provided balance to the image but evidently thought he had framed out the spittoon in the corner. Pictured c. 1925 are, from left to right, Wesley Billings, Lester Pratt, Arthur Henderson, Harry Lynch, and John Waters.

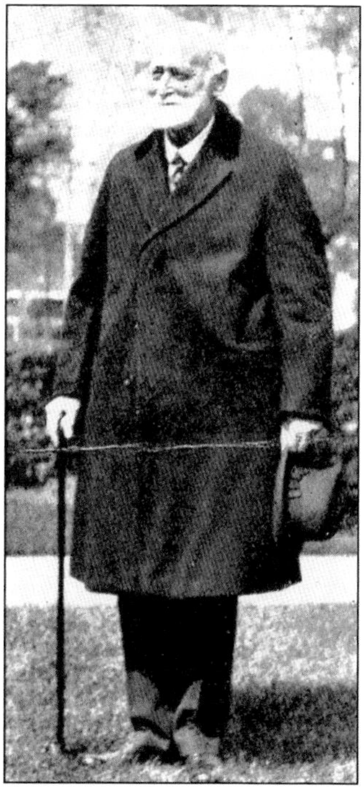

When this gentleman died in 1926, he was the subject of a three-page funerary tribute. Anson Tyler Hemingway was important to the Oak Park, Illinois, community as a Civil War veteran, realtor, YMCA leader, Congregational church deacon, friend, and good father of six. His son Dr. Clarence E. Hemingway was the father of the Nobel Prize–winning author Ernest Hemingway. Anson's sister Mary was married to George Stoughton (page 28), establishing another Thomaston-Hemingway connection. Anson Tyler Hemingway was born in East Plymouth, Connecticut, in 1844 and went to Chicago in 1854 with his father, Allan, who was sent West by Seth Thomas. Allan Hemingway of the Seth Thomas Clock Company was reportedly the first clockmaker to go West from New England.

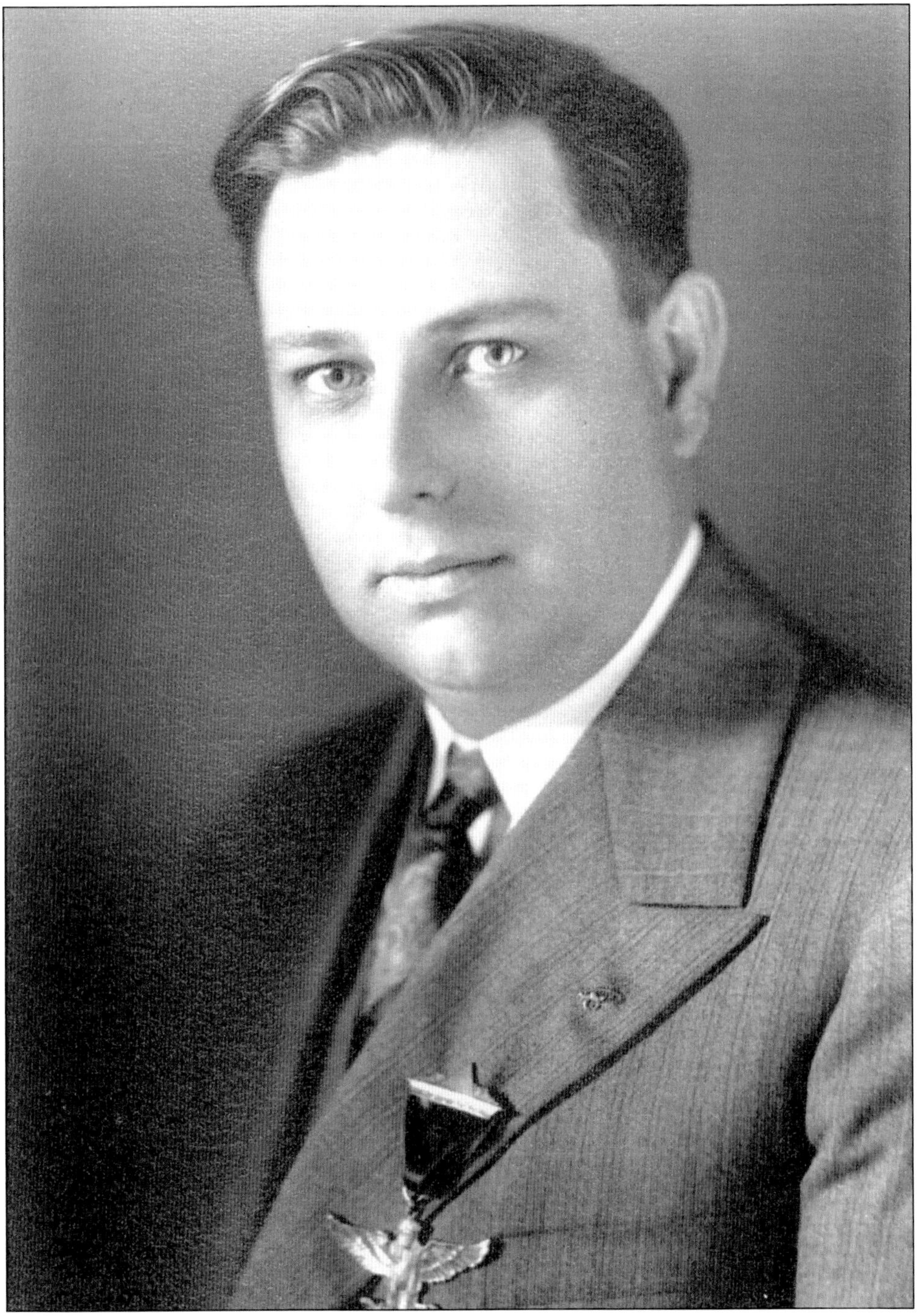

In 1922, Dr. Winfield E. Wight (1895–1977) bought the Dr. Ralph Schuyler Goodwin house, at 55 Elm Street. The physician-surgeon, who was born in Milan, New Hampshire, and educated at Bowdoin College in Brunswick, Maine, began a career in medicine and community service that made him one of the most respected and admired men of his generation. The Thomaston Savings Bank president and an original member of the board of finance, Wight is portrayed here in 1929. (Courtesy of Marion W. Conklin.)

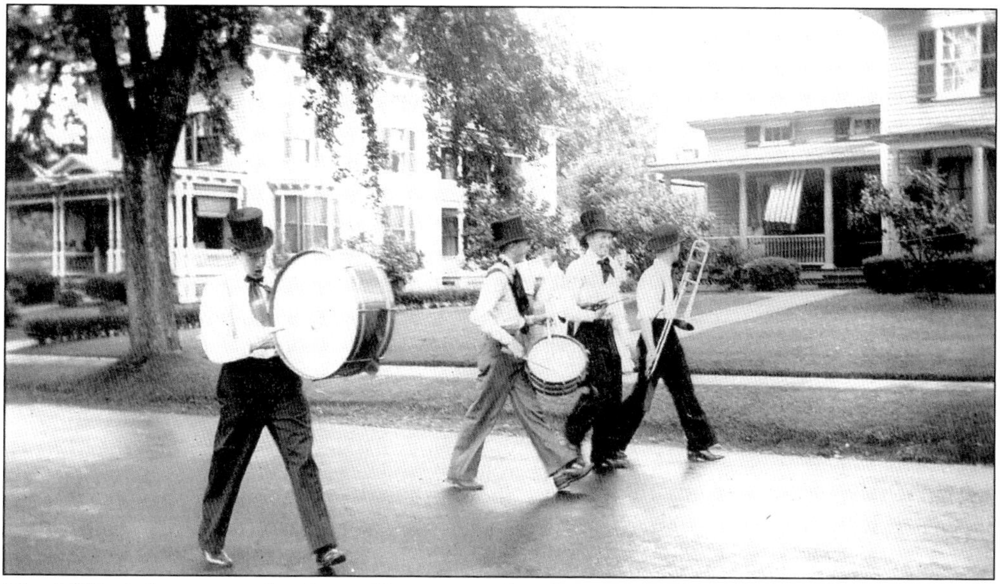

The 1930s is known as the Great Depression decade, a time of privation and pain. Into the White House in 1933 came Franklin Delano Roosevelt, and with him the New Deal. One element of the New Deal was the National Recovery Act, and NRA parades were held nationwide. Thomaston has always loved parades, and this one was certainly lively. The boys march along Elm Street. The house at the left, No. 65–67, was formerly on the front lawn of the Goodwin-Wight house, having been moved in 1928.

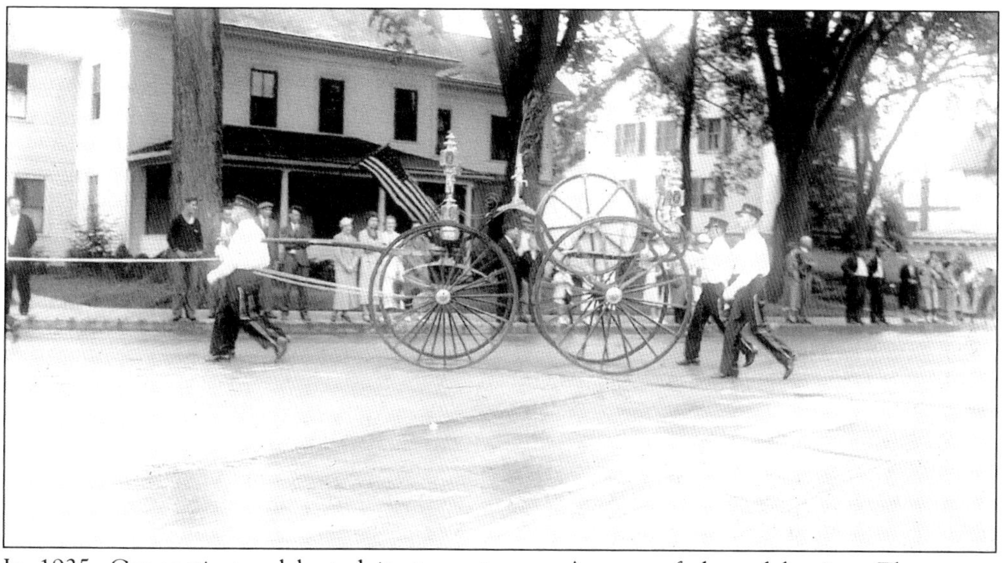

In 1935, Connecticut celebrated its tercentenary. As part of the celebration, Thomaston held another parade. In this image, we see the Crescent Hose parade wagon in front of the St. Thomas Church rectory, now gone. It was June 22, a Saturday, but the crowd was dressed in Sunday clothes.

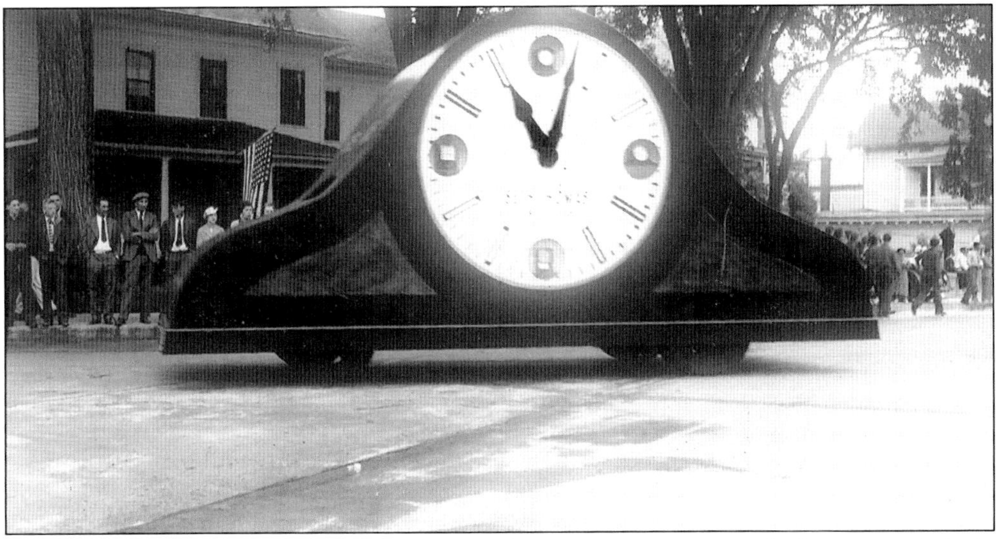

The Seth Thomas float in the tercentenary parade was a representation of a large mantel clock. The vantage point is the same as on the previous image. The photograph was taken as the float turned into the street on the north side of Kenea Park in front of the St. Thomas rectory.

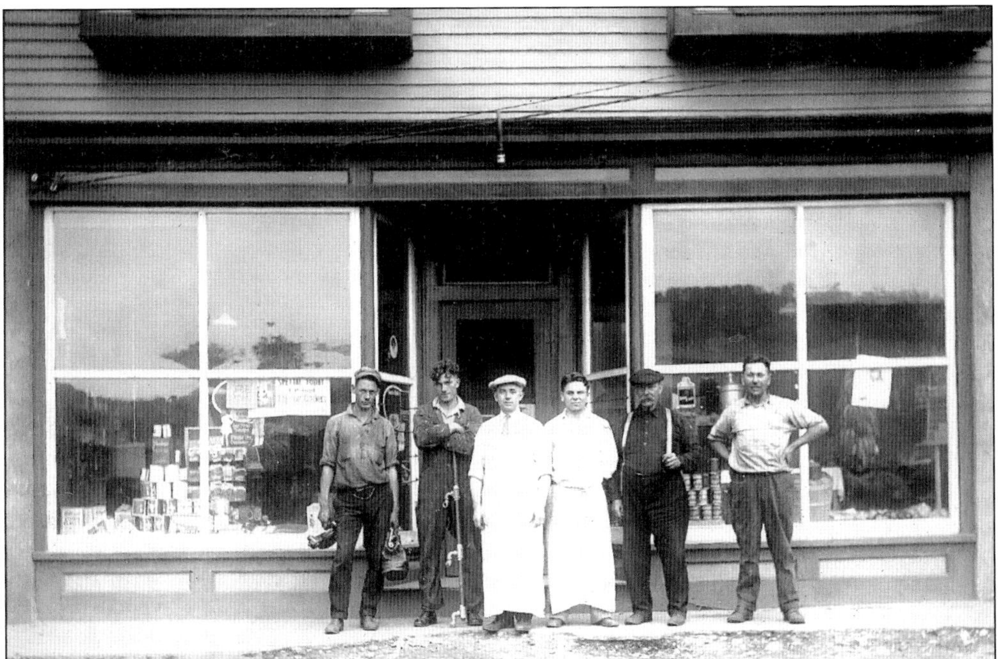

In the 1930s, small markets were the norm. Some served a neighborhood and some a wider range of customers. One of the former was on the east side and was owned by Enos Ptachcinski. He and his wife, Helen, lived upstairs in this Railroad Street house. Pictured here with the hat and apron is Ptachcinski; to the right in white is his brother-in-law Alexander "Cappy" Krayeski. (Courtesy of Dorothy P. Vigeant.)

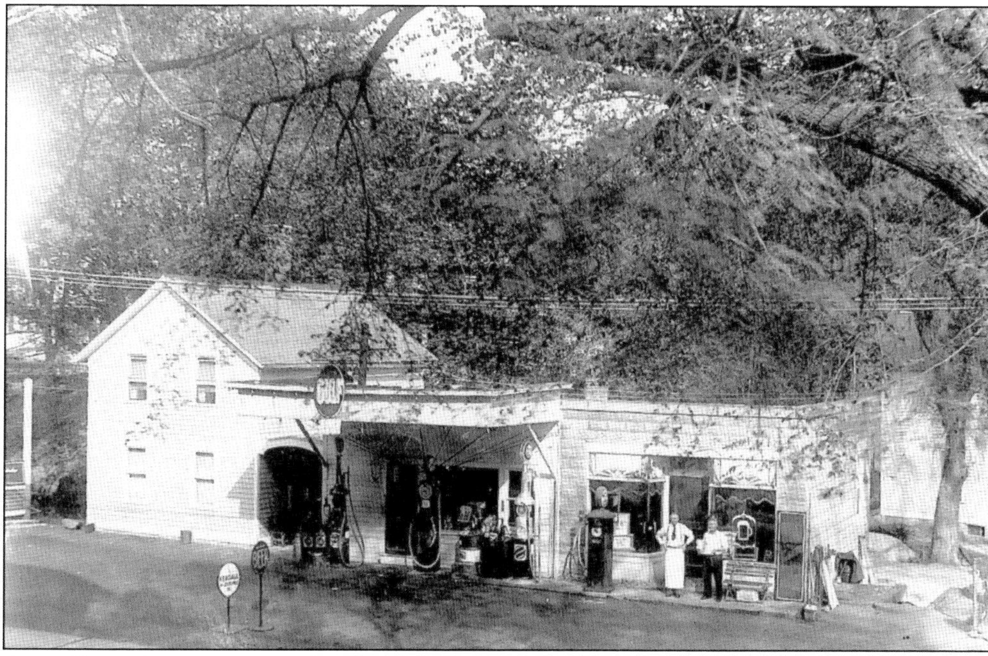

A small gasoline station on South Main Street, this business was owned by Aurelio Ghiaia. Located immediately south of the Mobil station today, it is still recognized by viewers as the popular KC's Package Store.

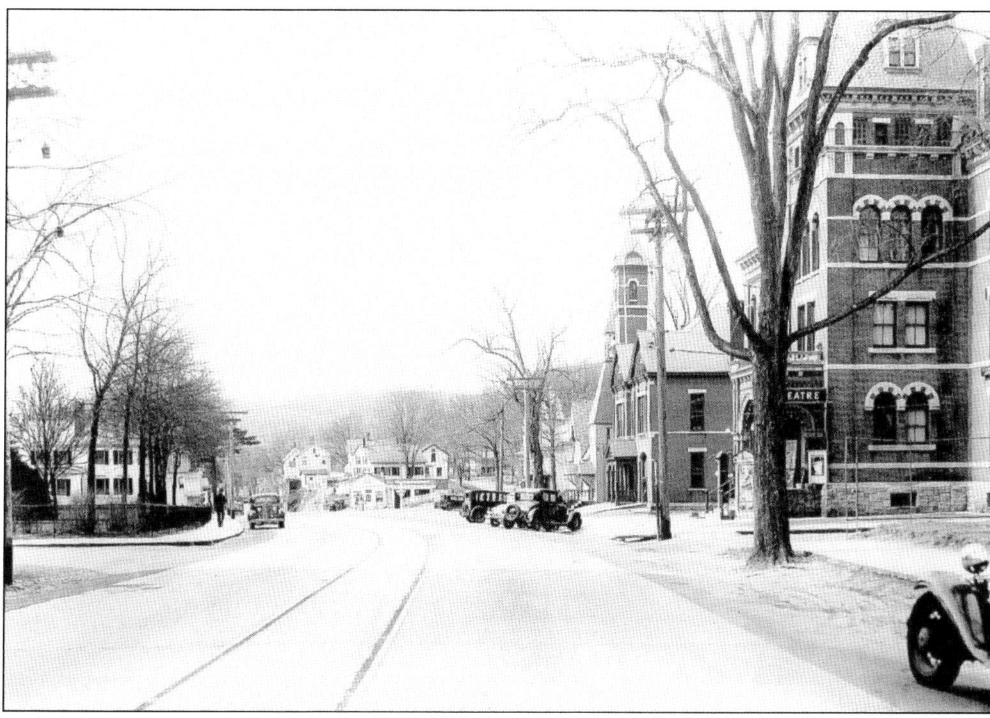

In 1936, the intersection at the town hall had no traffic light. Seen here are the trolley tracks, the angled parking, and the Paramount Theatre in the opera house.

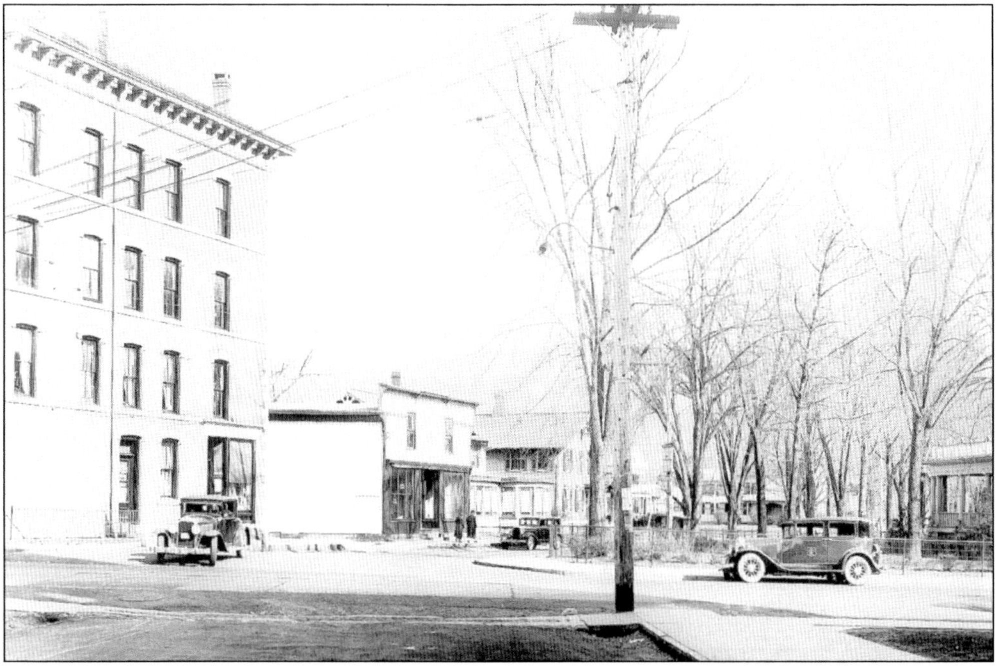

Looking down Union Street from Clay, we notice that the entire north side of the street is gone. Webster Bank has replaced the Bradstreet Block, and on the south side, Thomaston Savings Bank has replaced the Woodruff-Upson house. The photograph is dated 1935.

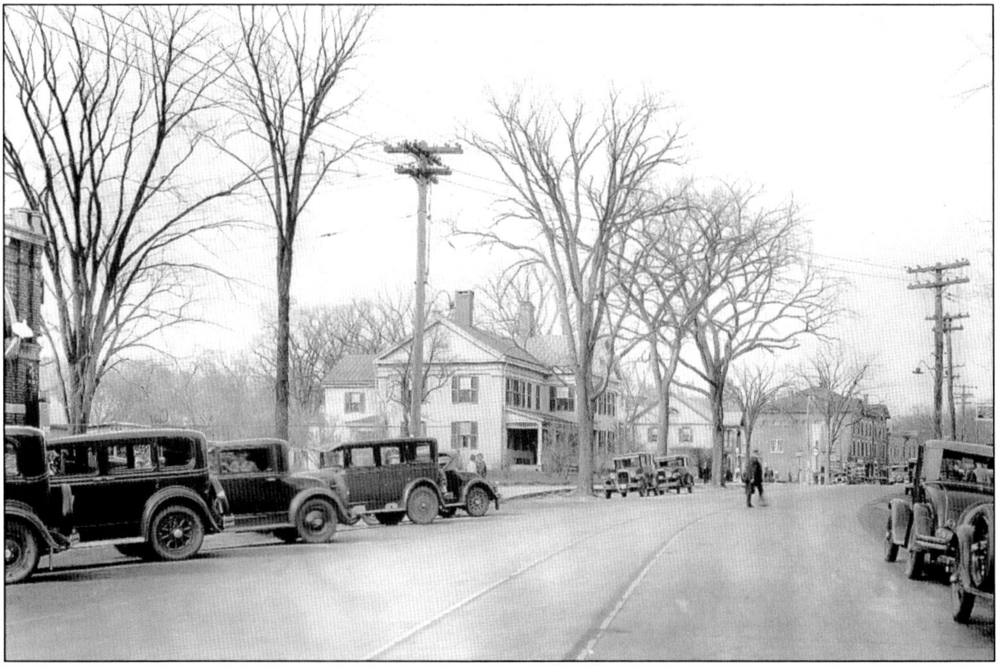

At about the same time, this view to the north reveals lots of activity: many cars, people chatting, a pedestrian crossing the street. The Seth Thomas house appears in the center rear; Seth Jr.'s house is just to the north. Both are dwarfed by elm trees, later victims of Dutch elm disease.

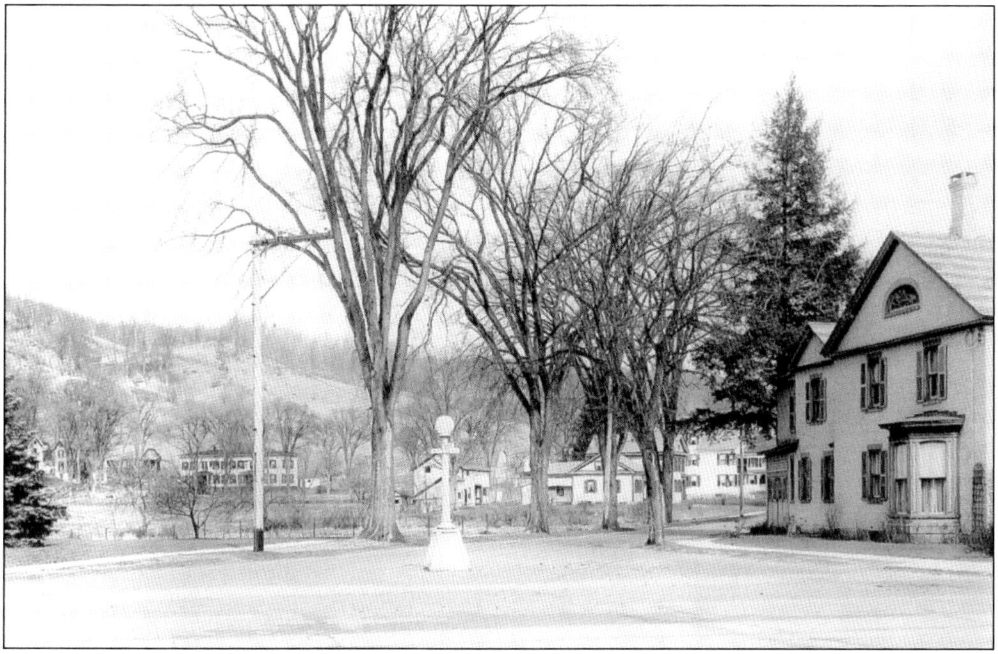

In this view up High Street from Main, the Seth Thomas Jr. house, on the right, occupies the site now held by the Country Grocer. Absent from the photograph is the Thomaston Center School. The signpost admonishes drivers to "keep to the right."

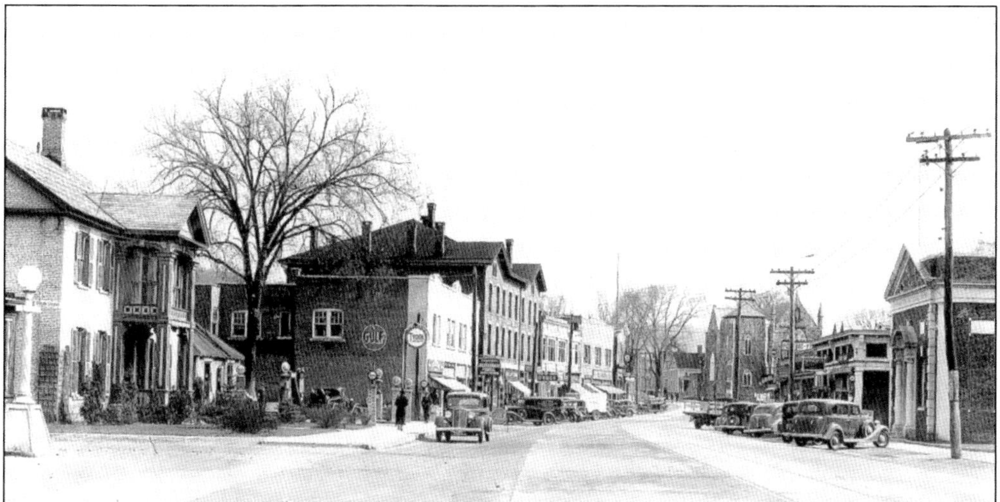

Pictured in this view of Main Street looking north are, from left to right, the Thomas house, Donovan's gasoline station, the Fulton Market, Anderson's Restaurant, a drugstore, W.T. Grant's, and the telephone company. Across the street and south are, from left to right, the St. Thomas Church (which has no bell tower), signs for a grill and a Pontiac dealer, Candyland, and Thomaston National Bank. The businesses have changed. Main Street has not.

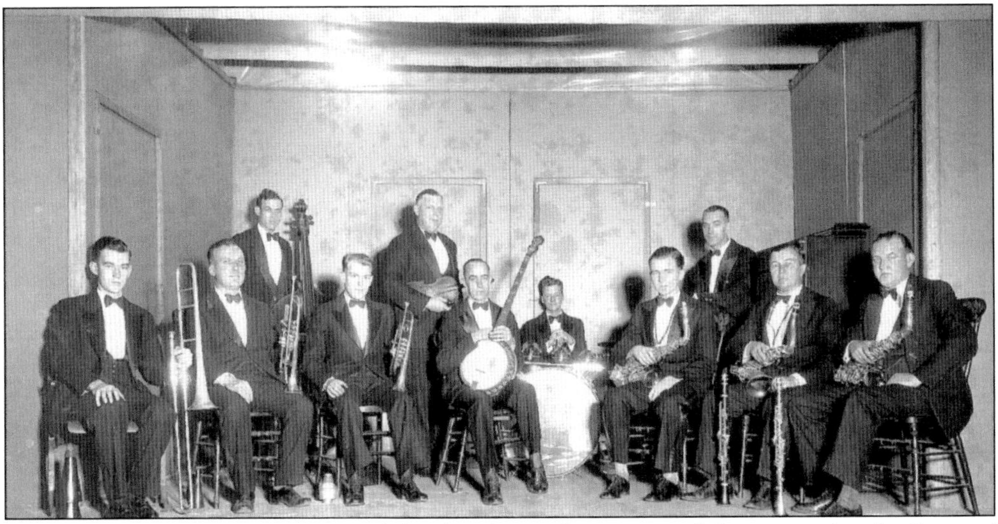

One of the inexpensive pleasures of the decade was listening and dancing to bands. Some of Thomaston's finest musicians are represented here. From left to right are Walter Dickinson, Gus Marks, Ray Cleveland (bass), Lev Tanner, Wesley Billings, Floyd Martin, Bobby Jones, Chet Foerch, Bill Pettijean (piano), Emil Marks, and Gene Terrill.

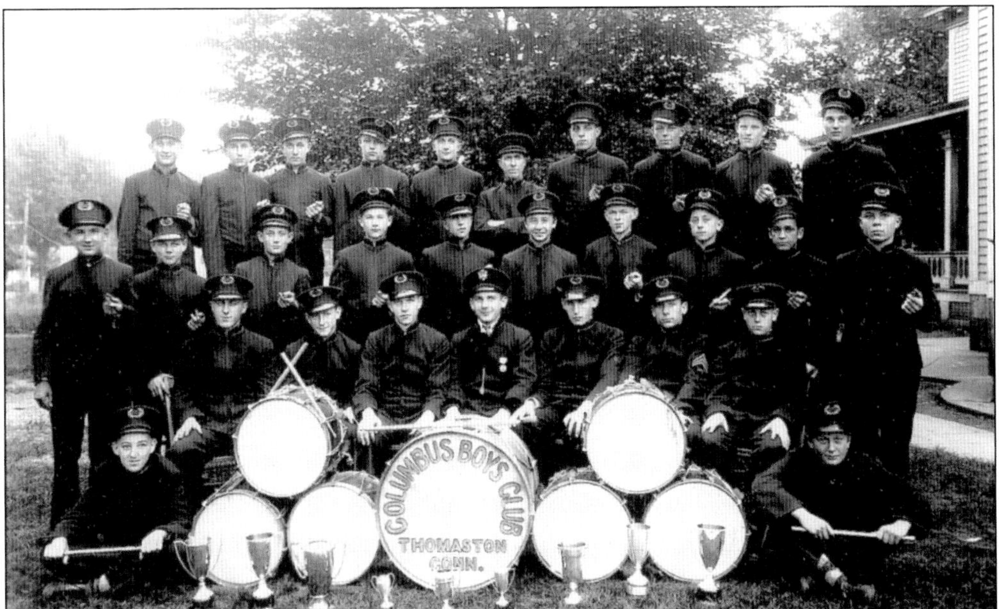

The Knights of Columbus served the young men of Thomaston. The award-winning band members in 1932 are, from left to right, as follows: (front row) Eugene Torrence, Francis Drunsic, Paul O'Brien, John Lyons, John Bycoski, Vincent Doran, John Moskaluk, Jim O'Halloran, and Fred Postic; (middle row) William Perchuk, H. Kuharski, unidentified, Telsford Nest, ? Chizmas, Joe Bycoski, unidentified, Stanley Czyz, unidentified, and Merle Petlak; (back row) Leo Puzacke, Ed O'Connell, Chris Martin, Joe Wojciehowski, Edward Mezocowski, Roy DeForrest, Harold Olcese, Robert Elty, William Sullivan, and ? Gurski.

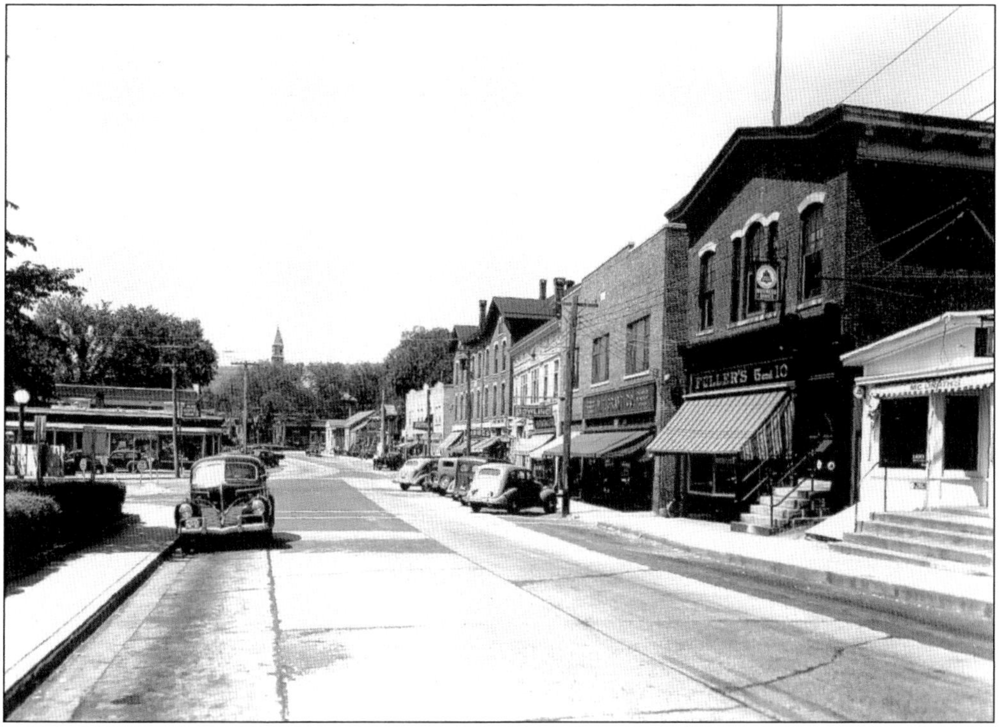

Vintage cars are parked along Main Street one morning in this southerly view. This quiet Main Street scene *c.* 1940 was soon to be shattered by the Japanese attack on Pearl Harbor. McGrath's Restaurant (on the extreme right), Fuller's five-and-dime store (housed in Thomaston's first brick building), and W.T. Grant are among the businesses pictured. The bowling alley, First National market, Latimer's Drug, Anderson's Restaurant, and a Gulf station are seen to the right. Opposite, signs for the Park Hotel, MK Liquors, and the A & P appear. Along with the majestic elms, all are gone except for Fuller's, now located on the site of the former First National store. (Courtesy of Matthew Monahan.)

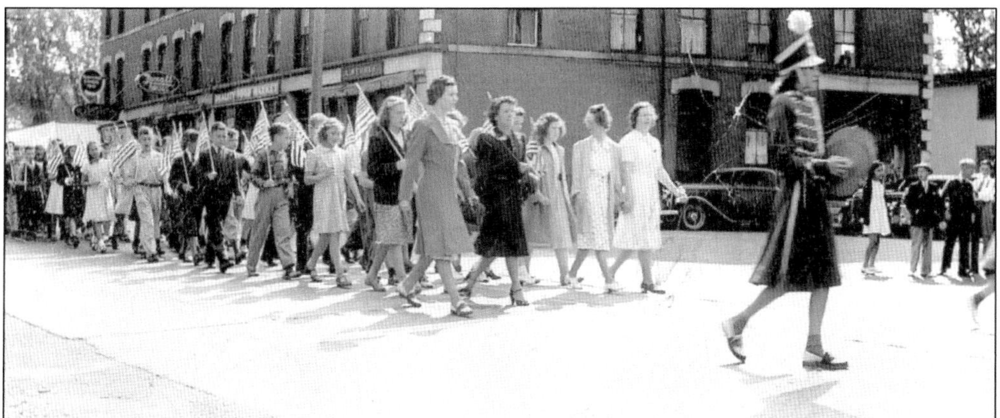

In the Memorial Day parade on May 30, 1941, schoolchildren march along holding flags. Doris Waters is the second teacher from the left (in the dark coat), and Hazel Ames is the second from the right (head turned). Europe had been at war since September 1939.

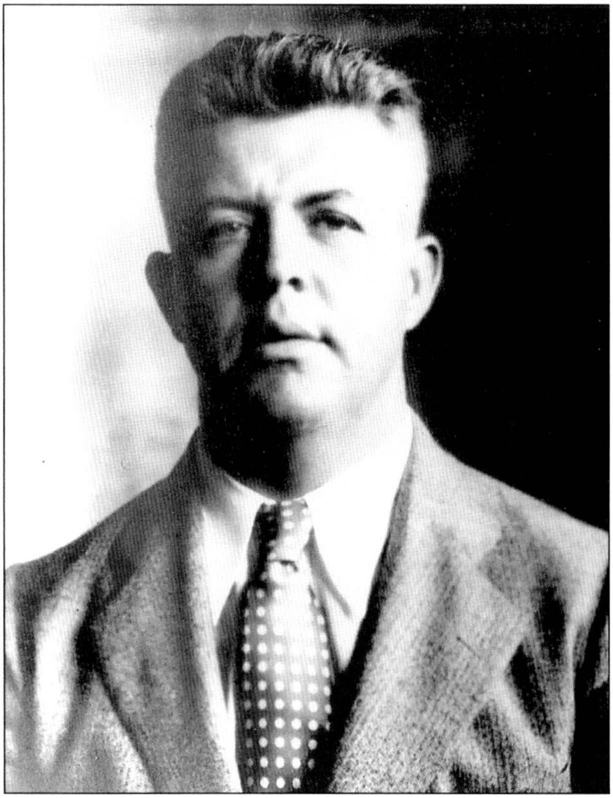

Pearl Harbor shocked America. This picture of Thomas Reeves gives no indication of the patriotism, bravery, and determination of Thomaston's greatest hero. On December 7, 1941, the day of the Japanese sneak attack, Chief Radioman Thomas J. Reeves died aboard the *California* while passing ammunition to his shipmates in a burning corridor. The 45-year-old career navy man received the Medal of Honor posthumously for "extraordinary courage." The medal is displayed with great pride on the Reeves Memorial Wall in the town hall. (Courtesy of the U.S. Navy.)

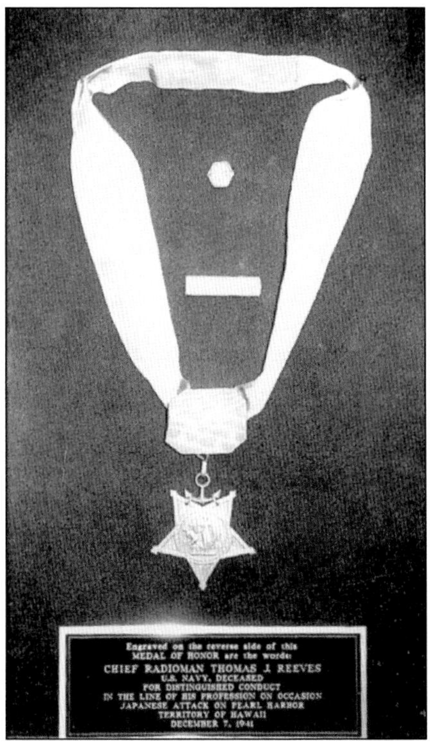

Pictured here is the Medal of Honor awarded posthumously to Thomas J. Reeves. Created for the Civil War, the Medal of Honor was made a permanent decoration by Congress in 1863. Only 57 were given to members of the navy in World War II. Of the 464 awarded in the course of the war, 266 were awarded posthumously.

Paul V. Lyons was a sophomore at the College of the Holy Cross when he was drafted. Serving in the Pacific, Corporal Lyons was killed by a Japanese sniper on the island of Leyte in the Philippines. It was November 22, 1944. He was 21. (Courtesy of Rosemary L. Martin.)

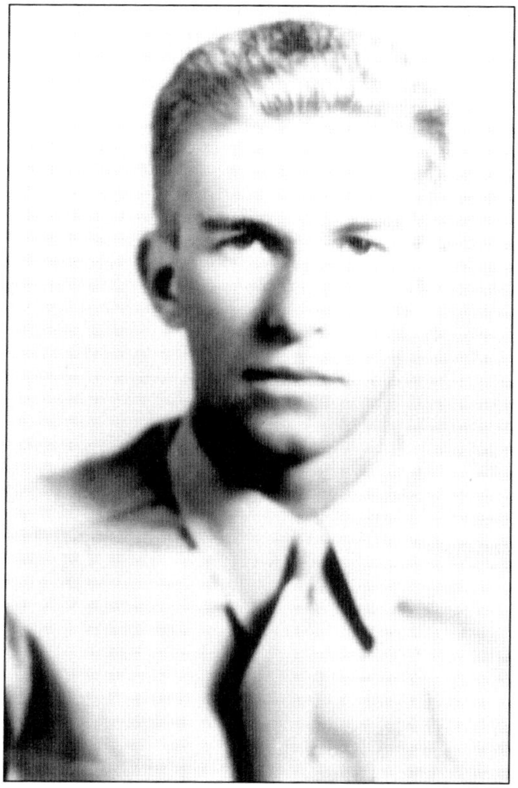

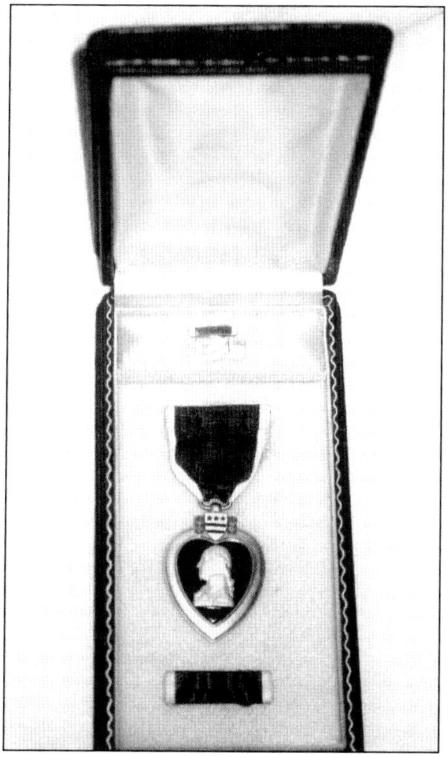

Paul V. Lyons was awarded this Purple Heart posthumously.

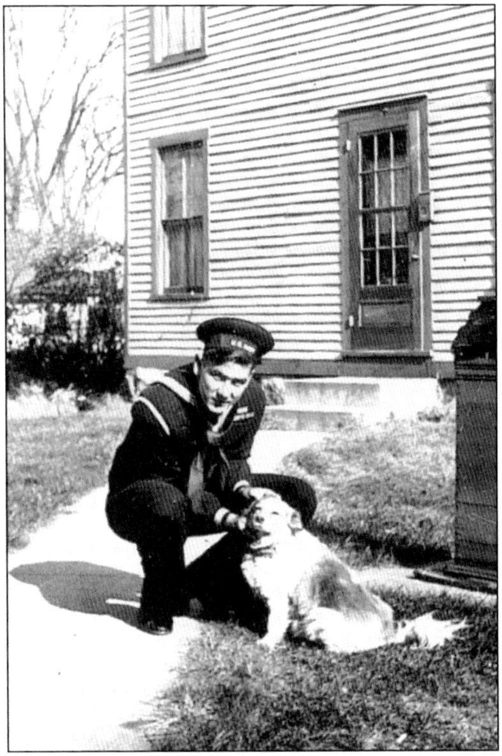

Lester Handlowich plays with Snookie at 72 River Street. His friends, the Dilgers, lived there, and Lester lived on Sanford Avenue with his parents, Stephen and Hazel. Enlisting at 17, he was on the submarine *Grayback* when it was sunk by a Japanese plane in 1944. He was 19. (Courtesy of Adeline Dilger Bolton.)

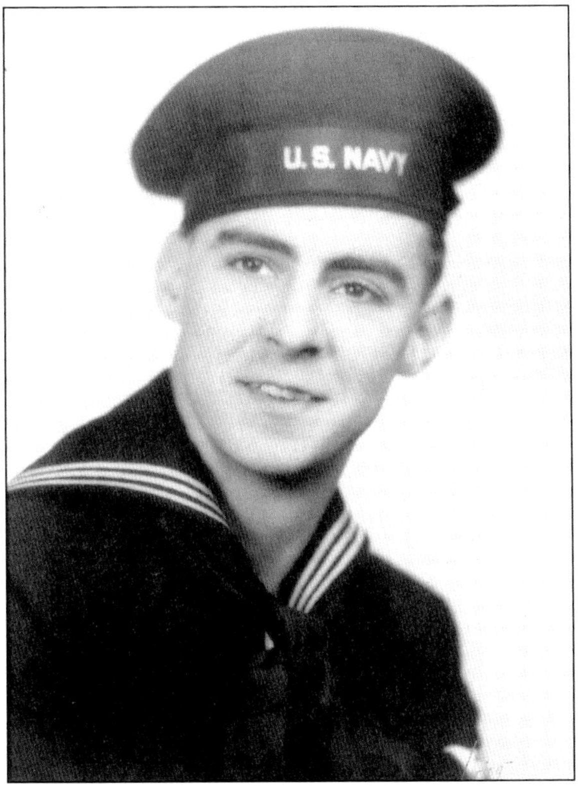

This handsome portrait of Frederick Dilger was taken after his 1943 enlistment. The son of Albert and Violet Dilger, Fred took part in the Normandy invasion aboard LCT-569. After the war, he became a plumber and was involved in many community activities. (Courtesy of Adeline Dilger Bolton.)

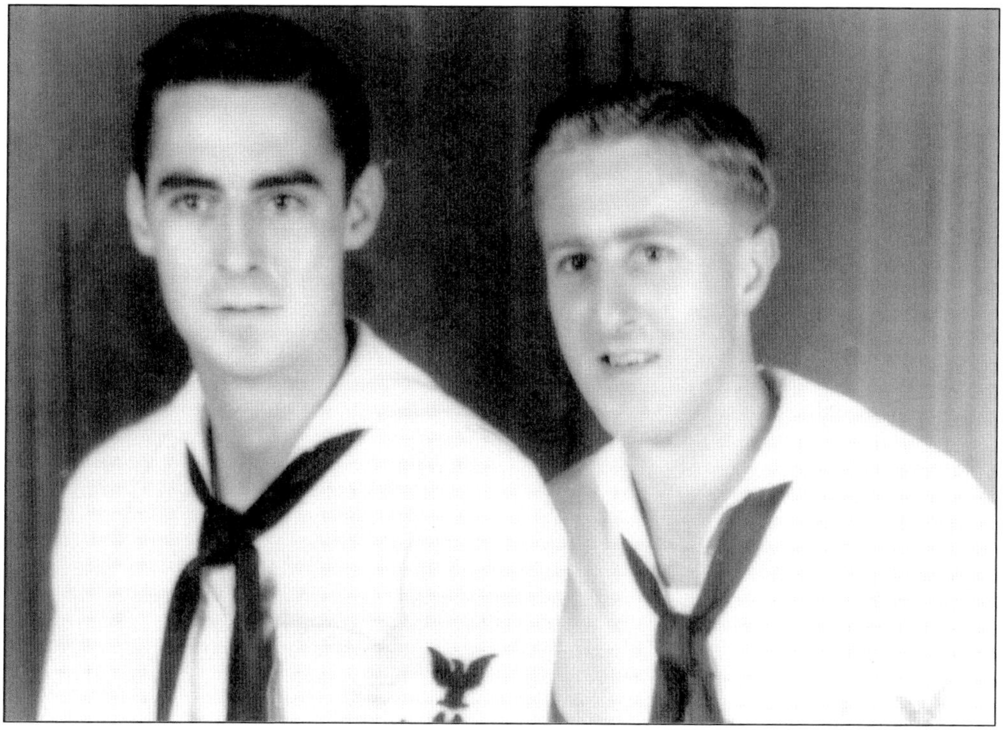

Good fortune does sometimes happen in wartime. While waiting in Panama for his next assignment, Fred Dilger (left) accidentally met his brother Roy, whose ship was en route to the Pacific. They had not seen each other for two years. Both sailors eventually came home to Thomaston. (Courtesy of Adeline Dilger Bolton.)

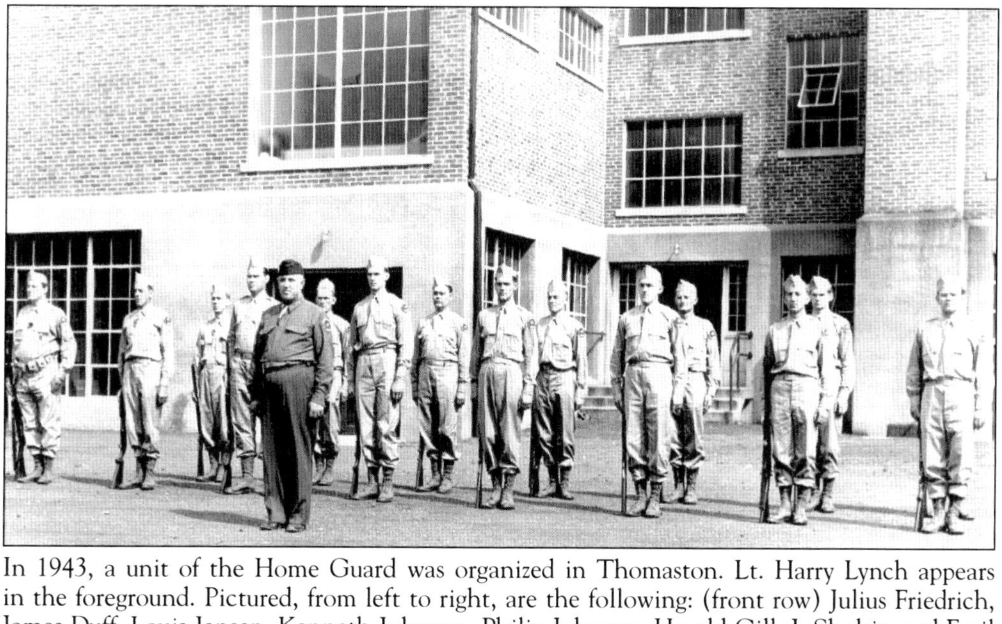

In 1943, a unit of the Home Guard was organized in Thomaston. Lt. Harry Lynch appears in the foreground. Pictured, from left to right, are the following: (front row) Julius Friedrich, James Duff, Louis Jensen, Kenneth Johnson, Philip Johnson, Harold Gill, J. Sholtis, and Emil Konopasky; (back row) "Bucky" Nygren, Jack Salamanter, Harold Skilton, Calvin Woods, Bill Moran, and ? Paczkowski

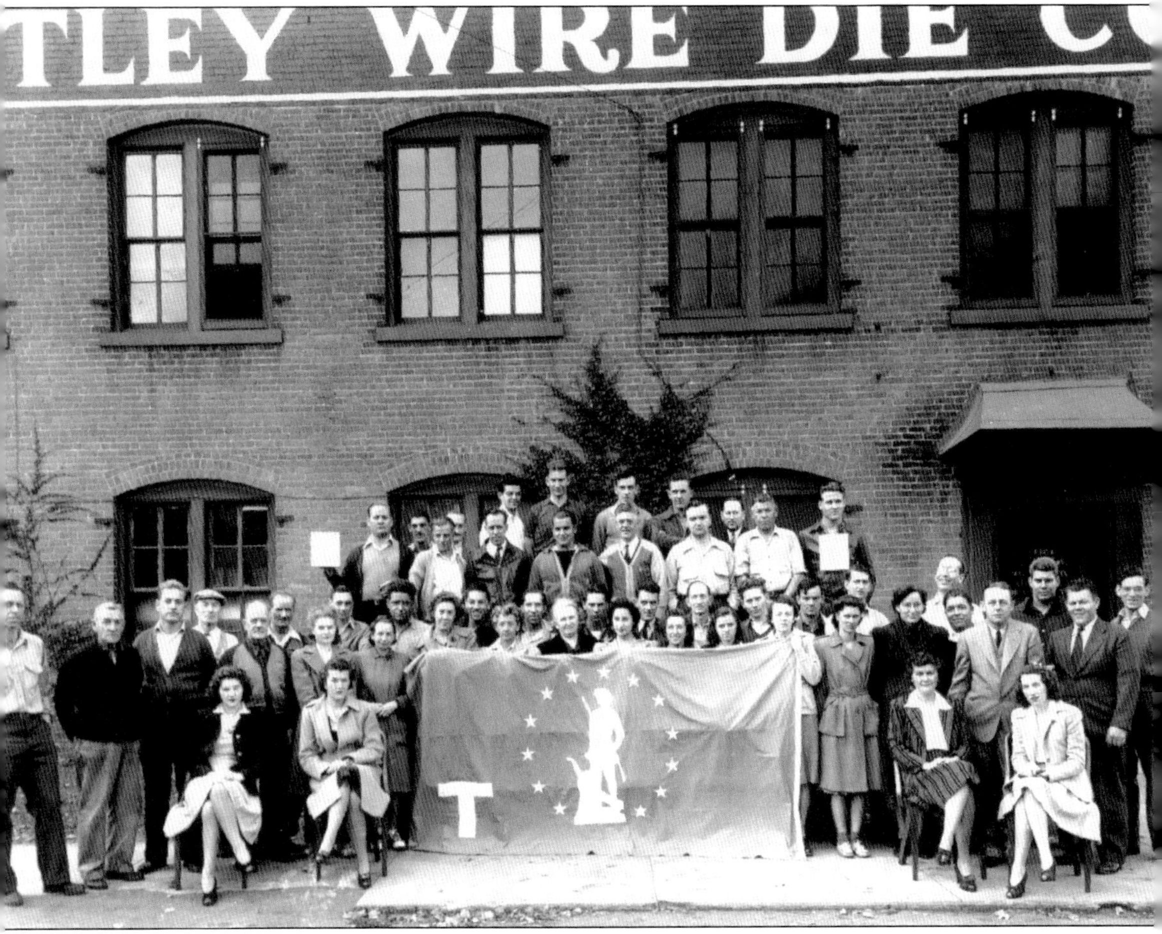

An example of the "all for one and one for all" spirit was the contribution to the war effort of Hartley Tool & Die Company employees. The symbol of the Concord Minuteman was used to sell war bonds. Employees pictured c. 1942 are, from left to right, as follows: (first row) Ruth Sarasin, Mary Landers, Gladys Hartley, and Mary Ryan Hanley; (second row) Roy McWhorter, Karl Neistroy, unidentified, Harold Bidwell, two unidentified workers, Kate Hanny, Raymond Petke, two unidentified workers, Margaret Miles, William Rogozinski, two unidentified workers, Lena Morton, Al Dovitski, Mary Zappala Edmonds, Tom Sanderson, Margaret Lowther, Tyler "Tighe" Stuart, unidentified, Leonard Burghardt, Frieda Miller Hildebrand, William Coss, unidentified, William Hanny, Florence Bushnell, two unidentified workers, owner Earl Hartley, Clarence "Pop" Fredlund, plant superintendent Anton Berg, and unidentified; (third row) unidentified, James Edmonds, unidentified, Ken McCallum, Ed Reed, Steve Garber, unidentified, Jack Waters, Les Raymond, unidentified, and Doris "Doc" Stringer; (fourth row) three unidentified workers and Charles Budney.

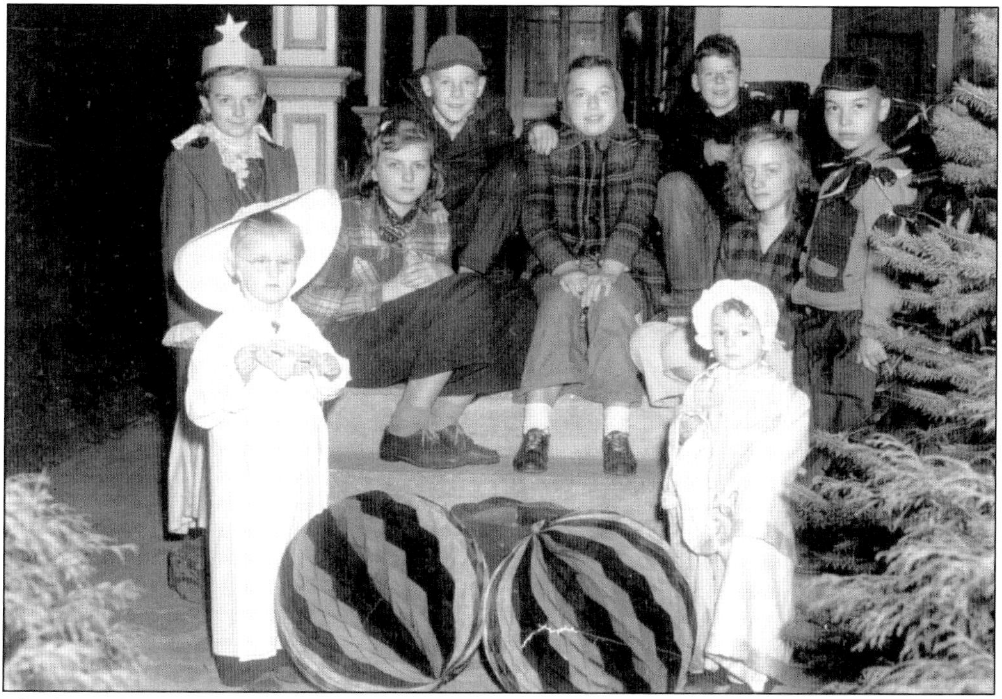

The homefront endured rationing and other restrictions during World War II, but children could still enjoy happy times, such as this Halloween in 1944. The setting was 67 Marine Street, and the photographer was Gunther Mathes. The children are, from left to right, as follows: (front row) Patricia McDonald and Robert McDonald; (back row) Barbara Sanderson, Jean Sanderson, Ted Johnson, Dorothy Golden, Robert Devino, Joan Sanderson, and William Polowy. (Courtesy of Patricia McDonald.)

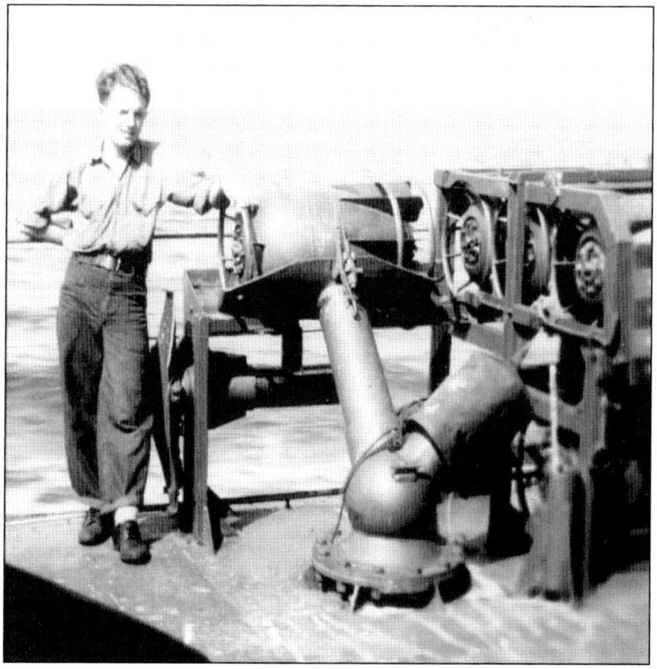

One of three brothers to serve in the U.S. Navy, Mario DePecol stands next to his ship's depth charges. The *Hollis* was the flagship for underwater demolition in the Pacific. This was May 1945, and soon he would join his younger brothers, Ben and Bruno, back in Thomaston. Our town sent almost 500 men to war. (Courtesy of Mario DePecol.)

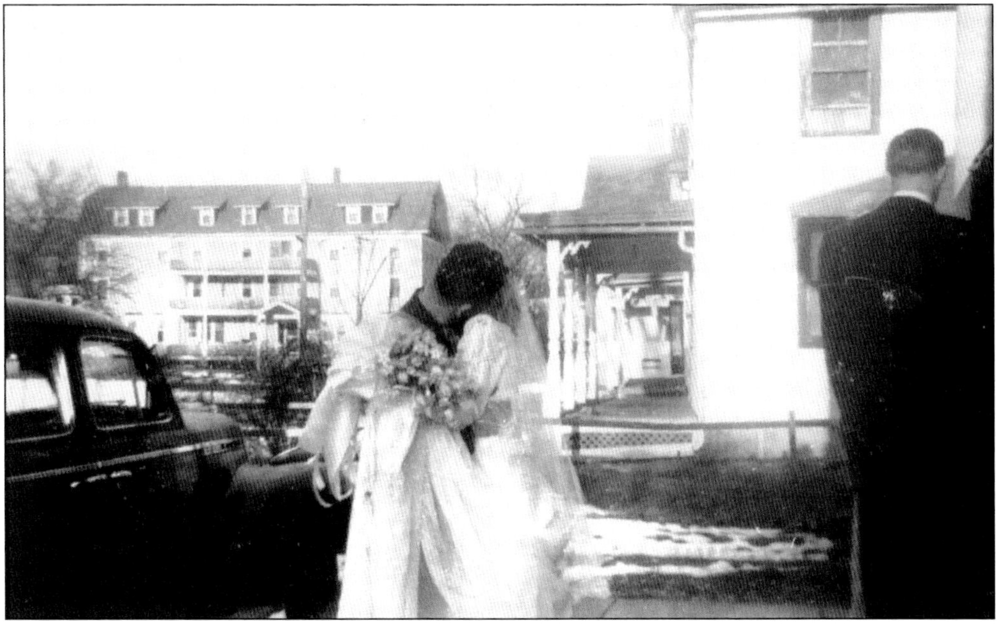

When the war ended, the Dilger brothers had a wedding to attend. Here we see their sister Adeline and her husband, Wallace Bolton, on their wedding day, December 8, 1945. The wedding reception was held in the Old Center School. (Courtesy of Adeline Dilger Bolton.)

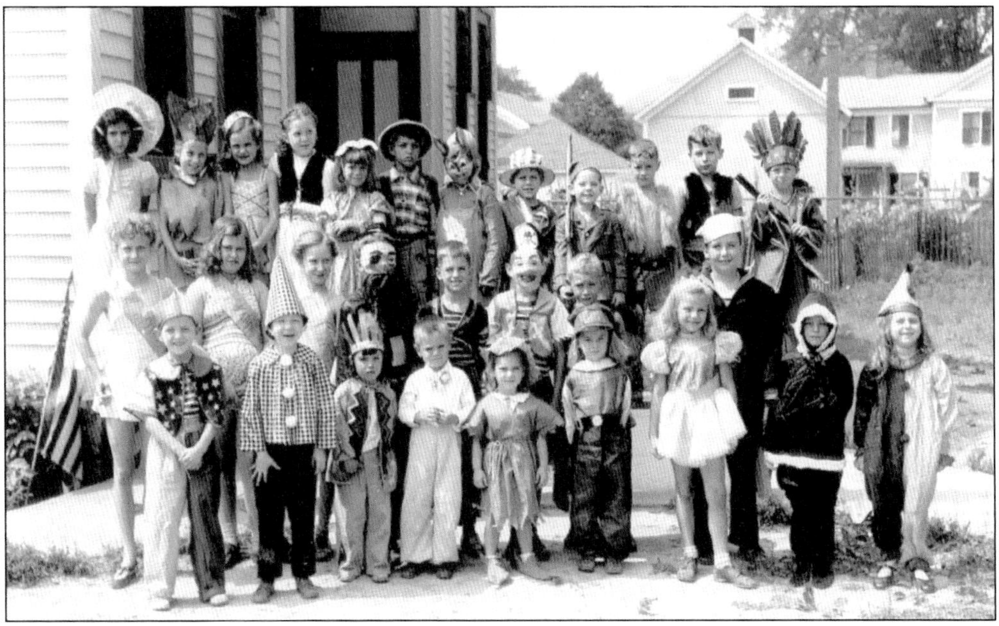

The summer playground began when the war ended. Seen here at the Old Center School grounds in the summer of 1946 are, from left to right, the following: (front row) William O'Connor, Charles Wysocki, Louis ?, Curt Atwood, Mary Ann Gesmondi, Robert Smail, Irene Talley, Barbara Smith, and Nancy Potter; (middle row) three unidentified people, Raymond Smith, Louis Gesmondi, James Smith, Robert Brink, and Luke Vincent Lauretano; (back row) Ann ?, Genevieve Gesmondi, Beverly Dick, Sylvia Wysocki, Judy Atwood, Mike ?, Donald West, James Debisschop, William Heffernan, Bruce Brink, Tyler Stuart, and Donald Kiely.

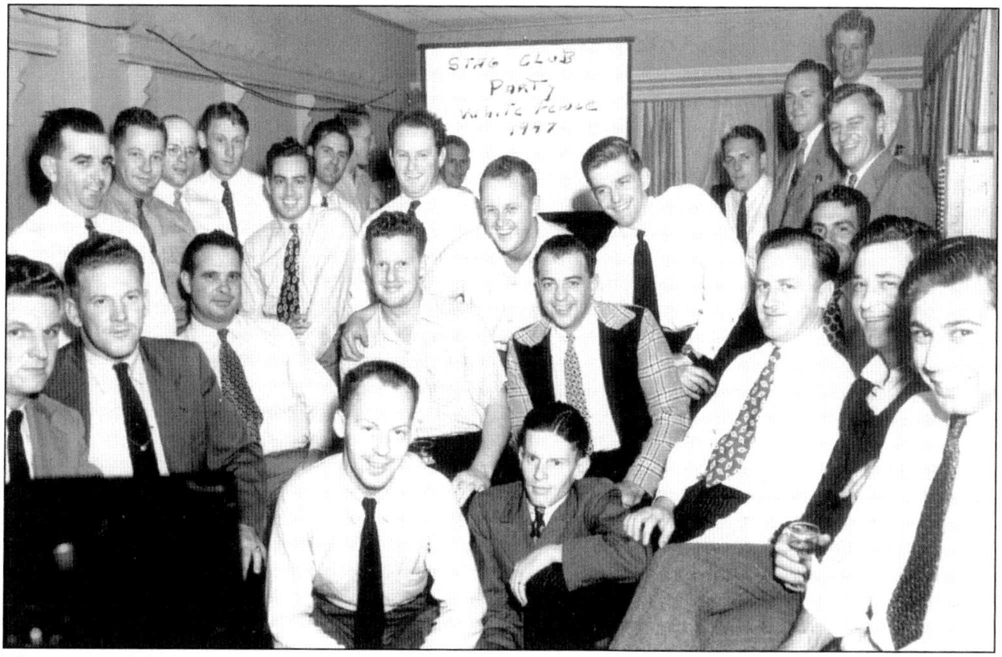

The Stag Club was a men's club whose annual minstrel show was a showcase for local talent. Here, Stag Club members are gathered at the White Fence Inn for a party on September 23, 1946, not 1947. Pictured, from left to right, are the following: (front row) John Monahan and Joseph Sullivan; (middle row) William Beardslee, Luke Martin, Jack Shearer, "Buck" Sullivan, ? Lumpkin, Edward O'Brien, Richard "Pop" Kane, and Albie Ciafardone; (back row) Fred Flynn, John Ashak, Robby Morton, Richard Ober, Robert Anderson, George Benedict, Paul "Peck" O'Brien, Vincent Doran, Ted Beardslee, John Lyons, Mario DePecol, Andy Fraleigh, Larry Volovski, and Bill Kane (rear). (Courtesy of Mario DePecol.)

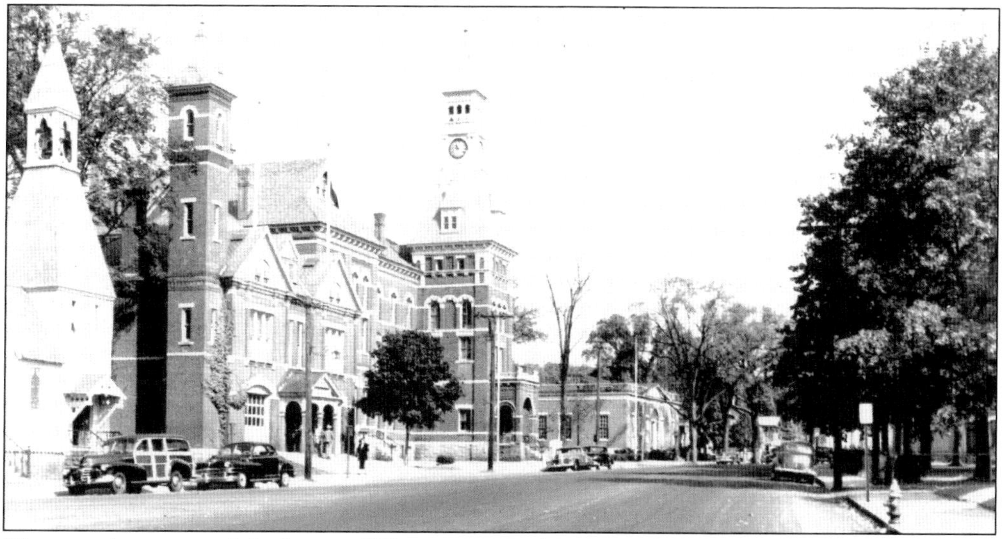

This was the image of the heart of Thomaston in the years after World War II. The town hall and opera house, the old firehouse, and the Episcopal church towers are as recognizable now as they were in the era of Harry Truman. The wood-paneled station wagon in front of the church adds a touch of nostalgia to the picture.

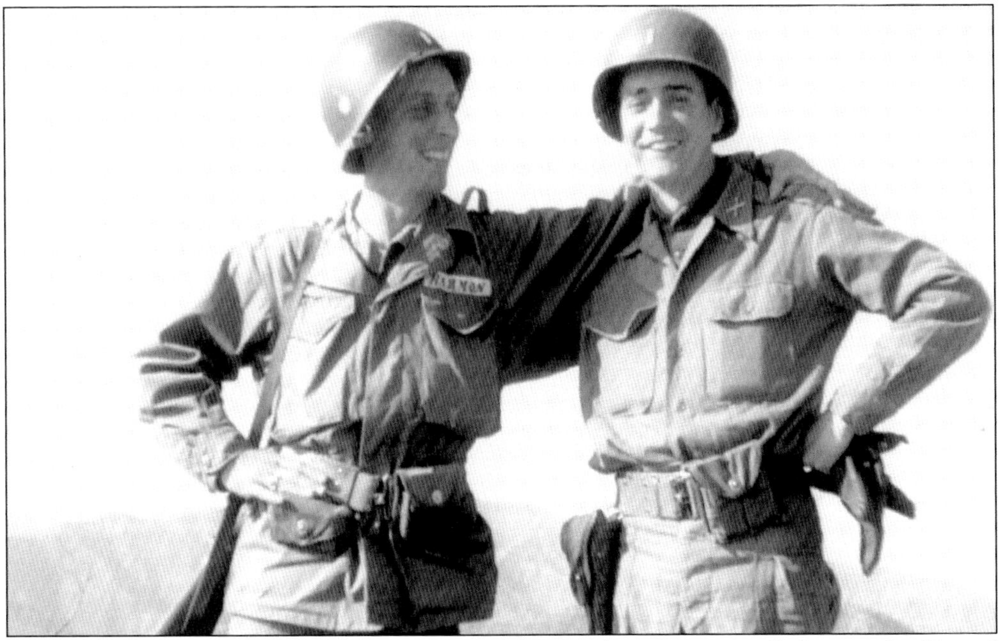

In June 1950, North Korea invaded South Korea. President Truman called upon the United Nations to resist, and they did so under American leadership. Almost 200 served from Thomaston. The young second lieutenant on the right is Walter Robinson, who served with the 981st Field Artillery Battalion of the 40th Infantry Division from 1952 to 1953. After the service, the Fordham graduate returned to Thomaston, where he had a very successful career as a history teacher. (Courtesy of Walter Robinson.)

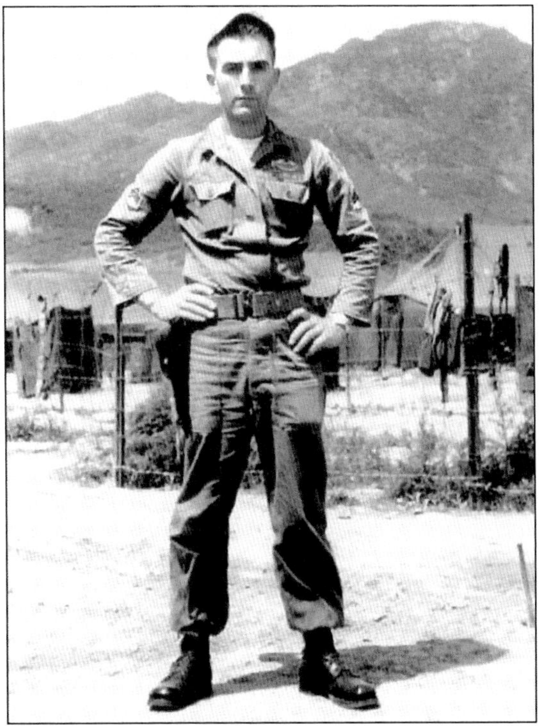

Sgt. Roger Gangloff served in Korea from 1953 to 1954 with the 25th Infantry Division. The rugged terrain and the barbed wire enclosure hint at the danger. After the war, he came back to Thomaston, where he worked at the Hallden Machine Company for 37 years. (Courtesy of Roger Gangloff.)

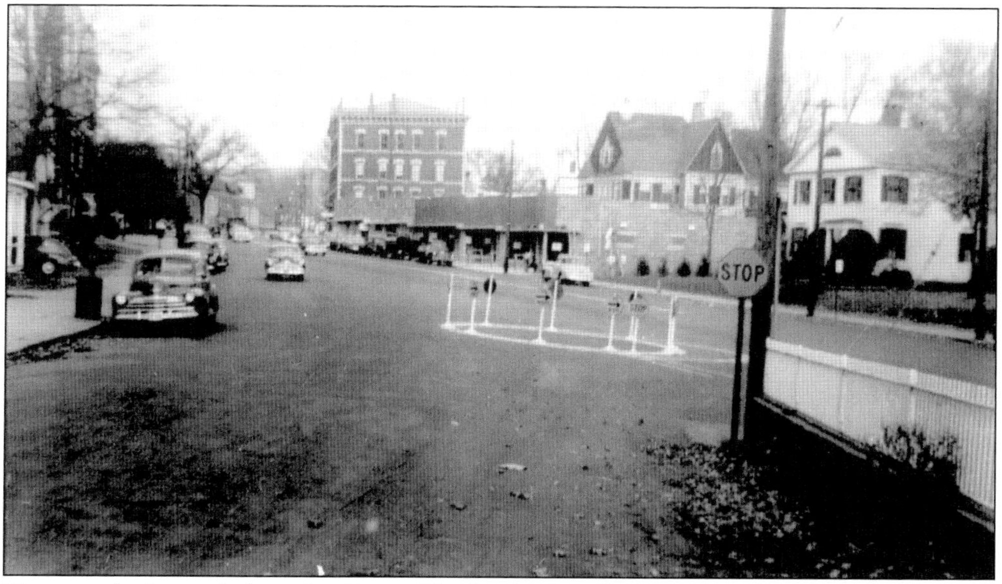

This view looks north from the library. The Bradstreet Block is in the center background, and to the right is the Woodruff-Upson house. In front of the house is a block of stores that existed for four decades. Pictured here *c.* 1951, the site is now occupied by the Thomaston Savings Bank's main office.

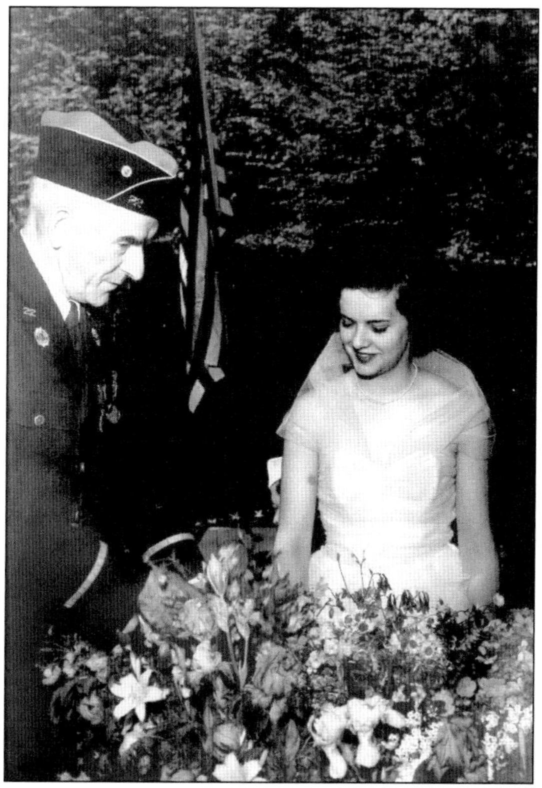

Sheldon Koops of the American Legion, a World War I veteran, and Clarice Bernatchez, a senior at Thomaston High School, collaborate in a ceremony to honor Thomaston's departed sons and daughters. Bernatchez was Miss Columbia for Memorial Day in 1954, and Hillside Cemetery was the setting.

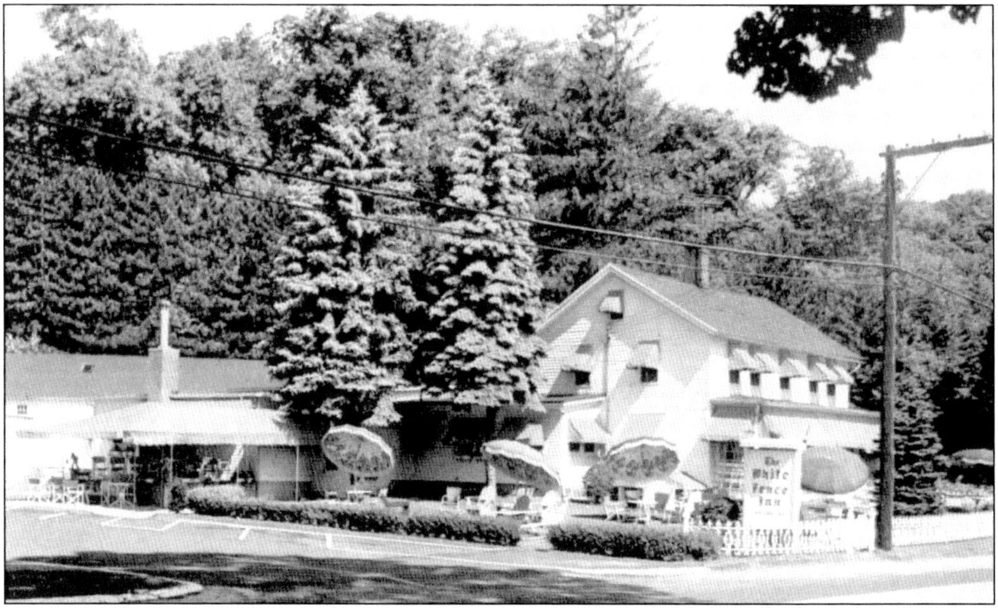

The busy intersection of Routes 6 and 254 was more tranquil in the 1950s. In a converted house, Koegel's Korner Kottage was an earlier restaurant on this site. Fred Denis owned the White Fence Inn, pictured here on this postcard. After a fire destroyed the restaurant in 1965, the site was occupied by the Flammias' Clearwater Pool Company. Now it is home to Cam Motors. (Courtesy of Robert Magdziarz.)

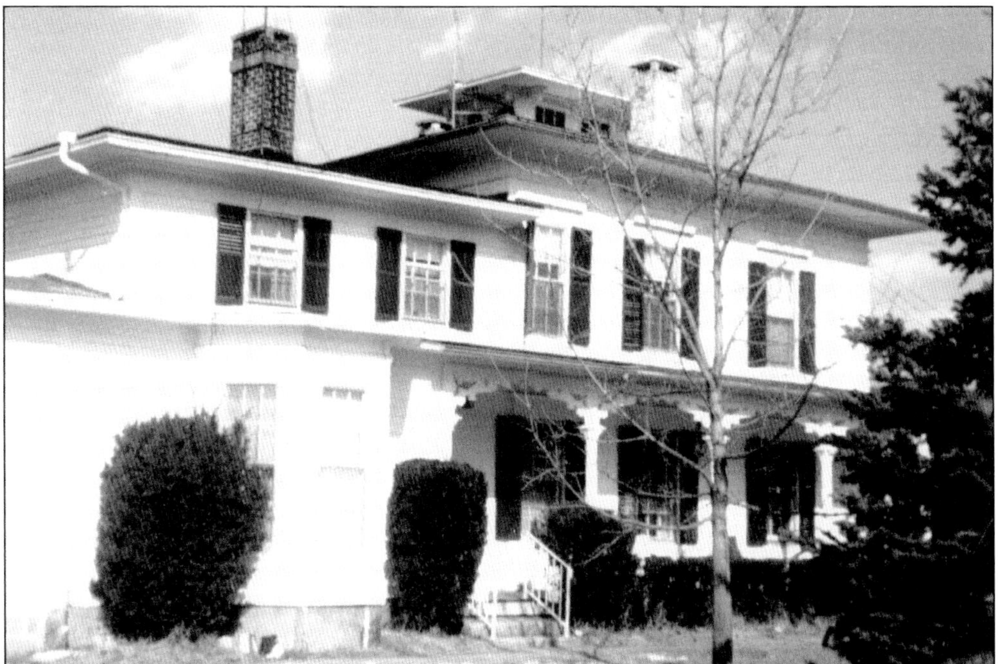

The Warners gave their name to Warner's Corner. Charles Norman lived in this house for many years on the south side of the intersection of Routes 6 and 254, while his paint business flourished across the street. Modern Motors now occupies both sites.

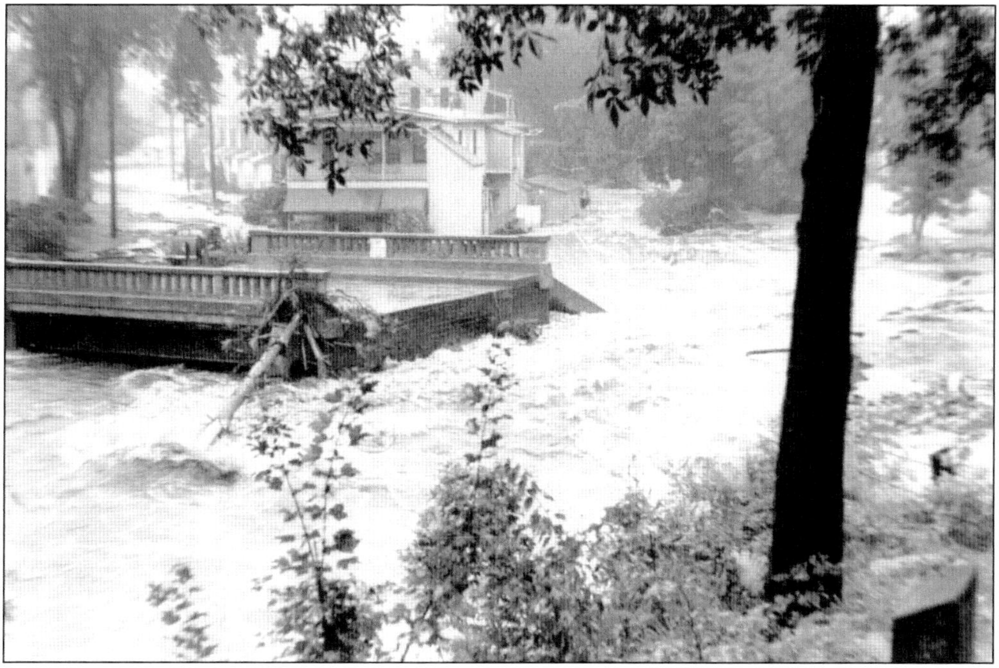

Hurricane Diane caused the Great Flood of August 19, 1955. The Naugatuck Valley suffered massive devastation. In Thomaston, Northfield Brook washed away this bridge at Center and Meadow Streets, where Route 254 passes over now. There was no electricity for three days; teenagers, including the author, were deputized for guard duty to prevent looting.

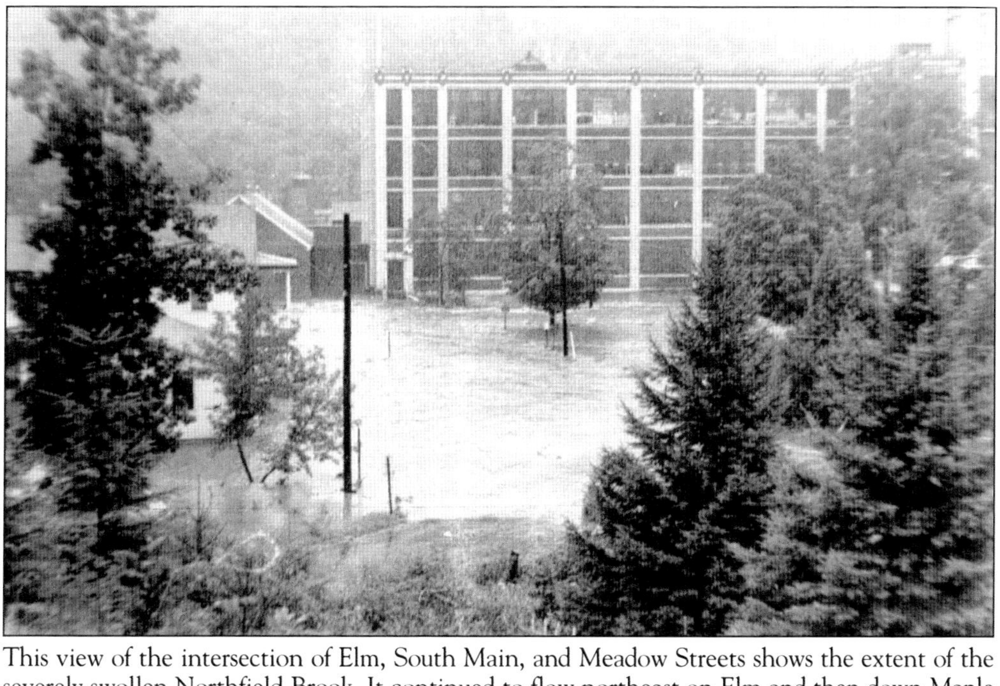

This view of the intersection of Elm, South Main, and Meadow Streets shows the extent of the severely swollen Northfield Brook. It continued to flow northeast on Elm and then down Maple Street to the river. Thousands of clocks that were damaged when the factory was flooded were later buried in the Elm Street parking lot. The vantage point is from high above Center Street.

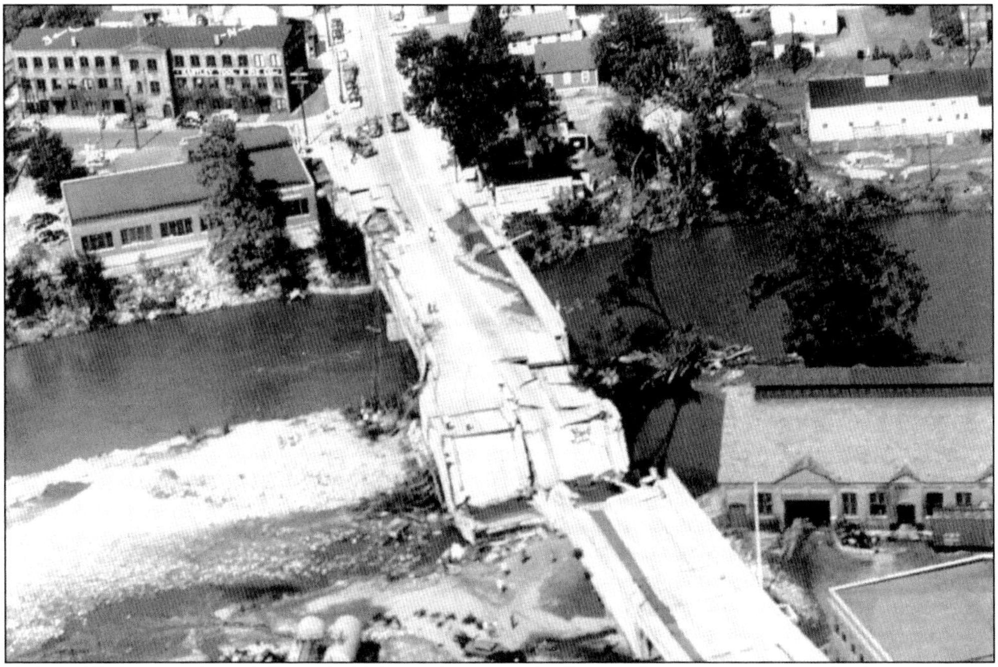

An aerial view shows the damage to the East Main Street Bridge. Traffic was rerouted to the southern side of the bridge, next to the railroad station, while the bridge was repaired. The Lyons Pontiac dealership appears on the west side of the river on the site of the old movement shop. There was no St. Thomas School, which would alter the landscape in the upper right of the photograph. With regard to fatalities, Waterbury lost 19 people, while one woman was killed in the Weeksville section of Thomaston.

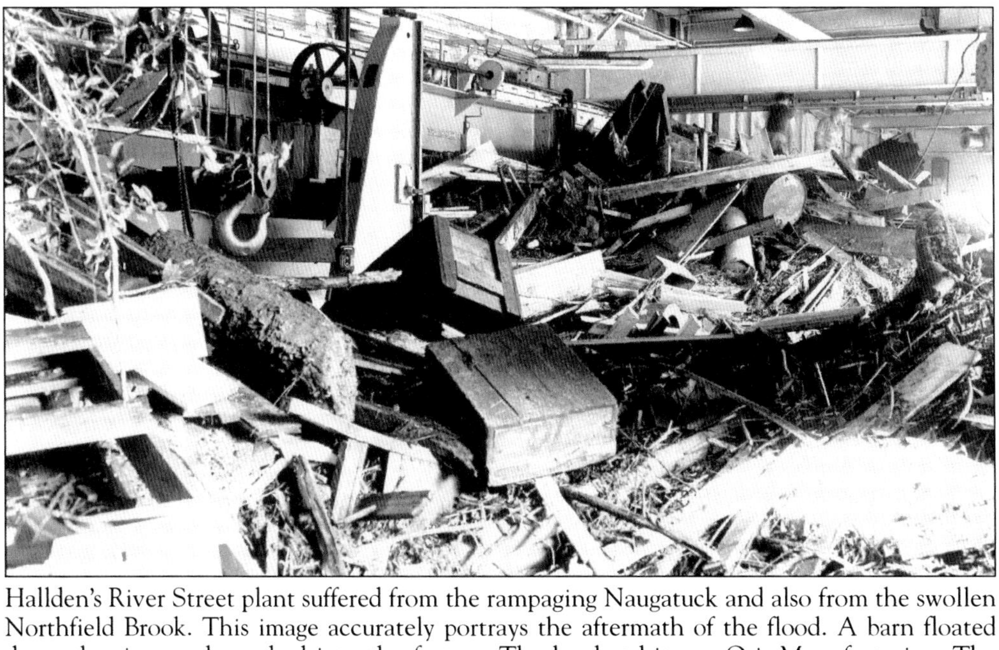

Hallden's River Street plant suffered from the rampaging Naugatuck and also from the swollen Northfield Brook. This image accurately portrays the aftermath of the flood. A barn floated down the river and smashed into the factory. The hardest hit was Oris Manufacturing. The factory and nearby Terry's Bridge were both totally swept away.

The example set by Dr. Winfield E. Wight was followed by two physicians 20 years later. Contemporaries, Dr. Daniel P. Samson (1917–1987), to the right, and Dr. Clifford T. Conklin Jr. (1914–1998), below, were both veterans of World War II. Samson, a native of Brockton, Massachusetts, graduated from Tufts University and the College of Physicians and Surgeons at Columbia University. He came to Thomaston in 1947 and established his family practice in his home at 147 Elm Street. His civic interests included the Rotary Club, the board of education, the Black Rock School Committee, the Thomaston Public Library, and a leadership role on the board of directors of the Thomaston Savings Bank. Pictured with him are his wife, Evelyn (Hagen), and children, Daniel Jr., Linda (left), and Claudia. Conklin was born in Columbus, Ohio, and graduated from Middlebury College in Vermont. The next step was medical school at the University of Vermont. After the army, he came to Thomaston in 1946. His family practice was established at 16 Grand Street. He, too, was a longtime member of the Rotary Club, chairing its scholarship program. In his 52 years of service to the community, he became the dean of physicians in his adopted hometown and was much loved, much respected.

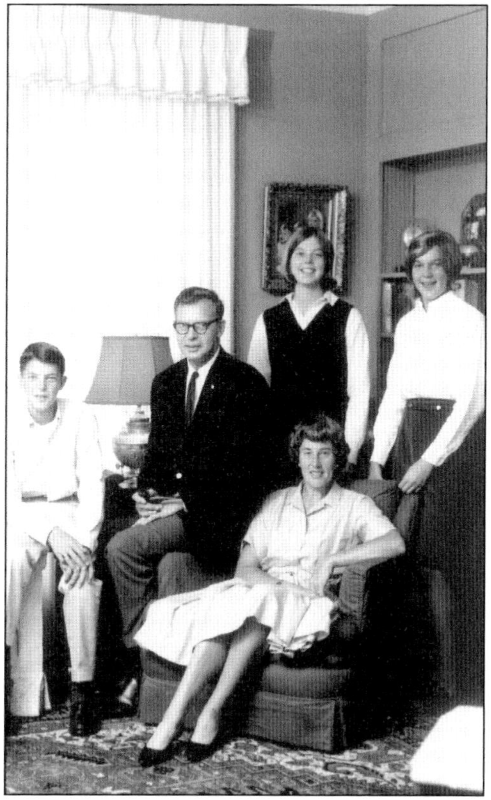

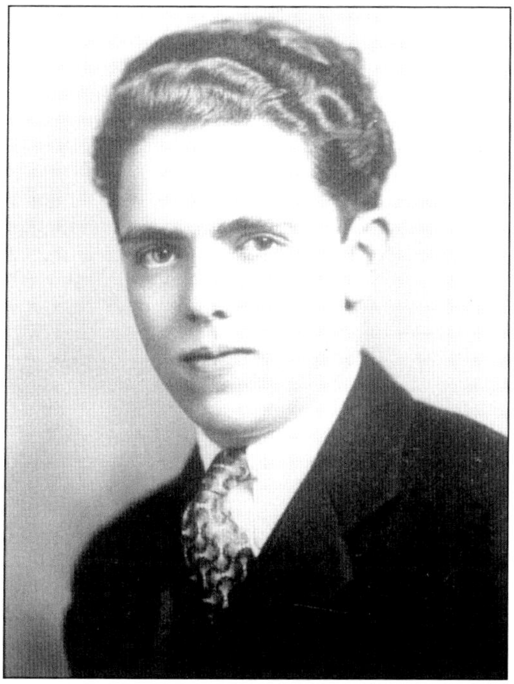

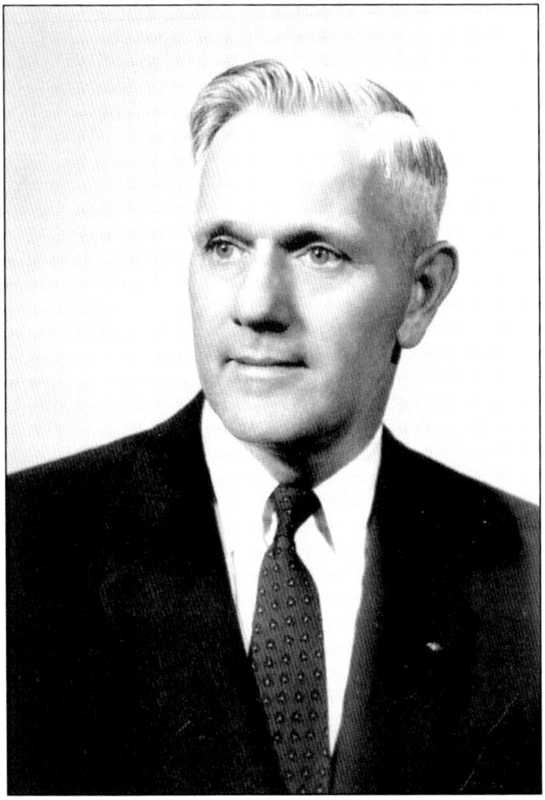

Allan C. Innes (1901–1980) was one of the most respected and admired men of his generation. Prominent in the business world, he contributed greatly to the town of Thomaston. Elected to the state legislature as a Republican, he took a leadership role at the state level. In town affairs, he served on civic committees, such as the high school building committee. In 1935, he was an original member of the board of finance, serving for decades. (Courtesy of Marion Innes DePecol.)

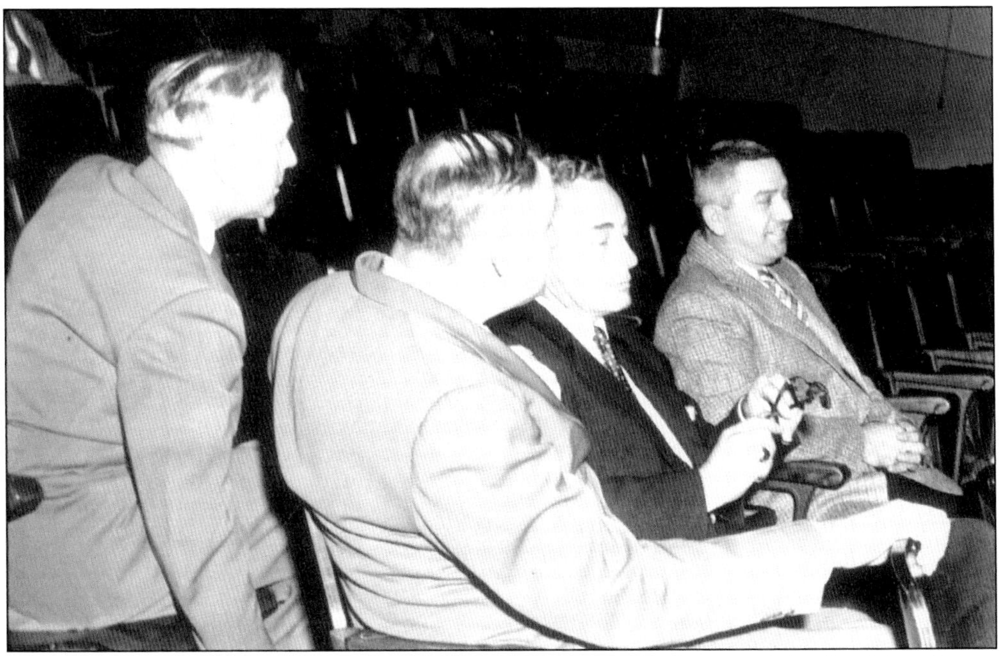

At a 1957 town meeting held in the high school (now the Center School), Allan Innes, chairman of the board of finance, sits behind the board of selectmen. The selectmen are, from left to right, Joseph Johnston, first selectman Charles "Chick" Eggleston, and Henry Gancos.

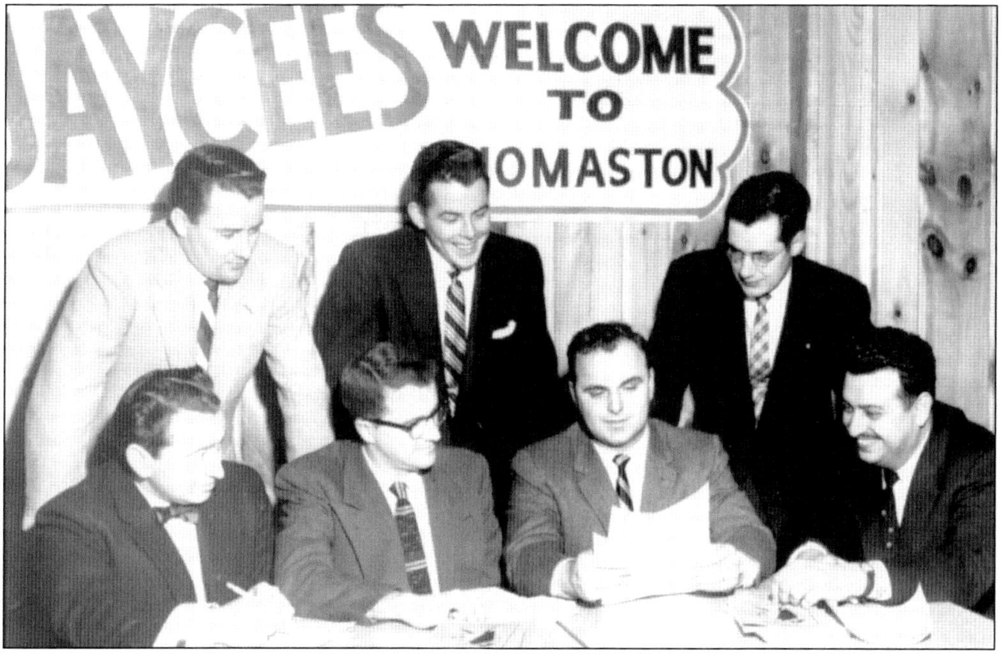

The interest exhibited by these business and professional leaders for their new organization makes this an engaging photograph. The members of the Junior Chamber of Commerce are, from left to right, as follows: (front row) studio photographer Milo Pawlechak, optometrist John Gould, men's clothier Roger DuPont, and publisher of the *Thomaston Express* Cesare DelVaglio; (back row) postmaster Matthew Monahan, attorney Richard Gilland, and Curtis Art Company owner Paul Tracy. The gathering took place at the Thomaston House c. 1962. (Courtesy of Matthew Monahan.)

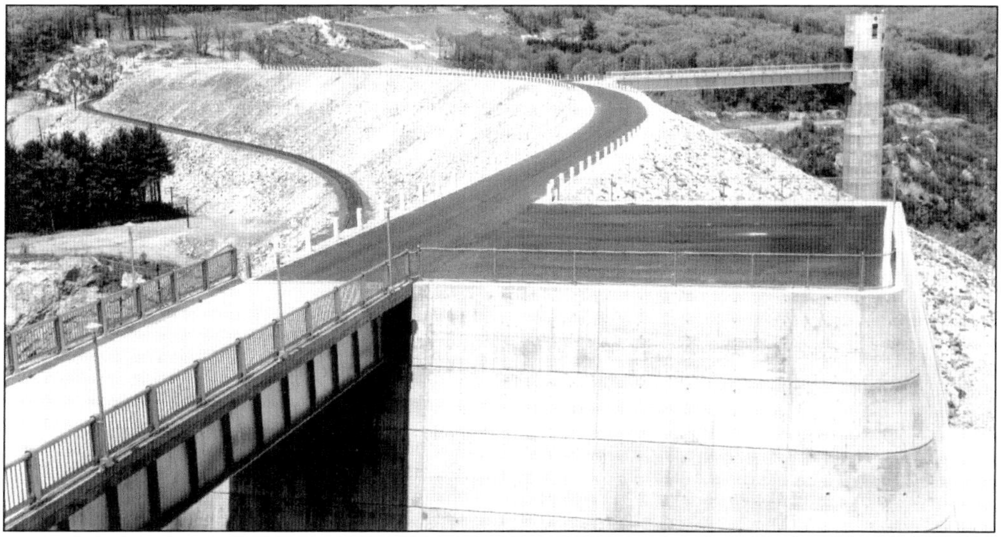

A project that would permanently alter the landscape was the U.S. Army Corps of Engineers' flood-control dams. The Thomaston Dam (pictured), on the Naugatuck River, cut off North Main Street just above Eclipse Glass. Riders to Torrington would henceforth travel on the new Route 8. This is a view looking west; the intake tower is at the right. In addition to flood control, recreational facilities were created: a picnic area and a trail bike area.

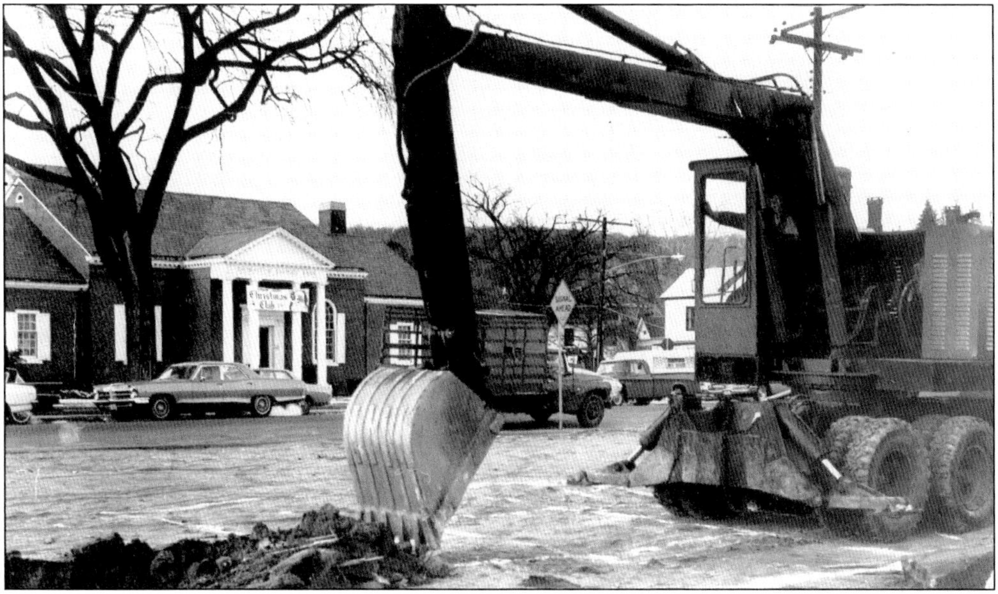

The appearance of Main Street was changing, too. In 1967, the Bradstreet Block was demolished and replaced by the Colonial Bank and Trust Company. At the right is the former Seth Thomas Jr. house, which would be demolished in the next decade. Across the street, the Thomaston Savings Bank appears. In 1990, the bank would move into new, spacious quarters. The Colonial Bank and Trust would give way to the Bank of Boston, Connecticut, and later, the Webster Bank.

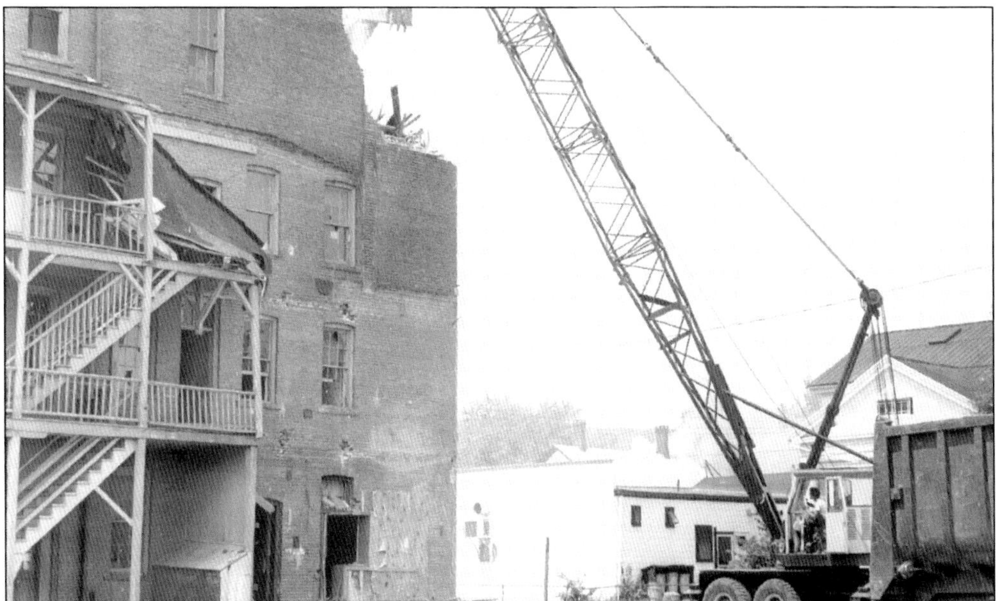

The Bradstreet Block stood as a landmark in town for 90 years. It was one of the first masonry structures, it bore the name of a prominent Victorian, and it anchored one of the four corners of the principal intersection. At the right of the picture is Talley's Restaurant and, partially hidden, the Canfield house. Both are now gone.

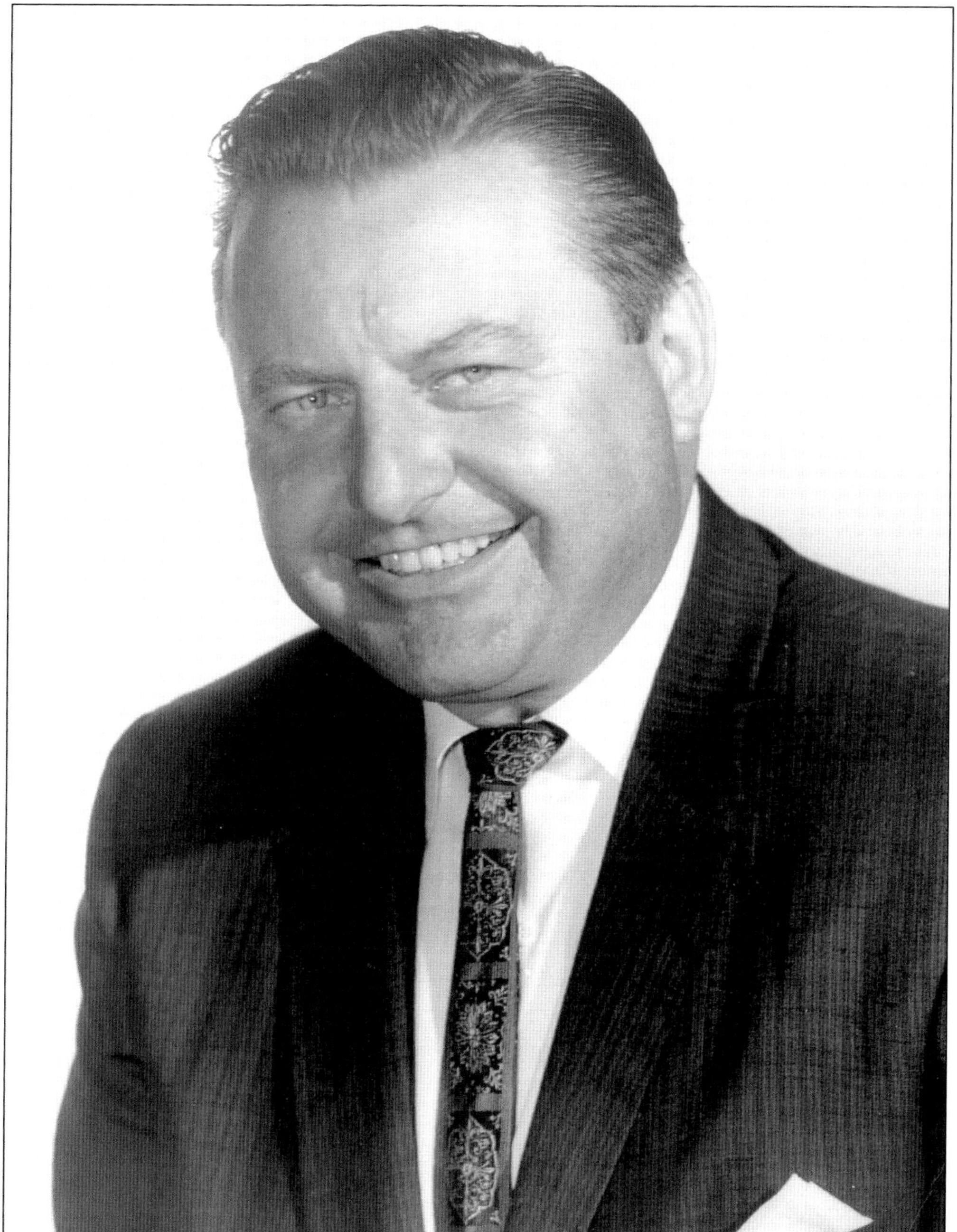

One of the most popular political figures in town during the 1960s and 1970s was George W. Johnston (1917–1996). A Republican, he was elected to the Connecticut General Assembly and then to the office of first selectman. His service to Thomaston spanned more than 25 years.

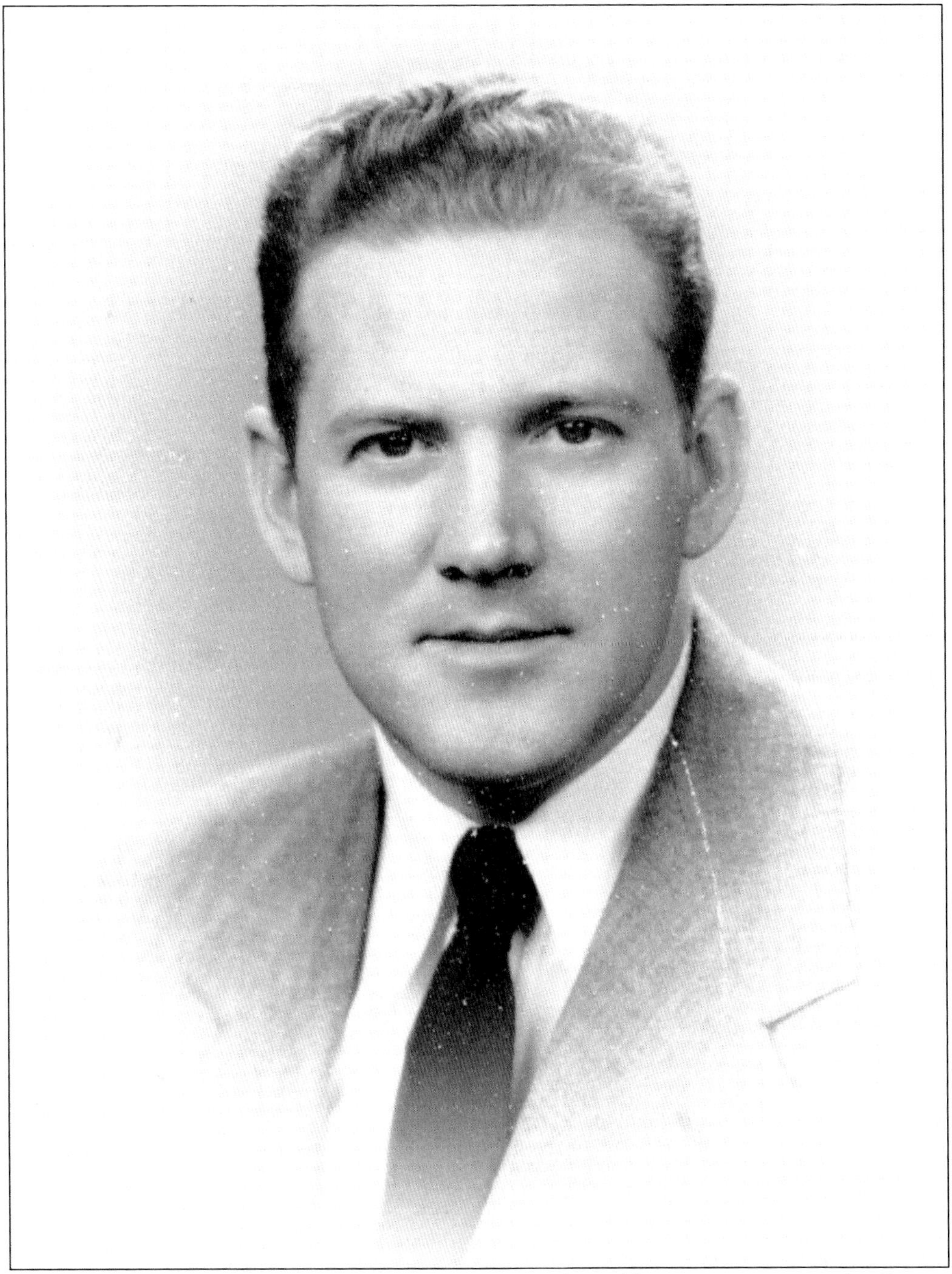

Luke Martin (1920–1980) was a decorated veteran of World War II, receiving the Bronze Star "for meritorious achievement" and the Purple Heart during his service as a lieutenant with the 94th Infantry Division in the European theater. A graduate of Trinity College and the University of Connecticut Law School, Martin became town clerk and a Democratic state representative. In 1961, he was named one of the original 44 Circuit Court judges. After promotion to the Court of Common Pleas, he was elevated to the Superior Court bench in 1975. (Courtesy of Rosemary Lyons Martin.)

The Vietnam War consumed much of the nation's attention during the 1960s and 1970s. Despite the controversial nature of the war, Thomaston sent nearly 200 young men, as it had in previous wars. This Marine served in Vietnam during 1965 and 1966. Richard O'Connell was a corporal with the 3rd Marine Division, 3rd Engineer Battalion, leaving the service as a sergeant E-5. A starting guard on the 1962 state championship basketball team, he has subsequently served Thomaston on the board of education, recreation commission, board of finance, and board of selectmen. (Courtesy of Richard O'Connell.)

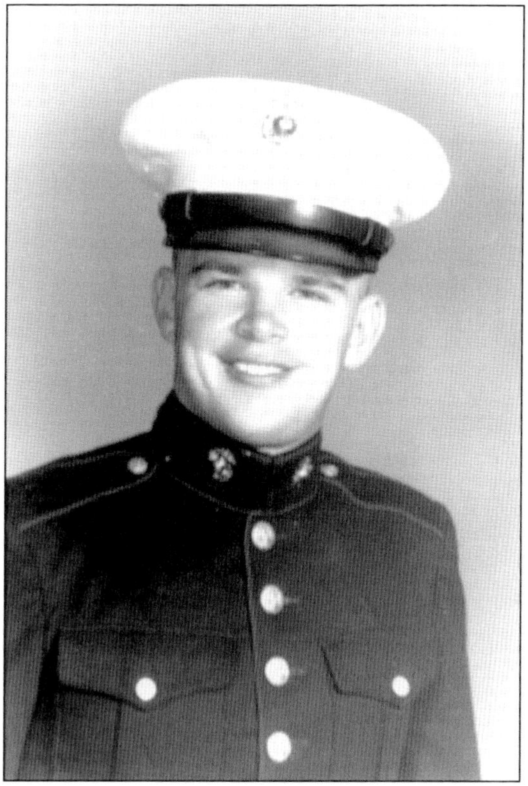

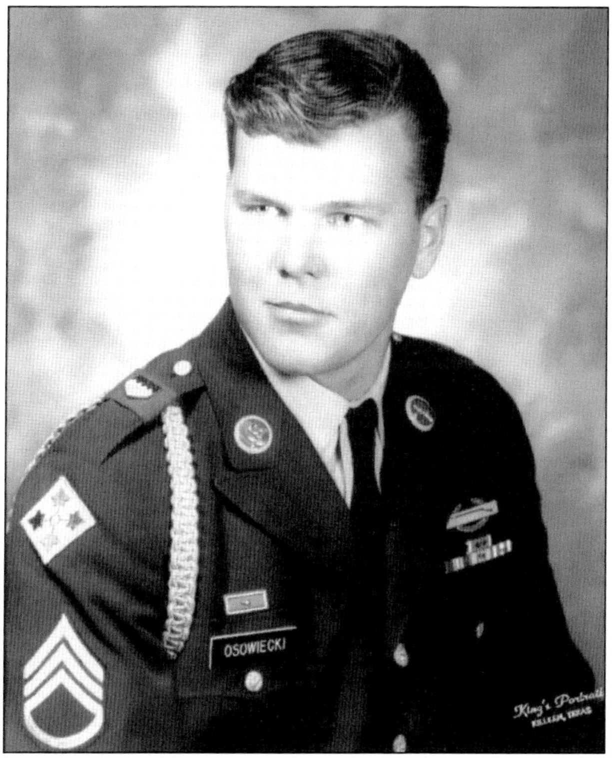

Henry M. Osowiecki Jr. was a sergeant with A Company, 2nd Battalion, 12th Infantry, 3rd Brigade, 4th Infantry Division. Receiving three Purple Hearts because of wounds suffered in the line of duty, he served in 1966 and 1967. In addition, he earned the Bronze Star, the Combat Infantryman's Badge, the Presidential Unit Citation, the Republic of Vietnam Campaign Medal, and the Republic of Vietnam Gallantry Cross. Currently, he is the leader of his unit's memorial activities. A successful businessman, he chaired the Town Hall Building Committee and is now a member of the Schools Building Committee. (Courtesy of Caroline Osowiecki.)

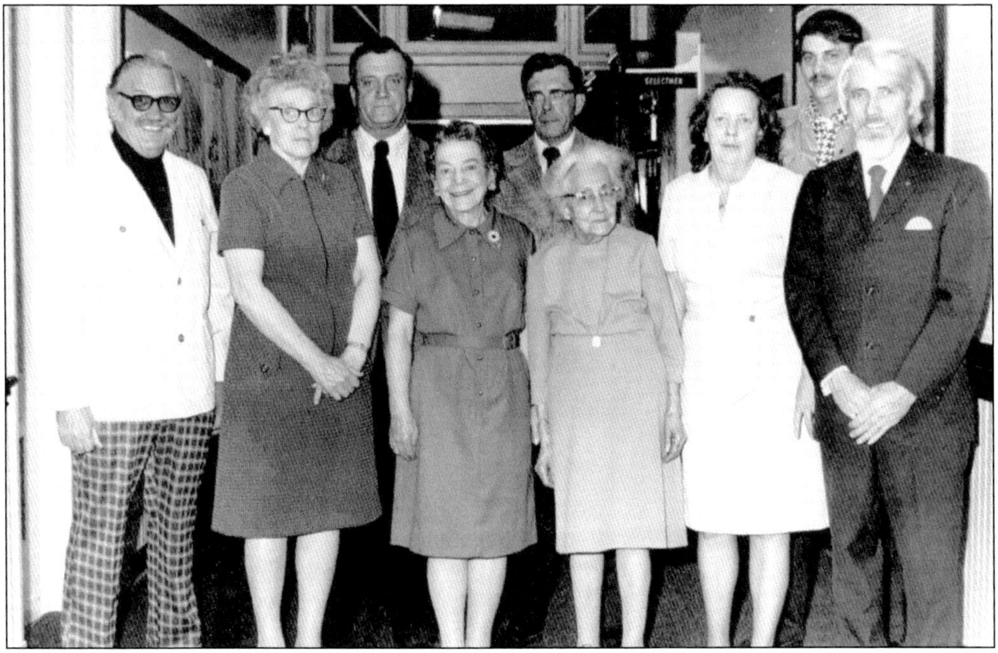

In 1975, Thomaston celebrated the centennial of its incorporation as a town. A huge week-long celebration was held with a variety of events. The committee responsible for much of the organization included, from left to right, "Lolly" Klaneski, Agnes Innes White, Bernard Hoyt, Rosa Gangloff, Thomas Reynolds, Clara Lake, Leona Sheldon, unidentified, and chairman Ransom Young.

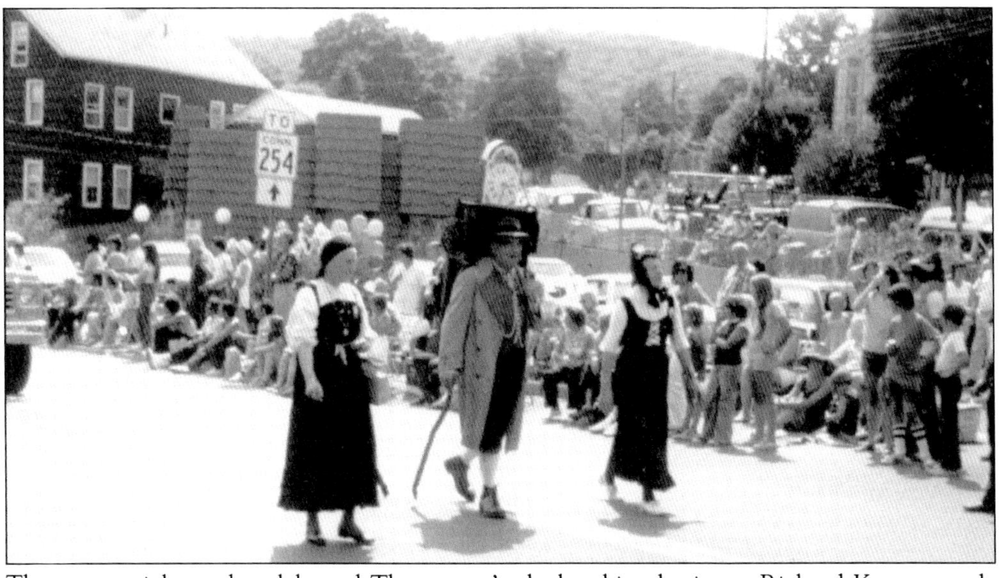

The centennial parade celebrated Thomaston's clockmaking heritage. Richard Kramer made and carried a reproduction of a clock peddler's rack, which the Thomaston Historical Society has in its collection. In traditional Black Forest dress, the marchers are, from left to right, Selma Kramer, Richard Kramer, and Frieda Hildebrand. It is fitting that in a town that has enjoyed so many parades and in which clocks have played such an important part, we conclude this book with both. (Courtesy of Richard Kramer Jr. and Thelma K. Snyder.)